CAREER DECISION MAKING FOR ADOLESCENTS AND YOUNG ADULTS WITH LEARNING DISABILITIES

To prepare youth and young adults with learning disabilities for entering adult occupational life, this author presents the theoretical and research foundations as well as the practices necessary to establish an appropriate model for understanding and assisting these individuals in making qualitative career decisions. Included in the text are the traditional trait/factor and developmental explanations of career decision-making behavior, but also presented is the concept of decision making based on social learning theory. Key sections of this text include an indepth analysis of the long-term effects of learning disabilities on educational and occupational attainment and specific guidelines for assessing and improving career decision-making skills.

CAREER DECISION MAKING FOR ADOLESCENTS AND YOUNG ADULTS WITH LEARNING DISABILITIES

Theory, Research and Practice

By

ERNEST F. BILLER, PH.D.

Assistant Professor of Rehabilitation Counseling
Kent State University
Kent, Ohio

CHARLES C THOMAS • PUBLISHER
Springfield • Illinois • U.S.A.

Published and Distributed Throughout the World by
CHARLES C THOMAS • PUBLISHER
2600 South First Street
Springfield, Illinois 62794-9265

© *1987 by* CHARLES C THOMAS • PUBLISHER

ISBN 0-398-05276-X

Library of Congress Catalog Card Number: 86-14455

With THOMAS BOOKS *careful attention is given to all details of manufacturing and design. It is the Publisher's desire to present books that are satisfactory as to their physical qualities and artistic possibilities and appropriate for their particular use.* THOMAS BOOKS *will be true to those laws of quality that assure a good name and good will.*

Printed in the United States of America
Q-R-3

Library of Congress Cataloging in Publication Data

Biller, Ernest F.
    Career decision making for adolescents and young
adults with learning disabilities.

    Bibliography: p.
    Includes index.
    1. Learning disabilities--United States.
2. Vocational guidance--United States. 3. Career
education--United States. I. Title.
LC4705.B545   1987   371.9   86-14455
ISBN 0-398-05276-X

PREFACE

Career Decision Making for Adolescents and Young Adults with Learning Disabilities: Theory, Research and Practice, is organized into three parts following the introduction. Part One of the text (Chapters 1-3) is a compilation of the major career theories posited by psychologists and sociologists to account for the formation of career patterns and outcomes in American youth and adults. Part Two of this text (Chapter 4) details the research and analysis of fifteen learning disability follow-up studies with respect to this special population's educational and occupational attainment. Part Three (Chapters 5 and 6) includes a chapter on the practice of assessing career development and decision making, while the final chapter outlines a model for understanding and teaching career decision making to adolescents and young adults with learning disabilities.

I wish to thank Ellen Horn for her meticulous efforts in editing this text and for her great patience through the completion of the project.

For assistance in typing the manuscript, I wish to thank Janice and Gregg McCullough, Virginia Ernstmann, Debbie Marks and my wife, Judy Biller.

Finally. I wish to thank the tremendous support and encouragement of my family—Judy, Cindy, Jeff and Christine.

E.F.B.

INTRODUCTION

"THE LEARNING DISABILITY PREMISE"

Premise (prĕm´ĭs): "A proposition upon which an argument is based, from which a conclusion is drawn."

IN THE LATE 1960s American educators were witnessing a repositioning of Special Education that had the academic underachiever moving into the mainstream of the Special Education System with what were, at that time, unpredictable events. Specific Learning Disabilities (SLD), as a new category of special education, had influence beyond its numbers during these early years because it looked like the new kid on the block. No one knew how big this kid would be, how rough he or she would be, or how compromising this kid would be. On the other hand, the mildly mentally retarded category of Special Education, which dominated the ranks of school aged handicapped since before the beginning of the middle of the century, had its energies spent trying to maintain quality programs in the face of its own declining enrollments all the while its new cousin, learning disabilities, was doubling and tripling in student enrollment. What was the premise upon which this new kid on the block became accepted? What was the proposition upon which the argument that a child who falls significantly behind in his or her achievement can be considered handicapped? What was the basis for which the conclusion "academic retardation is cause for identifying a child as handicapped?" And what were the logical constants and fixed truths representing the concept "specific learning disability?"

It seems not only logical, but imperative, to ask these questions for in order to make appropriate recommendations regarding the career futures of these young people identified as having a "specific learning disability," we should be able to establish and validate the premise upon which this "condition" is predicated, as well as be able to pinpoint the logical constants and truths that have permitted this newest category of special education to expand so quickly and in such great numbers (from 792,213 SLD pupils in 1976-77 to 1,811,489 SLD students in 1983-84). The SLD premise and its validation, however, remain elusive. For instance, since the first national attempt to provide a common definition for learning disabilities in a 1966 National Institute of Health Task Force report, there have been at least 50 SLD related terms published and at least 38 definitions suggested to describe what we now refer to, under P.L. 94-142, as "specific learning disabilities" (Lerner, 1981). Further complicating this issue are results such as one United States Office of Education (USOE) sponsored research institute on SLD which concluded, in part, that under the 17 criteria most commonly used by schools to identify learning disabled students, over 80% of "normal" students could be classified as learning disabled by one or more definitions (Ysseldyke, 1982). Similarly, the final report of a USOE supported work group charged with the task of finding a valid and reliable model for determining discrepant academic achievement, resulted in the conclusion that no current model could be fully recommended (Reynolds, 1985). Considering the $1,135,145,000 spent on special education (1985 allocation) and the fact that SLD populations now represent 42% of the total special education population (USOE Seventh Annual Report to Congress on the Implementation of The Education of the Handicapped Act, 1985), it becomes a quite questionable practice that we allow this newer category of school, defined handicap, to continue operating without establishing a valid premise. During 1985 there was a USOE Special Education Task Force initiated by U.S. Secretary of Education, William Bennett, to directly address this growing SLD dilemma.

Ultimately, however, it will be up to the SLD professionals, school administrators, regular educators, and parents to chart and implement a logical course for serving academic underachievers. The greatest obstacle is to bring about the validation of the SLD category. Adelman and Taylor (1985) have aptly pointed out these obstacles in a recent issue of the *Journal of Learning Disabilities:*

> The field of learning disabilities is in a state of flux. Some people even question (unthinkingly, we believe) whether there is an LD field at all. Those of us who identify with the field do so because we believe there are individuals whose problems should be differentiated from others who have learning problems. That's what unites us. But that's seemingly about all that unites us. We argue about definition; we argue about theory; we argue about how certain data should be interpreted;

we argue about corrective interventions and we argue about future directions for the field (p. 422).

Yet, despite the unclear premise and the lack of validation for justifying the existence of learning disability as a handicapping condition, and the arguments that ensue and will continue to ensue over the "premise issue," our efforts to meet the legal mandates to serve these special persons, must and will continue. Furthermore, and in the nature of this text, we must accurately identify, and explain just what the long range implications are for the person who has been identified as having a learning disability so that appropriate school curricula can be developed.

CONTENTS

CAREER DECISION MAKING FOR ADOLESCENTS AND YOUNG ADULTS WITH LEARNING DISABILITIES

PART ONE

THEORIES OF CAREER BEHAVIOR

CHAPTER 1

CAREER BEHAVIOR THEORIES

Career (kə-rir'): "A chosen pursuit; life work"

Assumptions and History of
Career Behavior Study

IN ESTABLISHING the roots of a best-practice model for assisting SLD persons in the task of career decision making, two initial concerns must be addressed: (1) What is a desirable or positive occupational outcome? and (2) How do most people achieve these career outcomes? Addressing these concerns entails looking not only at how or what career choices a person makes, but also what factors influence one's career decisions over time. Answering concern number one can be accomplished quite directly, while explaining the varied theories of how careers are thought to form will take the greater portion of this chapter.

Recognizing that formulating any opinions about what constitutes a successful adult career outcome is contained in making "value judgements," it is nonetheless suggested here that there can be a "minimal career expectancy" mode. It would be hoped that all SLD persons who want to participate in remunerative employment would be able to do so and that satisfaction, whether financial or work-related, would be inherent in that employment. Included in this minimal occupational expectancy is the hope that the person with SLD could maintain his/her employment as long as desired, that is, would not be dismissed due to an inability to perform the job duties over time or be terminated because of social or attitudinal problems related to their learning disability. The maximum occupational expectation would be that all SLD persons could achieve whatever occupational goal a similarly statured, nonlearning, disabled person could achieve, over and above a particular job

5

related disability that with "reasonable accomodation" still could not be performed satisfactorily by virtue of the specific learning disability; for example, a nonreading adult desiring employment as a newspaper copy editor. With these "value based" occupational "expectancy" outcome parameters stated, the theoretical issues of how careers are formed is discussed. Brief discriptions of each area are presented first.

Career Formation Concepts: Career Choice, Development and Decision Making

The Historical Markers of Career Theory Development

Over the last 75 years the study of career behavior has encompassed three major focuses: (a) that making career decisions is a one time "matching" event (1900-1950), (b) that there are specific developmental career stages over the lifetime and they include a succession of career stage/tasks concerns (1950-present), and (c) that people invoke specific strategies or processes in making career decisions and are influenced in their career formation by the interaction between the person's career decisions and the environment's response to those decisions (1979-present). Theories or models associated with explaining specific occupational "one time matching decisions" are represented by two distinct categories: Trait/Factor Theory and Sociological Theory. Before presenting these career theories, a caution needs to be made about their practicality in guiding one's individual career life. This caution concerns the maturity of the career psychology field. Beginning in the early 1900s with the trait/factor model, and the midcentury origin of the developmental career behavior perspective, with the career decision-making theory only just recently emerging, it can be said that predicting adult career outcomes is far from a well developed and perfected science (Carkhuff, Alexik, & Anderson, 1967). When applying these career behavior theories to special populations, there is even greater need to exercise caution in generalizing their applicability and/or suitability (Osipow, 1975). However, the need to assist SLD individuals in the formation of their careers remains enough of a concern (ACLD, 1982), that finding a best practice approach is believed to be well worth the effort, despite the limitations inherent within this young field of career psychology. The alternative would be to do nothing or attempt to make career decisions for these young people, neither of which can really be deemed acceptable.

Trait/Factor Models of the Period 1900-1967

The basic premise underlying the trait/factor approach, when discussing career choice, is that individuals seek occupations with requirements that are consistent with their personality traits, that is, their vocational interests and aptitudes. One of the most well-known developers of the trait/factor career counseling approach, John Holland (1985), asserted that people choose work environments that are congruent with their personality types. In Holland's approach, career behavior is considered to be observable and measurable and thus can be guided. Some variations of the trait/factor approach, however, use inferred theoretical behavior constructs (Bordin, 1968; Roe, 1956) and thus are criticized for their lack of measurability. One aspect that most all trait/factor theorists have in common is that they focus on the person side of the person-situation match. The early proponents of the trait/factor approach include the original pioneer of the concept, Parsons (1909). These letter career psychologists' (Dawis & Lofquist) "work adjustment" theory of the trait/factor approach, has been used extensively in the field of vocational rehabilitation.

Sociological Theories of Career Choice: 1967-Present

In contrast to the above career trait/factor approach, but still in the career choice perspective, is the sociological perspective. The sociological viewpoint stresses the cultural and social determinants side of career choice and attainment. The sociological theory of career choice, according to Brown and Brooks (1984), stresses that "social class boundaries may either facilitate or truncate choice, but in any case, they act as a critical filter to the kind of information, encouragement and opportunities available to the individual. Sociological theorists believe that people are steered by socioeconomic factors toward occupational roles that match their social status" (p. 5).

Theories of Career Development: 1950-Present

In the early 1950s a number of career behavior theorists began to describe individual career formation, not so much in terms of making a singular career choice or a person-job match, but rather in the perspective that career formation is an ongoing process or evolution of career related choices. Career formation is thought of by the developmental career theorists as an unfolding of behaviors within a framework of career life stages over the life span. The principal pioneer of developmental career theory is Donald Super, (1951, 1957).

Theories of Career Decision Making: 1965-Present

Finally, there were also career behavior theorists such as Harren (1966) and Krumboltz (1979, 1986), who realized that the specific decisions individuals make, must be viewed in the perspective that career decisions, and the strategies utilized to make decisions, are enveloped in an ongoing interaction between self and environmental expectations. In order to fully understand individual career behavior, we must also understand the decision-making strategies and the outcomes that occur throughout each of the several life stages.

For illustrative purposes, models from each of the above areas of career choice, development, and decision making are described over the ensuing chapters in more detail. Recall that under the first area, career choice, there are two categories, trait/factor and sociological; therefore, examples will be given in this chapter representing each of these two perspectives.

Career Choice: Trait/Factor and Sociological

Each of these two areas, trait/factor and sociological, depicted under the career formation genre of "understanding the nature and determinants of career choice," represents both sides of the coin with reference to the what, why and how of career choice. The trait/factor perspective, in the examples cited here, is concerned primarily with studying the career choice behavior of the individual, while the sociological viewpoint stresses the cultural and social environmental determinants that influence career choices. It is obvious that one must consider each of the above two categories to obtain a global perspective about the nature of career choice.

Trait/Factor Models of Making Vocational Choices

Behavioral traits of individuals were at one time thought of as "enduring psychic and neurological structures located somewhere in the mind or nervous system" (Hogan, DeSoto, & Solano, 1977, p. 255). Based on this assumption, psychologists developed instruments and computer analytic methods that they thought could isolate, identify and classify specific behavior traits, such as one's intellect, aptitude and interests. By virtue of this process, the hypothesized concept of a behavioral trait also became known as a factor, primarily because of the factor analytic techniques used in the study of such traits (Brown, 1984).

Despite the earlier beliefs that traits reflected the innate properties of the individual, others have posited that traits are learned entities that have validity only with regard to a specific task or situation (Anastasi, 1983; Tyron, 1979). In other words, traits "are not underlying entities or causal factors but descriptive categories" (Anastasi, 1983, p. 177). The traits, whether innate or learned, of most interest to career psychologists are vocationally related interests and scholastic aptitudes (Brown, 1984). Each of these appear to be fairly stable traits, as well (Hogan, De-Soto, & Solano, 1977).

Extending the general study of traits, to the understanding of career choice determinants, has led to the formation of several propositions or statements within the trait/factor framework: (a) each person has a unique set of traits that have validity with reference to a specific task or situation; (b) occupations require that, in order to be successful, workers possess certain traits; (c) the choice of an occupation is a rather straightforward process, and matching person and job is possible; and, (d) the closer the match between personal characteristics and occupational requirements the greater will be the likelihood for productivity and satisfaction (Klein & Wiener, 1977). In the trait/factor perspective, errors in career choice can possibly result in job dissatisfaction, unsatisfactory job performance and misguided job changes. In addition, changes in the occupational environment resulting in a person-situation mismatch can also result in undesired job changes (Brown, 1984). Holland (1985) took the perspective that job satisfaction occurs when personality traits are congruent with the job environment. Maintaining an ongoing correspondence with self and the changing work environment, has been postulated by Dawis, Lofquist and Weiss (1968) in what has been referred to as the "Work Adjustment Theory." The Holland Theory is presented first under the trait/factor perspective of career choice determinants, followed by Dawis et al.'s "Work Adjustment Theory."

Holland's Theory of Vocational Choice

Holland (1985), in his most recent update on understanding the nature of making vocational choices, stated, "the intellectual roots of the theory [Holland's] lie mainly in the traditions of differential psychology—especially the interest measurement literature and of typologies of personality. The interest literature provided the stimulus for assuming that people with different interests and in different jobs were in fact different people with different life histories." Holland further noted that he saw a typology of persons and occupations as a useful way to organize the vast information acquired about people and occupations.

More specifically, Holland stated that his theory of vocational choices provided explanations for three common and fundamental questions: (a) What personal and environmental factors lead to satisfying career decisions, involvement and achievement, as well as indecision? (b) What personal and environmental characteristics lead to stability or change in the kind of level and work a person performs over a lifetime? and (c) What are the most effective procedures for assisting people with career problems? Finally, Holland stated that the primary concern of his theory "is to explain vocational behavior and suggest some practical ideas to help young, middle-aged, and older people select jobs, change jobs and attain vocational satisfaction" (p. 1).

Components of Holland's Theory of Vocational Choice

The basic tenets of the Holland theory is that each individual to some degree resembles one of six basic personality types: (a) **Realistic** — prefers explicit, ordered or systematic manipulation of objects and tools, while having an aversion to educational or therapeutic activities, (b) **Investigative** — prefers activities that involve the observational, symbolic, systematic, and creative investigation of physical, biological and cultural phenomena, while having an aversion to persuasive, social, and repetitive activities, (c) **Artistic** — prefers ambiguous, free, unsystematized activities that entail the manipulation of physical, verbal, or human materials to create art forms, while having an aversion to ordered activities, (d) **Social** — prefers to act in manipulation of others to inform, train, develop, cure or enlighten, while being adverse to systematic activities involving materials, tools or machines, (e) **Enterprising** — prefers manipulation of others to attain organizational goals or economic gain but is adverse to observational, symbolic and systematic activities — such tendencies lead in turn to acquisition of leadership and persuasive competencies and deficits in scientific competencies, and (f) **Conventional** — prefers activities that involve explicit, ordered, systematic manipulation of data, such as keeping records, filing materials and so forth, while is adverse to ambiguous, free, exploratory activities (Holland, 1985). Within this six part personality typology, Holland asserted that the more one resembles any given type, the more likely one is to manifest some of the behaviors and traits related to that type (Weinrach, 1984). Similarly, there are six types of work environments described by the people who occupy them, for example, the work environment of a school teacher is different from the office environment of a file clerk.

Using these typologies to explain career choice behavior, Holland (1973) stated that "persons search for environments that will let them exercise their skills and abilities, express their attitudes and values and take on agreeable problems and roles. . . . A person's behavior is determined by an interaction of his environment" (p. 4). With respect to using the theory in applications with special populations, Holland (1985) concluded that "the roles of social class, special advantage or disadvantage, intelligence, and special aptitudes are incorporated only indirectly in the typology, so these personal and environmental characteristics must also be weighed" (p. 120).

Work Adjustment Theory: Dawis and Lofquist

The essential component of this trait/factor theory is that "each individual seeks to achieve and maintain correspondence with his environment" (Dawis et al., 1968, p. 3). According to Brown's (1984b) interpretation of the theory, "correspondence occurs when the individual and the environment are corresponsive—that is, the needs of the individual are met, and the individual meets the demands of the work environment. Correspondence is not the result of a one-time match but is rather a dynamic process because both the needs of the individual and the demands of the job change. If correspondence is maintained, the result is job tenure" (p. 23). Furthermore, if the individual's work-related needs change, and they are not met, job dissatisfaction occurs; if the demands of the job change, but the individual no longer meets the ability requirements to perform under the new job requirements, the result is employer dissatisfaction and employee termination. With regard to applying this theory to special populations, it should be noted that the Dawis and Lofquist Theory of Work Adjustment has been used extensively in vocational rehabilitation settings across the country with positive results.

Career Choice: Sociological Models

As noted earlier, the essential difference between a sociological perspective on the determinants of career choice and that of the trait/factor models is that of its sole focus on the environmental conditions influencing choice. In this perspective it is believed that people are steered by socioeconomic factors toward occupational roles that match their social status (Brown & Brooks, 1984).

In contrast to career behavior psychologists, such as Holland, who emphasize the individual differences of persons for career prediction, sociologists are more apt to view work and the selection of it as a major variable in the analysis of the larger framework of family, social deviance, race and technological change (Hotchkiss & Borow, 1984). The social role of worker, therefore, is studied by the sociologist with respect to a broad category of concerns, such as occupational mobility, comparative work across cultures, the occupational structure as a social hierarchy, the measurement of occupational status and the occupational socialization process, to name a few. Essentially, none of the sociological viewpoints about work have evolved with the specific goal of assisting persons in making a career choice. Instead, sociologists stress the ways in which the current of institutional life shape the career behavior of individuals (Hotchkiss & Borow, 1984). By far the most comprehensive amount of emphasis on work by sociologists has been in the area of the status-attainment framework, according to the above authors.

Status-Attainment Models: Their Influence On Career Choice

Based on a combination of early surveys during the 1940s, a graded scale of occupational levels was developed by Duncan (1961) to describe the relative positions (prestige) of occupations. The scale is commonly referred to as Duncan's Socioeconomic Index (SEI). The publication of Blau and Duncan's (1967) *The American Occupational Structure* outlined for the first time a systematic procedure for describing and evaluating the process by which individuals attained their respective levels (position on the SEI) of career status. To illustrate how relative prestige rankings of occupations relates to a total classification system for equating social class position, a table (1) representing U.S. Census data for males by income, education and traditional social class labels is shown. Used to rank the occupational classifications in the following table is a variation of Duncan's SEI, called Bogue's (1969) Index of Socioeconomic Achievement (SEA) Scale, which delineates a relative measure of inequality among occupations by using a ratio scale, with a zero point and equal intervals, which allows the absolute and relative differences between occupational categories to be examined.

TABLE 1

OCCUPATIONAL CLASSIFICATIONS AND RELATED SES COMPARISONS

Occupational classifications	SEA	Income*	Education**	Traditional class labels used by social scientists and journalists
Professional, technical and kindred workers	39	$12,518	16.5	Upper and Upper-
Managers, officials, and proprietors, excluding farm	37	12,721	13.0	Middle Classes
Sales workers	29	10,650	13.2	Lower-Middle Class,
Clerical and kindred workers	26	9,124	12.6	White-Collar Class
Craftsmen, foremen, and kindred workers	27	9,627	12.1	Working Class, Blue-
Operatives and kindred workers	23	7,915	11.3	Collar Class, Upper-Lower Class
Service workers, excluding private household	20	7,111	12.1	
Private household workers	14	n.a.	n.a.	Low-Income Group,
Farmers and farm managers		4,308	11.9	Poverty Class, Lower
Laborers, except farm		6,866	10.0	Class, Lower-Lower
Farm laborers, foremen	12	3,752	8.1	Class

* 1971 Data: *Current Population Reports,* series P-60, no. 85, Table 55.
**Education is years of school completed by employed males twenty-five to sixty-four years old in March 1972, from U.S. Bureau of the Census, "Educational Attainment: March 1972," *Current Population Reports, series P-20, no. 243, Table 4.*

Once this framework for measuring occupational prestige was formulated, it became necessary to describe how individuals attain the various occupational levels that they do. Blau and Duncan (1967) expressed a theory of career status attainment using the statistical conventions of path analysis. In its original form, the Blau and Duncan status-attainment model is outlined by Hotchkiss and Borow (1984) as follows:

> In its most parsimonious form, the status-attainment model postulates simply that the social status of one's parents affects the level of schooling achieved, which in turn affects the occupational levels that one

achieves. An informal path diagram of this idea is (Duncan, Featherman & Duncan, 1972): parental status — schooling — occupational status. In this view, schooling is seen as an intervening variable between parental status and one's own occupational status. Thus, although education is one of the indicators of status, it is not parallel to other statuses; it plays a functional role in a model of process that occurs over time (p. 142).

At about the same time Blau and Duncan (1967) had presented their ideas on status attainment, Sewell, Haller and Portes (1969) published follow-up data from a sample of Wisconsin students that had been observed since 1957. This follow-up account of Wisconsin high school students expanded the original Blau-Duncan attainment model by including additional data on cognitive functioning, academic performance and social-psychological processes.

Shown in Figure 1 is a diagram of the expanded Blau and Duncan model using the variables added by Sewell and colleagues in describing the Wisconsin follow-up study.

Figure 1. Path Diagram of the Original Wisconsin Model of Status Attainment*

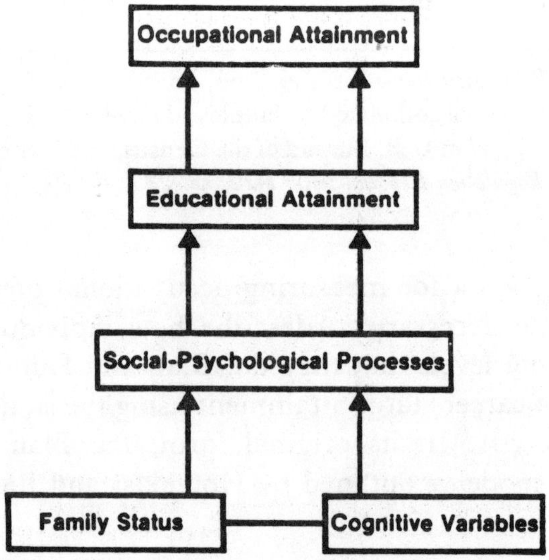

Adapted from Hotchkiss & Borow (1984) in Sociological Perspectives on Choice and Attainment, in Brown and Brooks, Career Choice and Development, Jossey-Bass Publisher.

The set of variables labeled social-psychological processes include educational and occupational aspirations of youth before leaving high school, parental encouragement to attend college, teacher encouragement to attend college and peer plans to attend college. Hotchkiss and Borow (1984) have referred to this parental and teacher encouragement and peer plans as examples of significant-other (SO) influences.

Summary and Review of Status-Attainment Studies

Reworking the data from earlier status-attainment research follow-up, Jencks et al. (1979) have presented some important findings within the status-attainment framework.

Nature of Jencks' Study and Findings

The Jencks et al.'s (1979) review was primarily concerned with ascertaining determinants of individual success within the existing economic system. More specifically, the Jencks et al. study was an effort to assess the impact of family background, cognitive skills, personality traits and years of schooling on occupational status. To accomplish this, Jencks et al. analyzed eleven different major surveys that studied the statuses of individuals as they moved through their education and work careers. Primarily, Jencks et al. investigated the relationship between personal characteristics and economic success among individuals aged 25-64. The study did not try to provide a complete picture of the determinants of individual success, but, rather, aimed to assess the effects of a person's characteristics when that person entered the labor market. As stated above, family background, cognitive skills, personality traits, and years of schooling were the four personal characteristics which were the focus in the Jencks et al. study. Brief definitions of the four characteristics or criteria are presented prior to summarization of the Jencks et al. study findings.

Definitions of the Jencks et al. Areas of Study

Occupational Status: Based on Duncan's (1961) Socio-Economic Job Status Index, an occupation's rating or score depended on the percentage of people working in the occupation who had completed high school and the percentage with incomes of $3,500 or more in 1950. A U.S. Census developed continuum of employment levels of unskilled to professional would roughly equate the Duncan scale, but in categorical rather than continuous data form. Since an occupation's (Duncan or

U.S. Census) score depends on its educational requirements, education inevitably influences a worker's score. Not just a methodological artifact, the above relationship reflects a social phenomenon; the average education of an individual in a given line of work is closely related to the **cognitive complexity** and desirability of the work. Duncan's scale runs from 0-96, roughly a one-point change in a person's Duncan score had the same effect on their "general (occupational) standing," as a 1.3 percent change in income.

Family Background: For the purpose of the Jencks et al. (1979) study, family background was defined as everything that makes individuals with one set of parents different from other individuals with a different set of parents. Principally, Jencks et al. used, as a measure of familiar influence, the degree of resemblance between brothers. Explaining this, Jencks et al. stated:

> Such resemblance can be due to common genes, common environment, or the influence of one brother on the other. But unless brothers deliberately become unlike one another, resemblance between siblings sets an upper limit on the explanatory power of their common environment and common genes . . . background characteristics seem to exert appreciable effects on both occupational status and earnings even among men with the same test scores and education" (p. 10).

Cognitive Measures: Note that most all status-attainment studies of the nature reviewed have relied on a single cognitive test score, usually designed to measure academic "aptitude" or "intelligence." There have been some studies, however, which administered cognitive tests that covered as many as 50 differing areas of academic ability. Using the results of the "multidimensional testing" study, Jencks et al. (1979) were able to explore the effects of different adolescent cognitive skills in greater detail than had been done in the past.

Personality Measures: Included in the Jencks et al. (1979) reviewed surveys were measures such as teacher ratings of high school respondents. The assessment tools included the *Thematic Apperception Test* (TAT), as well as specially designed assessment inventories to fit the needs of the individual studies. Questions were also elicited from students to describe their high school behavior, with the idea that such behavior presumably reflects differences to some extent.

Education: In the Jencks et al. (1979) study a primary interest was determining the highest grade of school or college completed. Attention was also given to differences in respondent's experiences while they were in school, particularly what kind of curriculum was followed and the institution attended.

Results and Explanation of Jencks et al.'s Report

Family Background

Family background accounted for 48% of the variance in attained occupational status and 15 to 35% of the variance in earnings among those aged 25-64 in the early 1970s. Apparently, those who do well economically, most likely, owe almost half of their occupational advantage and 55 to 85% of their earnings advantage to family background.

Cognitive Ability

The following summary statements can be made concerning the effects of cognitive ability, according to the Jencks et al. (1979) study:

a. Tests of academic ability predict economic success better than other tests. Tests that do not correlate highly with academic ability correlate poorly with one another and with later educational and economic success. Tests covering a wide range of academic abilities predict economic success better than tests covering a single ability. The academic ability factor explains 37.1% of the variance in education and 27.0% for occupational status.

b. Tests given as early as sixth grade appear to predict educational attainment, occupational status and earnings as well as tests given later suggesting that "it is not cognitive skill per se that affects later success. The stable motivations and aptitudes that lead to the development of cognitive skills also affect later success" (Jencks et al., 1979, p. 86).

c. Adolescents with more ability are successful partly because they possess family advantages that affect both their ability and their adult success.

d. Adolescents with greater academic ability succeed economically to a considerable degree because they are selectively encouraged to have higher aspirations and to attend school longer.

e. Even among people whose background, personality and schooling do not differ, those with high test scores are worth somewhat more to employers who hire, fire and pay them.

Summarizing the above findings on cognitive ability as it relates to family background, Jencks et al. (1979) noted that

> We have shown that, for example, a nontrivial fraction of background's effect on success derives from the fact that background affects cognitive skills. But it is not clear that cognitive skills are, or should be, synonymous with "merit." A large vocabulary seems to help a man get through school, and getting through school clearly helps him enter a high-status occupation and earn more money than most men do. But this does not prove that a man "needs" a large vocabulary in order to perform competently in most highly paid jobs (p. 83).

In explaining how academic ability exercises its influences on an individual's schooling, Jencks et al. (1979) noted that, "adolescents with high scores are more likely to be in a college curriculum, more likely to receive high grades, more likely to report that their parents want them to attend college, more likely to say their friends plan to attend college, more likely to discuss college with teachers and more likely to have ambitious educational plans" (p. 106). Finally, in summary of the occupational implications of cognitive ability, Jencks et al. (1979) stated that

> The most important reason why individuals with high scores end up in occupations of higher status than individuals with low scores is that they get more schooling . . . however, that unless these students (high scores) get more schooling, they derive little occupational benefit from their ability . . . the findings are similar with regard to other characteristics measured in high school. Curriculum placement, grades, encouragement, plans and personality explain why adolescents with higher ability get higher status jobs largely because they explain why adolescents with higher ability go to school longer. After controlling education, these characteristics explain very little of the effect of ability on occupation (p. 112).

Personality and/or Noncognitive Traits

While many persons assume that noncognitive characteristics such as "ambition," "good attitudes," "high aspirations," or "good judgement" are associated with educational and economic success, few studies have validated the hypothesis. The Jencks et al.'s (1979) report stated that:

> . . . individuals possess stable personality characteristics that influence economic success. Measures of personality based on high school student's self-assessments, personal behavior, attitudes, and ratings by others are related to subsequent occupational statuses and earnings, even after we control for family background and cognitive ability. . . .

Talent [one of the reviewed surveys] data suggest that the social skills or motivations which make a student see himself as a leader and hold positions of leadership in high school are critical to later achievement. . . . We found little support for the idea that any single personality trait is of critical importance in determining individual success. Rather, each trait that influences success seems to have a small and for the most part separable effect. In general, the personality characteristics that predict success are not closely tied to family status or to cognitive ability (p. 156-157).

Education Findings

The economic outcomes of schooling depend on three factors: (a) the level of schooling attained, (b) the measure used to assess economic success, and (c) the population studied. Accordingly, the following outcomes of the effects of education on occupational status are noted with regard to using the range and standard deviations of Duncan's (1961) occupational status index. Jencks et al. (1979) concluded that:

Completing high school rather than elementary school is associated with an occupational advantage of close to half a standard deviation among men 25-64 years old. Among men from the same homes and with the same test scores, the expected advantage is only a quarter of a standard deviation. The occupational benefits of secondary education do not appear to vary systematically by cohort or test score. The benefits are larger for whites than nonwhites and larger for nonfarm sons than for farm sons. Completing college rather than high school (only) is associated with an occupational advantage of more than one standard deviation among 25-64 years olds. The advantage is almost the same when family background and test scores are controlled. Nonwhites and farmers' sons appear to benefit more than others if they complete college. The occupational advantage of completing college does not vary systematically with test scores (p. 87).

Final Summary of the Jencks' (1979) Study

Overall, the following points may be made:

1) Family background explained 48 percent of the variance in occupational statuses.
2) With all aspects of family background controlled, a one standard deviation difference in adolescent test performance is associated with an occupational difference of one quarter to one third of a standard deviation (Duncan's scale) in all of the studied samples. "From

    60-80 percent of the effect of adolescent cognitive skills on adult oc-
cupational status derives from the fact that adolescent cognitive
skills affect educational attainment" (Jencks et al., 1979, p. 219).

3) Using four different measures of personality trait assessment,
teacher ratings, self-assessments, attitude measures, and reports of
actual behavior, it was concluded that "while no single, well-defined
trait emerged as a decisive determinant of economic success, the
combined effects of many different measures were typically as
strong as the combined effects of the different items that we used to
measure cognitive skills" (Jencks et al., 1979, p. 222).

    In adolescent groups, teacher ratings of tenth grader's executive
ability (planning, etc.) predicted adult earnings better than their
"industriousness." "About a third of this association derives from the
fact that both executive ability and earnings depend on background
and sixth-grade test scores. A third of the remainder is explained by
the fact that executive ability affects educational attainment"
(Jencks et al., 1979, p. 222).

4) In describing the association of education with occupational status,
it was found that " the highest grade of school or college he has completed is the best single predictor of his eventual occupational status" (Jencks et al., 1979, p. 222). Four years of secondary schooling
are worth an increase in occupational status of one half of a standard deviation. Four years of college are associated with increases of
more than one standard deviation. Overall, education explains
about 50 percent of the variance in occupational status.

A Recent Update by Jencks et al. (1983) or
Status Attainment

    More recently, Jencks, Crouse, and Mueser (1983) did an updated
comparison study on status attainment. Because of the extensive analysis on academic achievement factors, it is also included in this overview
of status attainment theory.

Validation on the Status Attainment Model: A Focus on
Abilities, Aptitudes and Aspirations

    Knowledge of the results of other follow-up studies that contrast the
Wisconsin model research analysis should lend or reject support for the
generalizability of the Wisconsin high school follow-up data. In this regard, Jencks et al. (1983) have provided such a validation. Summarized
below by Jencks et al. (1983) are their primary findings based on analyzed data from two other similar follow-up studies.

A 1972 follow-up of eleventh graders surveyed by Project Talent in 1960 yields results broadly similar to those reported by Sewell and Hauser for their Wisconsin follow-up and by Alexander, Eckland and Griffin for their EEO follow-up, suggesting that neither the geographic and educational restrictions of the Wisconsin survey nor the low response rate of EEO systematically biases their conclusions. The Talent data also provide more detailed information on teenagers' cognitive skills and educational aspirations than the Wisconsin and EEO surveys. The Talent data show that (1) conventional academic "aptitude" tests predict later success **less** accurately than academic "achievement" tests administered at the same time, (2) detailed measures of educational plans beyond high school predict later behavior more accurately than questions that merely ask high school students whether they plan to attend college, and (3) measures of how much money high school students hope or expect to earn have a very weak relationship to actual earnings (p. 3).

The Wisconsin, EEO and Talent Surveys Compared

The initial Explorations in Equality of Opportunity (EEO) sample covered tenth graders in predominantly white high schools with graduating classes of more than 20 throughout the nation in 1955. The initial Talent sample covered eleventh graders throughout the United States in 1960. The initial Wisconsin sample covered twelfth graders in Wisconsin high schools in 1959. The EEO follow-up took place 13 years after the respondents' expected high school graduation, when they were primarily 30 or 31. Data was obtained from 50 percent of the initial respondents; only 5 percent were not in civilian occupations at the time. The Talent follow-up took place 11 years after respondents' expected graduation when they were mostly 28 or 29, and obtained data from 88 percent of the initial respondents; all but 4 percent were out of school and in the civilian labor force. The Wisconsin follow-up took place seven years after respondents' expected high school graduation, when they were mostly 24 or 25, and obtained data on 87 percent of the initial respondents; 26 percent were still in school or the military.

Results of Education, Occupation and Earnings

Educational Attainment

According to Jencks et al. (1983), measures of parental socioeconomic status (SES) explained approximately 15 to 18 percent of the variance in education in all three surveys. Academic aptitude had a substantial effect on education in all three surveys, even with parental SES controlled. School grades also had a noticeable effect on education in all surveys, independent of academic aptitude, and friends' plans had an observable effect on education in all surveys, independent of parental SES, academic aptitude and grades. This effect persisted even with the individual's **own plans** controlled. **Parental preferences** had a lessor effect than **friends' plans** and a greater effect than **teacher discussions** in all three surveys.

A major difference between the three follow-up studies is that academic aptitude had a larger effect in the Talent study than in the Wisconsin or EEO. The relatively small coefficient of aptitude in the EEO sample may derive from the unreliability of the EEO test. The small coefficient in Wisconsin was less explainable according to Jencks et al. A second difference between the two surveys is that grades had less effect — and accounted for less of aptitude's effect — in Talent than in the other two surveys, perhaps because the Talent study had poor measures for grades. A final difference is that an individual's **own plans** had more impact on education when measured in twelfth grade (Wisconsin) than when measured in tenth or eleventh grade.

Occupational Status Comparisons

Occupational status was recorded when the majority of Wisconsin, Talent, and EEO sample respondents were seven, eleven, and thirteen years out of high school, respectively, and a difference that did not appear to have any significant effect on the differing study results. Education is by far the most important determinant of occupational status in all three surveys. Individuals with high SES parents, high aptitude scores, high grades, and college-bound friends all enjoy appreciable occupational status advantages. They do so however, only if they obtain more schooling than average. This can be interpreted as meaning that the relative importance of parental SES, aptitude, grades, friends, parents, teachers, and own plans is nearly the same for occupational attainment as it is for education attainment levels.

Income Attainment Findings

The Wisconsin, Talent, and EEO measures cover annual earnings 10, 11 and 12 years after graduation respectively. Wisconsin, thus, should have the smallest coefficients and EEO the largest. Despite this difference, however, the earnings differ more from study to study than the education or occupation findings. Controlling for aptitude did not significantly reduce the coefficients of the SES measures in any of the studies, implying, therefore, that high SES families did not increase their child's earnings primarily by providing them with enhanced cognitive skills.

Overview of Effects on Attainment as Predicted by Aptitude and Achievement

The Scholastic Aptitude Test (SAT), used by the Talent study, emphasizes vocabulary, reading comprehension and arithmetic reasoning, therefore the measure of academic aptitude was the total number of correct answers an eleventh grader gave on reading comprehension, vocabulary and arithmetic reasoning tests. Some psychologists, according to Jencks et al. (1983), have asserted that the best measure of academic aptitude is the general intelligence factor common to a diverse battery of mental tests that all require some degree of abstract reasoning. In the Talent sample, however, general intelligence was not the best predictor of later success. In fact, Jencks et al. reported a striking finding when they included all of the major aptitude measures into their analysis. Reading comprehension, vocabulary and arithmetic reasoning usually had negative coefficients, and these coefficients were frequently significant. This finding implied that there is an overestimate of the importance of the aptitude tests relative to other tests. Conversely, the tests that measured knowledge of English literature, social studies and mathematics usually had positive coefficients, suggesting that there is an underestimate of the impact of academic achievement on later success. Taken together, these findings imply that neither a conventional aptitude test that emphasizes reading comprehension, vocabulary and arithmetic reasoning, or a general intelligence measure is ideal for predicting adult success. Mathematics scores were by far the best predictor of education, occupation and earnings. English literature and social studies also had significant positive effects on education and occupation, though not on earnings. Scores in biological science, physical science, reading comprehension, vocabulary or arithmetic reasoning aptitude scores were not significant for any outcome. In analyses predicting female eleventh graders' future education, the results were equal to that of males, except that social studies scores were not significant for females. Among employed women, however, vocabulary had as much effect as mathematics on both occupation and earnings. In sum, mathematics achievement is the best predictor of educational attainment for both sexes even with one's college plans controlled, and social science and English literature scores continue to have significant effects for males while the aptitude tests do not.

Hypothesis for Superior Predictive Ability of Achievement Scores Over Aptitude

While Jencks et al. (1983) offered several possible reasons why aptitude scores were less predictive of adult success than achievement measures, their final hypothesis for the finding was that achievement predicts later success better than aptitude because achievement tests measure academic aptitude better than aptitude tests do. Jencks et al. explained this as follows:

> Most people define "aptitude" as ability to learn something. When we claim a test measures academic aptitude we are, therefore, claiming that it measures academic ability to learn the kinds of things schools try to teach. Neither aptitude nor achievement tests measure this ability directly. They do not, in other words, give students academic material to study and measure how much they can learn in a specified interval. For the most part, both aptitude and achievement tests measure how much students have learned over their entire life. The two kinds of tests differ largely in the kind of past learning they emphasize. Aptitude tests measure skills that someone has decided are necessary for mastering academic subjects. Achievement tests measure mastery of the subjects themselves. Since it is hard to tell what skills are necessary to master academic subjects, the best indicator of ability to master a subject is likely to be past mastery of it, at least among those who have had the opportunity to master it and have been motivated to do so.
>
> The rationale for aptitude testing is that opportunities and incentives to master academic subjects are evenly distributed, so that past achievement is not always a good indication of future achievement in a given area. This argument is only valid if, in fact, opportunities and incentives to acquire vocabulary, reading comprehension and arithmetic reasoning are more equally distributed than, say, opportunities or incentives to learn about Hamlet, the War of 1812 or the quadratic formula. While intuitively plausible, this assumption is hard to support empirically. Jencks and Brown (1975) showed, for example, that attending one Talent high school rather than another had no more and perhaps less effect on changes in knowledge of Social Studies between ninth and twelfth grade than on changes in Vocabulary, Reading

Comprehension and Arithmetic Reasoning. Similarly, Scarr and Yee (1980) found that growing up in one family rather than another had no more and perhaps less effect on adopted children's Achievement scores than on their Aptitude scores. Available evidence suggests, then, that we should be very cautious in assuming that conventional aptitude tests are less affected by variations in opportunity and motivation than conventional achievement tests. It follows that vocabulary, reading comprehension and arithmetic reasoning scores may not measure academic aptitude as well as past achievement in academic subjects does.

Whatever the explanation, it seems clear that investigators who rely exclusively on conventional IQ or aptitude tests to measure cognitive skills in adolescence will underestimate the importance of such skills (p. 12-13).

Summary of the Jencks et al.'s (1983) Comparison Survey

One unexplainable finding was that academic aptitude had less effect on education, and hence on later success, in the Wisconsin study than in the nationwide Talent study. This, according to Jencks et al. (1983), could be because Wisconsin's IQ device measured different skills from the Talent aptitude measure. It could be that Wisconsin's system of higher education was more accessible and attractive to lower scoring students than systems in other states. The Talent findings suggest that occupational plans are interchangeable with occupational aspirations and that adolescents' financial plans or aspirations are of little predictive value.

Finally, measures of academic achievement, especially in mathematics, seem to predict later success better than do conventional aptitude tests, primarily because achievement tests measure academic aptitude better than conventional aptitude tests do.

Summary of Career Choice Related Theories

Career guidance programs serving secondary and postsecondary students are largely a phenomenon of the twentieth century. Such programs had their beginnings with the work of Parsons (1909), whose major tenet in describing career formation was outlined in three major steps:

First, a clear understanding is needed of yourself, aptitudes, abilities, interests, resources, limitations and other qualities. Second, a knowledge of the requirements and conditions of success, advantages and disadvantages, compensation, opportunities and prospects in different lines of work. Third, true reasoning on the relations of these two groups of facts (Parsons, 1909, p. 5).

While other approaches to career development have been advanced over the last 80 years, much of its history in this century can be derived from Parson's early trait/factor conceptualizations (Herr & Cramer, 1979).

Taken together, the trait/factor and status attainment models of explaining career formation behavior depict a much clearer picture of how individuals end up in the occupations that they do. Even though these two perspectives still hold prominence in current explanations of career behavior, there have been criticisms that they fail to take into account the developmental dynamics of human behavior. Omitted from theories of trait/factor and status-attainment models of career behavior are the concerns for developmental growth patterns, and the influence such patterns could have on career behavior. In the following chapter a review of developmental career theory is presented.

CHAPTER 2

DEVELOPMENTAL CAREER THEORY

Develop (dĭ-věl´əp): To come to have gradually; acquire

A Definition of Career Development Theory

SINCE THE middle of the twentieth century, theories of career choice have taken the direction that it is a developmental phenomenon, which generally covers a period of six to ten years, beginning at about age 11 and ending shortly after age 17 or into young adulthood. The developmental approach is in direct opposition to an earlier belief that the career choice process is largely confined to a specific point in time in the life of the individual, such as at the end of the senior year of high school (Herr & Cramer, 1979).

Definitions of Career Development

Donald Super, a well known career psychologist, recommended to the National Vocational Guidance Association in 1951 a definition for career development to support the developmental perspective. This definition stated that guiding career development is "the process of helping a person to develop and accept an integrated and adequate picture of himself and of his role in the world of work, to test this concept against reality, with satisfaction to himself and to society" (p. 88).

Career development was later defined in the Joint Position Paper of the National Vocational Guidance Association and the American Vocational Association (1973) as the "total constellation of psychological, sociological, educational, physical, economic and chance factors that combine to shape the career of any given individual" (Hoppock, 1976, p. 6). Four of these career development factors have been defined by Hoppock according to how each may interact with an individual's changing needs and values to influence occupational choices:

1. Economic factors affect career choice by helping to determine the age at which a person ceases his or her formal education and enters the job market on a full-time basis. The economic cycle, moving from periods of prosperity to depression and back again, helps to affect the number and nature of the employment opportunities available at the time a person is looking for a job.

2. Education influences career choice by opening the doors to some careers that would otherwise be closed, by making an individual aware of jobs of which he/she had no previous knowledge, by affecting their interest in them, by providing exploratory experiences which lead the student to anticipate success or failure in specific activities.

3. Psychological factors influence career choice by helping to determine the extent to which one views one's own needs, accepts or depresses them, faces the realities of job opportunities and of his/her own interests, abilities and values, and thinks clearly about all these facts.

4. Sociological factors affect career choice by helping to determine the jobs with which a person is familiar, by way of his or her contacts with family and friends. The cultural milieu of the social group in which a person has been raised, most notably the family interaction patterns, and of the social group in which one currently identifies oneself helps to determine the jobs which will be considered socially acceptable and preferred.

In addition to Hoppock's four areas, factors of chance and physical requirements need to be addressed in relationship to making career choices.

Chance Factors in Career Development

Also associated with the above sociological perspective of career development are chance factors. The sociological view of career choice recognizes the role of happenstance in career development theory (Miller, 1983). According to this perspective, emphasis is put on the importance of environmental or situational circumstances beyond the individual's control as major determiners of career decisions. Miller further suggested that a broader perspective is needed to account for chance factors of career decisions and indicated that the life-span viewpoint would fit this need. Using a life-span perspective, Miller viewed vocational behavior as being affected by a range of life events, some of which are a result of chance factors such as social events, biological events, accidents and economic conditions.

Physical Factors in Career Development

Physical factors associated with career development can be divided into the physical surrounding of the work environment and the physical attributes of the individual. Just as individuals have various preferences for different kinds of work, they also have differing preferences for work environments.

Life Stage Career Development: Super's Perspective

Observing growth and development from the life-stage perspective aids understanding of life events as they are likely to occur, dynamically and in a multidirectional and interactive fashion. Critical to the understanding of the life-stage perspective is that successful outcomes of tasks completed in previous life-stages enhances ability to cope in later ones. Implications of viewing growth and development from this life-stage perspective is emphasized by Havighurst (1976):

> A developmental task is a task which arises at or about a certain period in the life of the individual, successful achievement of which leads to his happiness and to success with later tasks, while failure leads to unhappiness in the individual, disapproval by the society and difficulty with later tasks (p. 3).

Havighurst's formulation of developmental tasks occurring at certain life-stage periods have also been adopted by career development theorists such as Donald Super (1953, 1957, 1980). In a recent clarification of the developmental characteristics of career, Super (1982) stated:

> Buehler, Havighurst, and my colleagues and I used the concept of life stages to highlight the developmental tasks that tend to dominate at certain stages, such as those of childhood, adolescence and early adulthood. All concerned have recognized that accomplishing the typical developmental tasks of one life stage make it easier for the individual to cope with those encountered next, as social expectations and personal changes bring about new confrontations with the environment (p. 255).

It is within this dynamic, multidirectional and interactive life-stage process that career development is defined.

A Developmental Definition of Career

Career is most commonly referred to as the process of making a living via a particular occupation. In the *Concise Oxford Dictionary*, career is also defined as the "course or progress through life." Differentiating between the term career and occupation, Super (1980) noted that career is a sequence of occupational positions held over the course of a lifetime. Putting this distinction of career and occupation into the life-stage perspective, Super and Harris-Bowlsbey (1979) have formally defined career as:

> The sequence of positions occupied by a person throughout his preoccupational, occupational and post-occupational life in both work related and non-work related areas. A career may also be considered the sequential and simultaneous coping with developmental tasks in the various major roles played by most people over the life span: child, student, worker, spouse, homemaker, parent, leisurite, citizen and annuitant (p. 7).

Commenting on the belief that people play several roles simultaneously, and that these roles impact on each other, Super (1980) further stressed, as has Havighurst (1976), that "success in one [role] facilitates success in others, and difficulties in one role are likely to lead to difficulties in another, although success bought at too high a price may cause failure in another" (p. 287). And roles participated in are, in many instances, dictated by which life stage is occupied. At the age of ten, the major role is that of student; however, at age fifteen, the major role is still that of student, but now may also include that of a part-time worker. In addition to participation in a role because of its regarded tradition within a life stage, individuals may also occupy specific roles as an expression of their self-concept.

Career Roles and the Self-Concept

Formation of one's self-concept occurs as a result of interactions with others and of observing their reactions to our own behavior. Through this interaction, we acquire some idea of who we are; and this idea, or category of ideas, defines the self; and our self-concept is simply the opinion that we have of ourself (Mead, 1934). In adolescence, it is expected that individuals will define themselves, in part, by the career they expect to enter. Throughout each life stage, the individual is developing, specifying and putting into operation his or her self-concept (Super et al., 1963). Relating the construct of self-concept to the occupational role one may participate in, Super (1980) stated that "the more adequately, in self-perception and in that of others, the adolescent plays preoccupational roles, especially those of student and part-time worker, the more likely are successes in occupational roles" (p. 285). Also, according to

Winer, Cesari and Haase (1979), it is these self-percepts or observed facts, that the student uses in constructing his or her level of self-concepts, which also differ in their level of cognitive complexity. Further explanation of one's occupational role and self concept development can be described according to the major career life stages.

The Five Career Stages of Life

According to Super (1957), and as derived principally from Bueler's (1933) theory of life stage development, there are five career life stages: (a) growth in early childhood, (b) exploration in adolescence, (c) establishment in young adulthood, (d) maintenance in middle age, and (e) decline in retirement age. These stages are shown in Table 2 along with their corresponding substages of development. Description of these vocational life stages is summarized by Jordaan and Heyde (1979) as follows:

> The primary task of the first stage is to develop a picture of the kind of person one is and understanding of the nature and meaning of work. In the second stage, it is to crystallize, specify and implement a vocational preference. The third stage involves making a place for oneself in the chosen occupation and consolidating and improving one's position. The challenge of the fourth stage is to maintain and preserve the status one has achieved. Finally, the task of the fifth stage is to decelerate, disengage and cope with the problems of impending or actual retirement (p. 34).

All of these five life-stages are seen as being characterized by specific tasks the individual in that stage faces and which can be considered as prerequisite in success to the next stage (Super, 1983). Of specific interest is the particular life stage period of adolescence, identified here as the exploration stage.

Career Exploration Stage in Adolescence

Exploration refers to "activities, mental and physical, undertaken with more or less conscious purpose or hope of eliciting information about oneself or one's environment, or at verifying or arriving at a basis for a conclusion or hypothesis which will aid in choosing, preparing for, entertaining, adjusting to or progressing in an occupation" (Jordaan, 1963, p. 59). As noted in Table 2, under the **tentative** substage, it is necessary, as a prerequisite in making meaningful career decisions, to be aware of one's needs or values, interests and abilities, as well as the requirements of anticipated careers.

TABLE 2

SUPER'S CAREER LIFE STAGES

I. Growth Stage Birth to age 14	II. Exploration Stage Ages 15-24	III. Establishment Stage Ages 25-44	IV. Maintenance Stage Ages 45-65	V. Decline Stage 65-Death
Phase of general physical and mental growth	Exploring the world of work	Desire to enter a permanent occupation	Progression in an individual's selected occupation	Lessening of career involvement
A. Prevocational substage Birth to 3 1. No interest career choice. B. Fantasy substage Age 4-10 1. Fantasy is basis of career thinking. C. Interest substage Age 11-12 1. Career thought is centered on one's likes and dislikes. D. Capacity substage Age 13-14 1. Ability becomes the basis for career thought.	A. Tentative substage Age 15-17 1. Needs, interests, capacities, values, and opportunities become basis for tentative occupational decisions. B. Transition substage Age 18-21 1. Reality increasingly becomes a basis for vocational thought and action. C. Trial substage Age 22-24 1. First trial job is entered after the individual has made an initial career commitment.	A. Trial Age 25-30. A period of some occupational changes due to unsatisfactory choices. B. Stabilization Age 31-44. A period of stable work in a given occupational field.	A. Continuation in one's chosen occupation.	A. Deceleration Age 65-70 1. A period of declining vocational activity. B. Retirement Age 71-on 1. A cessation of vocational activity.

The information is adapted from Super et al., 1957.

Longitudinal research begun in the 1950s on factors related to career choice of high school youth culminated in results indicating that while the majority of boys in the ninth and twelfth grades expected to accept responsibility for their career choices, their use of appropriate resources, their knowledge of the world of work, and their plans for achieving their goals, were seriously deficient (Jordaan, 1977). Similar research findings on the lack of readiness of adolescents to cope with career choice basics within the exploration stage, have been reported by Gribbons and Lohnes (1968, 1969), Crites (1973), and Westbrook (1976). As summarized by Super (1977), adolescents during the exploration stage "should know the options available when entering high school; they should look ahead to a variety of choices in curricula offering different types of training institutions and occupations" (p. 297). The degree to which adolescents have achieved these tasks have been referred to as career maturity (Super, 1957, 1977, 1980, 1983). See Biller (1985 a, b) for the relationship of career maturity to SLD youth.

Self-Esteem and Career Development

Relationships between an adolescent's level of self-esteem and career development have been extensively studied by Super (1957, 1963, 1983) and by Korman (1966, 1967, 1970). Korman and Super have developed models to define the processes underlying the relationship between self-concept, self-esteem and career decision making status (Barrett & Tinsley, 1977). According to research reviewed by Barrett and Tinsley, high self-esteem individuals more often display greater commitment to career choices, feel more certain about their choices, and more frequently select more satisfying goals than low self-esteem students. Korman and Super each offer differing theories, however, regarding the manner in which self-esteem is associated with career development.

Summation of Super's Career Development Model

Super's model is truly a segmental model that incorporates many components thought to affect career formation. The best summary, however, is provided by Super (1984) himself:

Current Status. During the past decades, this career development model has been refined and extended. Differential psychology has made technical but not substantive, advances. Operational definitions of career maturity have been modified, and the model has been modified with them. Our understanding of recycling through stages in a minicycle has been refined, but the basic construct is essentially the same as when first formulated thirty years ago. Ideas about how to assess self-concepts have evolved as research has thrown light on their measurement, and knowledge of how applicable self-concept theory is to various subpopulations has been extended, but this segment of the model has not greatly changed. Life-stage theory has been refined but mostly confirmed by several major studies during the past decade. The career development model is now in the maintenance stage, but maintenance consists not of stasis but rather of updating and innovating as midcareer changes have been better recognized and studied (p. 217).

Combining the knowledge of trait/factor, status attainment and now the developmental aspects of career behavior, attention is now given to the topic of the strategies and styles people use in making career related decisions.

CHAPTER 3

CAREER DECISION MAKING THEORY

Decision (dĭ-sĭzh´ ən): The act of reaching a conclusion or making up one's mind.

Career Decision Making Models by Harren and Krumboltz

DECISION MAKING can be divided into the areas of knowledge of and commitment to the principles of decision making, ability to apply these and styles of decision making. Considered by some as basic personality traits (Super, 1983), decision making strategies are more similar to one's career development than specifically to one's readiness to make career decision (career maturity). Important in sound decision making skill is to know how to apply these skills to career related objectives. It does appear, however, that decision making competence is successful to the extent that the individual has developed an adequate planning orientation, makes use of adequate exploratory resources and is able to apply principles of decision making to specific career problems (Phillips & Strohmer, 1982). Two models of decision making are provided here, one by Harren (1979) which emphasizes the above mentioned styles of decision making, and a more global model of career decision making formulated by Krumboltz (1979).

Career Decision Making: The ACDM by Harren

As family influences interact within the bounds of a child's environment, there exists a dynamic threshold for the process of decision making to occur. This process, as viewed by Harren (1979), consists of four interactive stages: (a) awareness of self in particular environments,

(b) the career planning process, (c) commitment to a career preference, and (d) implementation of career choice. This choice process takes place within a particular time perspective and is also affected by one's degree of self-concept, decision making style, and self-autonomy (locus of control). Family influence on these personality variables can be illustrated in the manner in which the home environment affects self-differentiation and self-concept development which, in turn, advances or retards the decision making process (Hesser, 1982).

The model to assess decision making strategies was formulated by Harren (1966) to measure the stages that a college student had reached with regard to decisions about the selection of a college major and an occupation using a test known as the *Vocational Decision Making Q-Sort* and later renamed the *Vocational Decision-Making Checklist* (VDC). In use, the VDC revealed the occurrence or significant progress in career decision making for students participating in a number of instructional and counseling situations (Buck & Daniels, 1985). Based on yet further analysis, the VDC was again renamed the *Assessment of Career Decision Making* (ACDM) (Buck & Daniels, 1985).

The roots of the original decision making model by Harren and of the current ACDM are grounded in Tiedeman and O'Hara's (1963) belief about career decision making being able "to link the person to career through concepts of personality and individual responsibility" (Tiedeman & Miller-Tiedeman, 1984, p. 11). In their formulations of career, Tiedeman and O'Hara chose Erickson's (1959) psychosocial theory of ego identity as the developmental framework for understanding the many differentiations and reintegrations individuals experience during career formation. According to Tiedeman and Miller-Tiedeman, differentiation commonly occurs in the process of considering a choice. As such, experiencing a choice invokes the beginning of rational differentiation, that is, "the individual becomes aware that his or her present situation is unsatisfactory or is likely to become unsatisfactory" (p. 287). The Tiedeman and O'Hara theory on decision making is one of "how people decide, not of what they choose" (Tiedeman & Miller-Tiedeman, 1984, p. 301).

Building off of this Tiedeman and O'Hara decision making framework, Harren, in the current ACDM, condensed the eight decision making styles reported by Dinklage (1969) into three decision making styles: "Rational (originally called 'Planning'), Intuitive and Dependent" (Buck & Daniels, 1985, p. 41). The basic purpose of the three styles is to operationalize a way to ascertain the strategy or combination of strategies a student uses in making decisions.

Description of the Rational, Intuitive, and Dependent Decision Making Styles as Provided by Buck and Daniels (1985)

The **Rational** style refers to the degree to which a student makes a realistic appraisal of self and the situation when making decisions. The highly Rational decision maker makes decisions deliberately and logically, based on the information available.

The **Intuitive** decision maker addresses attention to present feelings and emotional self-awareness in making decisions. Those who are highly Intuitive decision makers use fantasy, feelings and imagination as the basis for decision making rather than a logical evaluation of available information. Similar to the Rational type, the Intuitive also takes responsibility for his or her decisions.

The third type of decision maker, the **Dependent,** is represented by a lack of willingness or capability to take responsibility for decision making. The highly Dependent decision maker is heavily influenced by the expectations and desires of authorities and peers. They will also actively seek out significant others to make their decisions for them. Characteristics of the Dependent decision maker are noted by passiveness, complaint, a high need for social approval and a view of the world as manifesting restricted or limited options. While this style may reduce the tension associated with decision making, it is also most likely to result in a lack of personal satisfaction.

Overall, these decision making styles define the strategies that people incorporate to approach and resolve important decisions. Measurement of these styles reflect reported feelings at one point in time and thus, can be different at different points in one's career life span.

Career Decision Making: Krumboltz's Social Learning Theory

According to Mitchell and Krumboltz (1984), the Social Learning Theory (SLT) of career decision making is "designed to address the question of why people enter particular educational programs or occupations, why they may change educational programs or occupations at selected points in their lives" (p. 238). Furthermore, the SLT examines the impact on career decision making process of such factors as genetic predisposition, environmental conditions and events, learning experiences and cognitive, emotional and performance responses and skills. Each of these factors contributes to all career decisions made, however, the varied combinations of interactions of the factors produce the multitude of different career choices that different individuals make (Mitchell & Krumboltz, 1984). In summary of the SLT of career decision making, Mitchell and Krumboltz have stated:

> The social learning theory of career decision making can be used to recognize and predict environmental conditions and events that are likely to provide learning experiences that will either foster or inhibit the career planning of individuals. The theory does not advocate any one particular sequence of career-relevant activities, as do many developmental models of career choice. It is recognized that there are many routes to successful career planning, where successful is defined as the route which leads to satisfaction for the individual. When individuals or groups perceive the learning experiences or opportunities that exist in their environment as unfair or discriminatory, they may undertake to change those factors in their environment, either through individual or collective action. Such action in the United States has resulted in, among other things, affirmative action legislation, and some shifts in conventional values regarding occupations (for example, emphasis on low-stress work environments to promote physical and mental well-being).
>
> The social learning theory of career decision making suggests that, to promote maximal career development of all individuals, each individual must have the opportunity to be exposed to the widest possible array of learning experiences, regardless of race, gender or ethnic origin (p. 256).

It is important to note that Krumboltz, Scherba, Hamel and Mitchell (1982) have developed programs to assist in making **Rational** decisions.

Summary, Comparisons, and Critique of the Presented Career Formation Theories

Career Choice: Trait/Factor Models of Holland, Dawis and Lofquist

Characteristics of the Holland, Dawis and Lofquist trait/factor related theories, "is that each individual possesses certain psychological traits that are inhibited or develop as a result of person-environment interaction. . . . Satisfactory performance results in positive feedback and need fulfillment. The task of occupational choice making then, is to match persons to jobs, so that individual needs will be met and satisfactory job performance will result" (Brown, 1984b, p. 3). The Dawis and Lofquist Work Adjustment Theory asserts that job changes occur when either the job is being performed unsatisfactorily or the individual's needs are not being met.

Some of those concerns expressed on behalf of the use of trait/factor models of career choice is they have failed to consider and define sufficiently the breadth of variables that affect the occupational choice-making process (Brown, 1984b). Also noted by Brown as a weakness of the trait/factor models is the failure to deal adequately with the choice-making process itself. A major weakness of the Dawis and Lofquist model is that it does not explain the developmental process that applies to the entire life span. In summary, Brown (1984a) stated that "in its current state, the trait and factor models cannot stand alone as an explanatory system for occupational choice making and has not been reconciled with the career development model" (p. 319).

Sociological Perspective of Career Choice: Status-Attainment Theory

Sociological perspectives on career choice are not intended to be guiding principles for practicing career psychologists or counselors. Nor do they try to analyze the psychological processes that individuals go through while forming their careers. Because the sociological perspective tends to explain the complex variables that affect career choices, it cannot be totally criticized for its lack of focus on the "how" of career choice.

Clearly, education obtained plays a key role in affecting the level of occupation achieved, although it is less significant for income level. Also significant is the influence of career expectations held during the last years of high school on career attainments after leaving school, thus supporting the need for quality career guidance programs. Significant others, such as teachers, peers and parents meaningfully influence the development of career expectations of youth, but parents are particularly influential. Parent involvement in career guidance programs seems quite apparent as a need for occupational mobility. Hotchkiss and Borow (1984) concluded that "the chief contribution the sociological perspective can make to career guidance is to expand its recognition of complex societal and demographic influences on career choice and outcomes" (p. 167).

Career Development: Super's Model in Review

Super's model is considered by other career theorists to be the most comprehensive of all career behavior models. The model makes reference to individual differences that unfold over the life span but includes the tasks that each stage requires depending on the role required of that stage. Also included in the model are concepts of readiness for career decision making, as well as outlining the necessary steps to take beyond the readiness levels. A most important contribution is the concern for the formation of self-concept in establishing one's career identify as life stage development evolves. The criticism of the Super Model is that he has yet to fully integrate all of the parts of the model so that full understanding and implementation can occur. An attempt by Biller (1985b) to integrate all of the components should be reviewed by the reader as it pertains specifically to persons with SLD. Brown (1984a), stated that Super's model holds center stage with Holland's model, "however, of all available models, Super's holds the greatest promise of providing an ideal standard for the processes involved in career development" (p. 329). In an overall summary and evaluation of Super's model, Osipow (1975) has stated the following:

> The theory [Super's] is a well-ordered, highly systematic representation of vocational maturation. It has the virtues of building upon aspects of the mainstream of developmental psychology and personality theory and demonstrating how those two streams can come together to clarify behavior in one major realm of human activity. . . . In its current state, the theory has considerable utility for both practice and research in vocational psychology.
>
> Most of the research reported on Super's theory supports his model. The developmental aspects of the theory are well documented, though certain details have been modified as a result of empirical findings such as the specific timing of developmental tasks. . . . The data with respect to . . . self-concept generally agrees with the theory. . . . The future prospects for this approach to career psychology appear to be promising. Still needed are better ways to integrate economic and social factors which influence career decisions in a more direct way than the events described by the theory currently do, as well as to continue the development of specific and rigorous formulations about aspects of career decisions and ways to bring about appropriate behavioral changes which will facilitate [the development of] vocational maturity (p. 222).

Finally, in criticism of most typical career education curriculums, Super (1984) concluded:

> this is no place to attempt to develop the details of a sounder of career education based on career development theory, but such a program would recognize individual differences in career development and

avoid lockstep curricula; it would seek to foster curiosity (and thus exploratory behavior), autonomy and time perspective in the elementary years, at the same time that it exposed children to a variety of adult role models (pp. 223-224).

Career Decision Making Models: Harren's ACDM and Krumboltz's SLT

The concept of Harren's ACDM provides the means to provide a measurable definition of factors involved in the career decision making process. The ACDM measures a student's satisfaction with and adjustment to school, progress in the selection of both a major and an occupation and use of career decision-making strategies. The ACDM, according to Buck and Daniels (1985) is intended for use with adolescents and adults, particularly college enrolled adolescents and young adults. The ACDM does not have norms for applicability with nonstudents. Reading difficulty is set at a sixth grade level. Summarizing a number of studies lending to a prediction about the technical aspects of the ACDM, Buck and Daniels stated that "evidence of the ACDM's reliability and validity is extensive and adequately establishes the psychometric properties of the scales" (p. 73).

Career Decision Making: Krumboltz's Theory in Review

Enhancing many of the ideas of social learning theory, while at the same time deviating from the SLT concepts, the Krumboltz model has not had wide influence on career formation thinking or practice. A major weakness is that it does not take into consideration the developmental processes thought to influence career decision making. Based on this weakness, Brown (1984a) stated that "it would be difficult to construct a model of normative behavior and thus design career development programs based on the model" (p. 332). Career counseling materials that would be helpful to the same degree as have those developed by Holland and Super, have not yet been adopted for use with the Krumboltz decision making theory (Brown, 1984a).

Summation of Career Theories from Chapters 1-3

The framework within which each of the career formation theories has been presented was based on an approximate historical continuum consisting of: (a) the years 1900-1950 being a period of focus on career choice as a one time event in a person's career life, (b) the period 1950-

1965 representing the emergence of a developmental stage perspective on how careers are formed, and (c) the period from 1965 to the present representing explicit models describing specific career decision making processes.

Within the first phase, 1900-1950, the trait/factor approach as exemplified by Parsons (1909) posited a simple match between person and occupation would lead to a job satisfaction. Holland's (1959, 1973, 1985) derivation of the trait/factor concept led to a much more comprehensive and practical usage of the matching theory construct for obtaining job satisfaction. Dawis, Lofquist and Weiss (1968) added to the trait/factor concept by demonstrating the "dynamic" aspects of career choice when considering the need to maintain a correspondence between a changing work environment and the individual.

Beginning a second phase of career formation viewpoint (1950-1965) was the acknowledgement that career formation is not a "one time event" but, rather, takes place over time and in stages, with respective tasks to be completed at each stage. At any one stage, a "minicycle" of stages can occur equating the longer term cycle of growth, exploration, establishment, maintenance and decline. Inherent in the developmental perspective is the idea that by successful completion of the growth stage, readiness or maturity for making career decisions is adequate in order to benefit from the exploration stage learnings that will take place. The thread that weaves through this developmental concept of career is that the individual has an ongoing and dynamic identity as a result of their stage development. Often referred to as "self-concept," it has been suggested that it is through the stating of a vocational preference that individuals express one of the dimensions of their self-concept. This expression is also referred to as "crystallizing" a career choice, and individuals with clouded self-concepts or with a dimension of self-concept that is negatively formed can have interference with the ability to formulate (crystallize) a tentative career objective. The phase following crystallizing a career choice(s) is the process of implementation of career choice and then preparation for that career choice. While these events are often construed within a time frame of the adolescent years, they can, and do, occur throughout the adult life span.

Finally, the actual task of having to make decisions is only of recent career behavior study (1965-present). One approach, Harren's ACDM, deals directly with identifying how people go about the actual process of making decisions with the idea that one decision-making style is more advantageous than another, for example, a Rational type would make a better decision maker than a Dependent one. Knowing this, an individual can be counseled about the possibility of whether or not his or her decisions are well formed and executed.

Fortunately, career decision-making models such as the social theory of career decision making have formulated behavioral models which assist individuals who may be faulty decision makers. One of the strengths of the behavioral model is that it has always put more emphasis on how to correct a problem within the actual environment when it occurs, thereby providing solutions that other theories have only been able to classify as a problem. Krumboltz's decision-making model falls within this behavioral utility and in time should provide one of the more efficient approaches to solving career formation problems.

PART TWO

SLD EDUCATIONAL AND OCCUPATIONAL ATTAINMENT RESEARCH

CHAPTER 4

OCCUPATIONAL ATTAINMENT OF ADULTS WITH LEARNING DISABILITIES

Attain (ə-tān´): To gain, reach or accomplish by mental or physical effort.

A Review of Fifteen SLD Follow-up Studies

A NUMBER of societal ills have been causally attributed to America's growing number of functionally illiterate adults, that is, those functioning below a fifth grade level in academic related abilities (Kozol, 1985; Hunter & Herman, 1979), and it was also suggested at the introduction of this text that illiteracy and the condition known as "specific learning disabilities" (SLD) can have similar impacts on society. In general, the official definition for SLD indicates that this category of school impairment is reserved for individuals who are of average intelligence, have no physical or mental problems that would be the primary cause of the academic impairment, and the condition is not due to an adverse socioeconomic condition. When it comes down to the major criteria on who shall or shall not be given services under the category of SLD, it appears that currently the **amount of discrepancy** between a student's ability (IQ), and what they have actually learned (academic skills achieved) is the only clearly quantifiable and consistently verifiable factor in making such a diagnosis, although legally, other criteria must also be considered.

In order to actually evaluate whether or not persons with learning disabilities are less likely than their nonhandicapped peers to become economically productive citizens, we must objectively document the occupational histories of such persons. A major difficulty in conducting such a documentation is the fact that the United States Office of Education (USOE) did not officially recognize this impairment as a handicap until the late 1960s and waited even longer (1977) to specify objective identification criteria for it. Students identified as SLD under these 1977 USOE guidelines at grade 1 to grade 12 will not have reached adult midlife until about the year 2000 and 1994, respectively. Considering this needed maturation span to validly evaluate the hypothesis that SLDs are or are not at high risk for obtaining meaningful and productive lives, the actual testing of this hypothesis must await the beginning of the coming century. While awaiting this maturation period, the next best alternative is to address the issue by considering follow-up studies that have been conducted with varied populations, identified as having some type/degree of academic achievement problem but certainly not identified in any consistent or precise manner. Making any generalization from the data presented in this chapter is limited but none the less quite useful, in formulating prospective theories and possible hypotheses to test with the upcoming adults identified under the 1977 SLD guidelines. Even those (1977) guidelines are quite inconsistent across states (Reynolds, 1985) but are certainly more structurally organized than the studies currently completed and reported here. A few of the studies included in this current analysis do include post 1977 SLDs but because of their young adult age status the long term effects are only speculative.

A Comment on Three Previous SLD Follow-up Reviews

Previously conducted reviews of SLD follow-up studies (Herjanic & Penick, 1972; Horn, O'Donnell, & Vitulano, 1983); Schonhaut & Satz, 1983) have reported summary results indicating indecisive and contradictory findings (Herjanic & Renick, 1972), as well as positive vocational outcomes based on quite limited information (Horn et al., 1983). Only the Schonhaut and Satz SLD review generated a comprehensively derived outcome statement:

> First the academic outlook for children with early learning problems is poor, unless a child happens to come from a high SES family and/or is exposed to an intensive program such as the Orton-Gillingham program in which case the outlook may be good. Second, children with early learning disabilities are probably more likely to drop out of school, but seriousness of that risk is unknown. Third, it is probable that with the exception of high SES children, few learning disabled youngsters will enter occupations demanding extended education; however, what occupations these people enter and what level of job

satisfaction they enjoy have not been determined. Fourth, whether early identification and treatment of learning disabilities improves prognosis (and, if so, to what extent) is still unanswered (p. 560).

The focus of this SLD review is to attempt to answer Schonhaut and Satz's observation that occupational selection decisions are yet unanswered. And as family background, academic achievement, and educational attainment relate, it was necessary to report on those factors as well.

Educational and Occupational Attainment of Individuals with Learning Disabilities

The assumption that each person can enter an occupation that permits the implementation of his or her personality or that it is logical to expect satisfaction from careers in an increasingly technological society, is perhaps a more idealistic expectation than realistic one. Similarly, the assumptions that work maintains the central life role and that it is the ability of the individual that allows one to overcome the constraints of the social system and the demands of our economy and move into jobs that are rewarding, may also be a more optimistic than realistic point of view. Extending this concern of over optimism for career attainment, Warnath (1975) suggested that career psychologists and counselors broaden their theoretical models to general models of human effectiveness, such as in Super's definition of career, encompassing a variety of life roles being played out over the life span. Despite the logical inferences about work situations, it is difficult to deny the great importance American society places on the occupational status of individuals. To be sure, new acquaintance dialogue rarely begins without some conversation about what one does for a living. Montagna (1974), a sociologist, delineated the meaning of occupation in the American culture as follows:

> Peoples' occupations are generally regarded as the most important indicator of their positions in the social structure. Occupations provide income, social status and personal satisfaction. They are the most ubiquitous of all social and sociological factors used in the measurement of social class, political motivations, leisure time orientations and other work and non-work characteristics. Occupation is used as a category to measure changes in individual life patterns called occupational careers as a phenomenon explaining marriage and divorce patterns and as a political organization to protect workers engaged in similar work tasks and to develop a common consciousness among them (p. 1).

Taking the above description of occupation one step further, Montagna noted that economic relations of production in most societies lead to a dual labor market of primary occupations and secondary occupations based on distinctions of race, sex, age and most certainly, handicap.

Montagna also posited that the primary occupations are characterized by high job stability, clearly defined career patterns and a considerable degree of work involvement, while secondary occupations are highly unstable and alienating. For definitional purposes, primary sector occupations generally refer to upper tier occupations (professional and technical) and lower tier occupations (salepersons, clerical workers and skilled craftsmen). Secondary sector occupations refer to unskilled, semiskilled and service type occupations. As social status is largely derived from one's occupation, as well as providing opportunities for career stability and involvement, the seeking and obtaining of primary level occupations would be, to a measurable degree, a commonly valued goal. As the Status Attainment Model indicates, education is a primary determinant of occupational status and thus is a value parallel to the desire to achieve status in a primary occupation. In fact, holding this value may be more important than other variables traditionally associated with career attainment. Vanfossen (1979) offered an explanation of this viewpoint:

> . . . Education seems to affect what kind of job a person can get and thus where he or she will be located in the stratification system [primary or secondary occupational levels]. Yet it has also become clear that education is often unrelated to the skills needed on the job. While medical schools may prepare persons to become doctors and law schools prepare persons to become lawyers, for a large proportion of occupations, the skills learned in schools are not those used on the job. Nor does educational attainment correlate very highly with measures of general intelligence. It is increasingly apparent, then, that except for the most highly technical and professional occupations, education serves more as a credential than as an indicator of job performance skills (p. 19).

In the kind of educational training programs that do teach specific job skills, such as vocational education, those society members that need it most, often do not receive it. Summarizing the concerns with regard to students denied either an academic or vocational preparation curriculum and thus denied access to skilled or professional work, Montagna (1977) has noted that "schooling in America tends to weed out those students who perform poorly. Those who cannot afford higher (and even secondary) education are also forced to drop out. The graduates are those from the higher class families. Education maintains the hierachical structure and income distribution of the system" (p. 427).

In the research reported by Jencks et al. (1979, 1983), there are similar conclusions. Jencks et al. depicted the United States as a class-ridden society where being born into the "right" family is vitally important, especially because of its impact on educational attainment. Education is typically crucial to "getting ahead" in America. Successful early experiences in school shape people's aspirations as well as the expectations of others. What counts most is not what one learns in college, but the fact that one completes college and acquires the proper credentials. Hence, the factors making for success are interrelated; an individual who comes from the right family is more likely to acquire high aspirations, have high academic tests scores, complete college and have the personality attributes associated with success.

Importance of Education in Occupational Attainment

Individuals planning for a career should be aware of the continuing rise in the educational attainment of workers. Between 1970 and 1982, the proportion of the labor force aged 18 to 64 with at least one year of college increased from 26 to 39 percent. The increase in educational attainment reflects both the retirement of older workers, many of whom had little formal education, and the influx into the work force of young people who generally have a high level of formal education. Among workers aged 25 to 34, nearly half have completed at least one year of college.

The disadvantage that less educated workers suffer when seeking jobs is clearly shown in their unemployment rate. In 1982, the unemployment rate among 20 to 24 year olds with less than four years of high school was 32.2 percent. The rate for those with four years of high school was about half that, 15.5 percent. The rates for those with one to three years of college and four or more years of college were only 9.6 and 5.6 percent, respectively (Statistical Abstract of the United States, 1982).The connection between higher unemployment rates and low levels of education shows the importance of education in a job market that increasingly requires more training.

It is also important to note that a college degree does not guarantee success in the job market. Between 1970 and 1982, employment of college graduates grew 103 percent. The proportion employed in professional, technical and managerial occupations, however, declined because these occupations did not expand rapidly enough to absorb the growing supply of graduates. As a result, one out of five college graduates who entered the labor market between 1970 and 1982 took jobs not usually requiring a degree. Not all occupations requiring a college degree will be overcrowded, however. Good opportunities will exist for systems analysts and engineers, for example. Despite widespread publicity about the poor job market for college graduates, a college degree is still needed for most high paying and high status jobs.

Indeed, even many SLD students who do not drop out of high school are excluded from both the academic/college track and the vocational/technical skill preparation programs. Data most currently available from the U.S. Department of Education (1985) on SLD vocational class participation, show that SLD adolescents are the least participative in vocational education programs (only 24 percent participate out of all SLDs available to enter such programs) of all the other mildly handicapping conditions, for example, behavior disorders (34 percent) and mentally retarded (48 percent). And only recently have colleges and universities begun to accept the SLD student (Cordoni, 1981, 1982), and most of these SLD students are found to be from middle to upper class families. Data for the 1982-83 school year indicated that of the 5.4 percent of entering college freshman who were disabled, 6.0 percent were learning disabled (Astin, Hemond & Richardson, 1982). The number of examinees with learning disabilities who completed the American College Testing exam under special testing conditions increased from 1,406 in 1982-83 to 1,791 in the 1983-84 school year, an increase of 27 percent (Laing & Farmer, 1985).

Because postsecondary services are of recent origin for the SLD young adult, it will be several years before we can fully ascertain their successful/unsuccessful vocational outcomes with reference to vocational behaviors attributed to these newer postsecondary SLD assistance programs. However, there is much that can be learned from current and past SLD follow-up studies, realizing, of course, that known etiologies of the SLD subjects in these somewhat recent and older follow-up studies are quite vague when compared to the more stable identification practices that are now beginning to emerge in states such as Kansas, Colorado, California and Iowa.

Previous Findings on the Occupational Status of SLD Adults

In reviewing several follow-up studies of learning disabled students (Biller, 1985b), it was reported that those SLD persons coming from higher socioeconomic backgrounds and having above average IQ levels, were more likely to hold primary sector jobs, that is, management and professions, than compared to their SLD counterparts of average IQ and whose family backgrounds were considered to be in the lower middle socioeconomic range. It was suggested (Biller, 1985b), that if secondary sector level jobs (unskilled and semiskilled) were considered to be an acceptable employment outcome then all of the SLD follow-up studies reviewed could be construed as illustrating a successful vocational prognosis for these people, as the rates of employment were not significantly abnormal, for either high or low IQ/SES SLDs than those of their respective control groups.

The perspective taken here, however, is that if the dynamics for entrance into primary sector careers are better understood, along with greater discernment for the role of ability and family background factors in occupational attainment, it may be possible to move more SLD persons from the less desirable secondary sector jobs to the more desirable primary sector occupations. Provided, of course, that all else being equal, and over and above the specific learning disability, SLD persons are not entering occupational levels commensurate with their nonhandicapped peers. Presented in the remainder of this chapter is a more defined account of SLD career attainment, including several studies not included in former follow-up reviews of this population.

SLD Follow-up Research: Formulating the Hypothesis

In order to make best use of information collected in any series of follow-up studies, some working hypotheses are needed which will allow the study findings to be put into a framework for meaningful interpretation. It is expected that these hypotheses would be derived from past research and/or previously derived theoretical assumptions. This first set of hypotheses will be evaluated strictly on a subjective comparison; however, following this more subjective analysis will be a statistical evaluation of the eight studies that included control groups.

Hypothesis #1. The first hypothesis is stated in the form of: SLD individuals who come from more favorable socioeconomic status backgrounds (SES) will have done better in school, completed more schooling and consequently, will have achieved a higher occupational status than their lower SES, SLD peers. Research (as cited in Chapter 1) conducted over the last 20 years appears to substantiate, to a large degree, this hypothesis.

Hypothesis #2. A second hypothesis, related to the first, is stated in the form of: Having a specific learning disability(s) would have a negative impact on one's educational attainment and subsequently, on occupational outcomes. Research by Jencks et al. (1983) indicated that achievement is perhaps a better predictor of adult success than is reading comprehension, vocabulary and arithmetic reasoning ability. Arithmetic achievement is, according to Jencks et al., the most salient academic behavior for male attainment success.

Hypothesis #3. The third hypothesis is stated in the form of: SLD adults should fare better in occupational status outcomes than their counterparts identified as educable mentally retarded (EMR) or other related language disability groups such as the hearing impaired. For example, recent follow-up studies have shown that EMR and rehabilitated deaf adults have employment rates in competitive employment ranging as low as 60-70 percent and hold jobs primarily in unskilled and semi-skilled occupations (Crain, 1980; Marqalit & Schuchman, 1978; Schalock & Harper, 1978; Stabler, 1974; Lacey, 1975).

Hypothesis #4. A fourth and final hypothesis is stated in the form of: SLD adult populations, as a group, are not by and large, **functionally** illiterate, that is, are not reading, writing or calculating below a fifth grade level.

It is against these four hypotheses or criteria that the subsequent SLD follow-up studies included in this present analysis will be contrasted and evaluated. In the statistical analysis to follow this subjective comparison, the primary hypothesis will be stated in the form of: SLD follow-up subjects are not significantly different in the level of educational or occupational attainment from their nonhandicapped controls. SLDs are not significantly different from their controls in their rate of employment participation.

Criteria for Selecting SLD Follow-up Studies to be Reviewed

There are five major criteria considered essential in evaluating any follow-up study (Schonhaut & Satz, 1983). Among the most important of the five criteria are adequate follow-up periods and appropriate comparison groups. Sample size and method of the selection also rate as equally important. A final selection criteria would include a clearly defined etiology or definitional label of the disabled population, which in the field of learning disabilities, is probably the most difficult criterion to clarify. There are, however, many commonalities among these SLD study subjects, for example, below average in reading and spelling performances.

Selecting an Overall Disability Label

Given the predominance of reading and spelling deficits in the SLD population, and recognizing the varying labels used to describe these deficits, definitional terms, such as dyslexia, meaning "an acquired disorder of reading in which there may or may not be an associated disorder of writing (dysgraphia) . . . [and] include disorders of spelling" (Duane, 1979a, p. 6), may be considered for use as the definitional label of choice. A problem in the term "dyslexia" exists however, in that using it generally connotes a genetically determined basis for the deficits in learning behavior (Duane, 1979a), yet not all children will have this familial factor as their primary cause for reading failure. Therefore, another definition is often suggested in the form of "Specific Reading Disability" (SRD), likewise implying a reading problem but also including the implication that spelling problems co-exist (Duane, 1979a). As it is not known for certain if any of the subjects included in these follow-up reviews are learning disabled on the basis of a familial factor, it may seem most logical to use the SRD label. On the other hand, since the most commonly identified disabilities are usually of the reading and spelling variety, but do include others, for example, writing and arithmetic (Lerner, 1981; Kirk & Elkins, 1975), using specific learning disabilities (SLD) as the umbrella term throughout this follow-up review may be the most appropriate overall. Two remaining areas of selection criteria mentioned earlier still need to be clarified, that of follow-up study time periods and the use of control groups.

Follow-up Intervals and Control Group Uses

Ideally, the most well-designed follow-up would begin when a child begins schooling and, if concerned with occupational outcomes, culminate when the subject reaches at least age 35. For example, to accurately assess the significance of an early age learning disability on occupational attainment, the final follow-up period should allow the adult to have the opportunity to "establish" him or herself in the job market (Schonhaut & Satz, 1983). Thus, any study that included a follow-up period extending only to age 21 would not be nearly as explanatory. However, as the younger age SLD can provide insight into transitional level difficulties, they are also quite important. Studies included in this current review on limiting age basis were: Vetter (1983); Hartzell and Compton (1984; Humes and Brammer (1985); and Carter (1964). Some SLD follow-up studies were not included because of the paucity of occupational information, (Preston & Yarrington, 1967; Silver & Hagin, 1964). A most recent follow-up study by Levin, Zigmond, and Birch (1985) is not included as part of the 15 study review because of the age span factor and other limited data, however, it does have some important when-in-school findings. A major weakness of a number of the presently reviewed studies remains in that we do not know the precise SLD selection criteria used by the reviewers, thus further limiting generalizability of the data. Some studies have students that began in SLD programs at an early age while others did not, which may differentially affect adult occupational outcomes.

Finally, with respect to the highly desirable use of control groups, it should be noted that of the 15 studies available to be reviewed only eight contained such comparison groups. While the sampling techniques differed on selecting these control groups and their SLD subjects, overall, a most serious selection bias may be found in those studies compromising private school and clinical samples. With these above hypotheses stated, study selection criteria specified, limitations defined, and a title (SLD) for the population established, presentation and analysis of these follow-up studies is given.

SLD Follow-up Studies Order of Presentation

The studies presented in this review will be arranged in the order of the highest mean percentage of high school education completed within each study. Given the importance of education completed as a predictor of occupational attainment level, this seemed to be a logical way to order them. Shown (in Table 3 and 3a) are the key variables for each study. Control group studies (marked with an X) have data listed directly under their SLD group in boldface type. The SLD studies are identified in Tables 3 and 3a.

Rawson's SLD Follow-up Review

Background of Study

Rawson's (1978) Rose Valley Private School subjects came from the elite Swarthmore College neighborbood of Moylan, Pennsylvania, a small suburb of Philadelphia. This study included 56 boys and their families, of which 20 boys were identified during their Rose Valley School careers as moderately to severely learning disabled. The mean IQ of this SLD group was approximately 123. The Rose Valley School, begun in 1929, was privately operated and founded by a group of parents who had been studying child development and had developed strong agreement concerning modern educational objectives. The Rose

TABLE 3

ATTAINMENT OF SLD POPULATION RANKED BY HIGH SCHOOL COMPLETION RATE

| ID | N | Set | Age Span | SES | IQ | % H.S | Achievement | | | % Coll | % Grad | % Emp | U | Job Class | | | |
							R	S	A					SS	S	M/S	P
A.	20	PvS	26-40	H	123	100	*	*	*	90	70	100	0	0	10	30	60
B.	406	PvS	26-55	H-M	118	96	9.6	8.5	*	55	8	94	10	6	3	65	17
C.	44	Cln	17-28	*	120	94	*	*	*	56	17	98	18	17	11	29	25
D.	63	PS	19-25	L-M	!97	94	*	*	*	11	*	95	(SEI = 19.74)!!				
E.	114	Cln	15-27	H-M	107	91	*	*	*	17	*	*	*	*	*	*	*
F.	101	Cln	17-29	M	103	90	9.7	8.7	6.5	11	8	83	(4.08)!!!				
G.	562	Svy	18-50	*	*	88	*	*	*	19	17	82	24	27	24	10	15
H.	32	PS	20-26	L-M	100	84	10.2	*	*	31	3	100	29	14	38	14	5
I.	26	PS	*	*	*	83	*	*	*	0	0	90	6	63	19	11	0
J.	11	Cln	25-30	M	92	81	2.6	2.1	4.6	0	0	72	41	18	29	12	0
K.	91	PvS	21-39	M-H	98	70	10.4	8.4	6.7	38	29	60	23	41	3	13	13
L.	19	PS	19-35	L-M	97	68	6.3	*	*	0	0	95	26	37	26	10	0
M.	381	Reh	23.2	*	*	63	*	*	*	5	*	36	*	*	*	*	*
N.	27	Cln	24	L-M	92	36	7.0	7.0	8.5	12	0	54	41	18	29	12	0
O.	23	PS	19-25	L	104	30	*	*	*	0	0	91	14	67	19	0	0
P.	20	PS	19	*	104	10	*	*	*	0	0	99	17	55	28	0	0
SLD Mean			21-32		104	74	8.0	7.0	6.5	22	12	83	21	30	20	17	12

ID = Identifier for Study; A:Rawson, B:Gottfredson, C:Robinson & Smith, D:Vetter, E:Hartzel & Compton, F:Bruck, G:ACLD, H:Balow & Blomquist, I:Humes & Brammer, J:Frauenheim & Heckerl, K:Rogan & Hartman, L:Howden, M:Steidle et al., N:Spreen, O:Carter, P:Hardy. Set = Type of environment population was sampled in; PvS = private school, Cln = clinic, PS = public school, Sib = siblings as control, Svy = survey, Reh = data from state rehabilitation cases. SES = socio-economic status. Achievement = Reading, Spelling, Arithmetic scores by grade level at last follow-up. Job Class = U:Unskilled laborers; S = Semiskilled such as service workers, clerical, operatives and apprentices, truck drivers etc.; S = Skilled workers such as building and machine trades etc.; M/S = Managerial and Sales workers; P = Professional and Technical Occupations. ! = IQ mean was taken from recent Kansas Survey; !! = Job Class expressed as a Duncan SEI Score rather than broken down into specific Job categories; !!! = Similar to Duncan SEI but in Canada is the "Blishen Index"; lower number is higher status. * = data not reported in study.

TABLE 3a
ATTAINMENT OF SLD POPULATION WITH CONTROL GROUP STUDIES ONLY
AND RANKED BY HIGH SCHOOL COMPLETION RATE

ID	N	Set	Age Span	SES	IQ	% H.S	Achievement			% Coll	% Grad	% Emp	Job Class				
							R	S	A				U	SS	S	M/S	P
A.	20	PvS	26-40	H	123	100	*	*	*	90	70	100	0	0	10	30	60
X	36	PvS	26-40	H	137	100	*	*	*	83	58	100	0	8	0	42	50
B.	406	PvS	26-55	H-M	118	96	9.6	8.5	*	55	8	94	10	6	3	65	17
X	416	PvS	26-55	H-M	127	100	*	*	*	94	58	95	3	2	1	43	51
D.	63	PS	19-25	L-M	!97	94	*	*	*	11	*	95	(SEI = 19.74)!!				
X	63	PS	18-25	M	!109	99	*	*	*	70	*	89	(SEI = 33.26)!!				
E.	114	Cln	15-27	H-M	107	91	*	*	*	17	*	*	*	*	*	*	*
X	144	*	15-36	*	*	99	*	*	*	31	*	*	*	*	*	*	*
F.	101	Cln	17-29	M	103	90	9.7	8.7	6.5	11	8	83	(4.08)!!!				
X	50	Sib	17-29	M	*	94	13.7	13	10	20	*	92	(3.25)!!!				
L.	19	PS	19-35	L-M	97	68	6.3	*	*	0	0	95	26	37	26	10	0
X	22	PS	19-25	M	107	96	(All At Grade)			25	0	100	23	23	27	27	0
N.	27	Cln	24	L-M	92	36	7.0	7.0	8.5	12	0	54	41	18	29	12	0
X	51	PS	24	M	110	80	10	10	11.5	47	0	94	33	8	19	19	21
O.	23	PS	19-25	L	104	30	*	*	*	0	0	91	14	67	19	0	0
X	12	PS	19-25	L-M	105	83	*	*	*	25	0	100	33	33	34	0	0
SLD Mean			21-33		105	76	8.0	8.0	7.5	25	14	87	18	26	17	24	15
X = C Mean			22-34		116	94	11.9	11.5	11.3	49	23	91	19	14	16	26	25

ID = Identifier for Study; (X = Control Group), A:Rawson, B:Gottfredson, C:Robinson & Smith, D:Vetter, E:Hartzel & Compton, F:Bruck, G:ACLD, H:Balow & Blomquist, I:Humes & Brammer, J:Frauenheim & Heckerl, K:Rogan & Hartman, L:Howden, M:Steidle et al., N:Spreen, O:Carter, P:Hardy. Set = Type of environment population was sampled in; PvS = private school, Cln = clinic, PS = public school, Sib = siblings acted as control, Svy = survey, Reh = data from state rehabilitation cases. SES = socio-economic status. Achievement = Reading, Spelling, Arithmetic scores by grade level at last follow-up. Job Class = U:Unskilled laborers; S = Semiskilled such as service workers, clerical, operatives and apprentices, truck drivers etc.; S = Skilled workers such as building and machine trades etc.; M/S = Managerial and Sales workers; P = Professional and Technical Occupations. ! = IQ mean was taken from recent Kansas Survey; !! = Job Class expressed as a Duncan **SEI** Score rather than broken down into specific Job categories; !!! = Similar to Duncan SEI but in Canada is the **"Blishen Index"**; lower # is higher status. * = data not available.

Valley School tried to follow the then popular **Progressive Educational Movement** of balancing intellectual, emotional and practical approaches to child development, which gave great importance to a student's individual differences in ability. Originally, beginning reading instruction at Rose Valley was based on a sight word approach with some phonetic emphasis (Rawson, 1978). In the progressive education mode and following the first years of the school's beginning, through 1947, initial reading instruction was not begun until the second grade with the hope that students would benefit from increased maturity. Up to the year 1935, Rose Valley's students' reading problems were met with typical corrective techniques. However, in 1935 the school was introduced to the Orton-Gillingham approach to remediating reading problems. The first Rose Valley boy to receive this programming was seen by Dr. Samuel Orton and Dr. Paul Dozier, both well known pioneers in the field of learning disabilities at the time.

Background of the Rose Valley Subjects and Outcomes

Over 95 percent of the SLD boys' fathers had college degrees and were in predominantly professional and managerial occupations (50%). 82 percent of the mothers included in the overall study had college backgrounds as well, and 18 percent had graduate degrees. In the study overall, 10 (18%) of the fathers were lawyers, 13 (23%) were college faculty and administrators, 14 (25%) were researchers and engineers, 12 (21%) were in business management and sales and only 1 (1%) was listed as a skilled worker.

Data on the SLD Boys

Of the 20 dyslexic sons, two (10%) became medical doctors working in research areas, one (5%) became a lawyer, two (10%) were researchers, six (30%) were in business management, four (20%) were in education, and two (10%) were in the skilled trades. Twelve of the lower language ability students had a mean of 5.6 years of higher education; eleven had BA degrees, six had masters and three had earned doctorates by 1965. The highest percentage of Rawson SLD men were in "people" oriented careers (55%). Students at Rose Valley were classified as SLD if there was failure in learning to read during the first year or two of reading instruction, up to the levels which were consistent with classmate's performance and his own general intelligence (Rawson, 1978). For example, two Rose Valley SLD students were noted by their poor oral reading and work memory and the persistence of reversals of orientation and sequence. Reading comprehension was a problem only in the sense that there was a failure to decode the written messages, to recognize or work out words and phrases. Early and continuing speech delays and inadequacies in such areas as late talking, poor articulation and stuttering, were frequent among the Rose Valley SLD students, specifically for the poor language group, four of which were severe dyslexics. Of the remaining 51, eight (15.77%) were labeled severely handicapped with eight of the boys identified as moderately SLD. Overall, the dyslexic group had few differences from their controls except in IQ, however, controls had approximately 10 percent more subjects in professional/technical positions.

Two Case Histories in the Rawson Study: Henry and Dan

Henry, when in fifth grade and after two years of tutoring, was at 5.5 grade level in reading paragraph meaning, 4.1 in spelling, and 6.7 in arithmetic reasoning. Henry was classified by Rawson as a borderline (moderate to severe) dyslexic. Later, in high school, Henry found English and French more difficult than Math and Latin. At the time of the follow-up, Henry was completing a doctorate and had done some notable writing, had worked in public relations, and had worked as an assistant manager to a national trade association. At last follow-up Henry was starting up his own business. Rawson stated that despite these successes Henry still read slowly, remained a poor speller, and wrote legibly but not particularly well.

Dan had more difficulty than Henry due to extremely poor spoken language skills. Dan was a student who had relatives with a history of learning disability. After sixth grade he was one half year above grade level in reading but was below grade level in science and social studies. Arithmetic reasoning was marginal, but scores in computation, spelling, literature, and language usage were still well below average. Despite these deficits Dan graduated cum laude from high school, received excellent marks in a high standard college and law school, and was reported to be doing well in a law practice. The main comment made by Dan at follow-up was, "I don't have good memory for details but use reason instead. The law is based on reason so I generally come out with the right answers as I find when I check by looking them up in our law library" (Rawson, 1978, p. 55).

Commenting on the high maturation of these SLD persons, Rawson noted that:

> In the school as a whole "drive," "motivation," and emotional tone were very good, and the low language boys pretty much shared this state of affairs. . . . The problem of low self-concept was more prevalent and persistant among the boys who were diagnosed and given help after they had experienced failure. It was hard for them to believe that they were as capable and as likely to succeed as the accumulating evidence of their competence indicated. Low self-concept was, rather surprisingly, something of a general problem in this school, however. The writer has often encountered the problem in highly intelligent individuals whose life situations permit them to set their own standards.

Perhaps they are bright enough to know what could be but not experienced enough to accept human limitations (p. 58).

Hypotheses Comparisons of Rawson's Follow-up Study

Despite the fact that, methodologically, the Rawson (1978) follow-up study was considered well done, Schonhaut and Satz (1983) criticized it for having an unclear basis for classifying a child as SLD. Rawson, in her text, does give a detailed definition for SLD, but it is hard to reconcile it when trying to determine what grade level deficits these students actually had when they began the program and when they left it, these detailed kinds of data were not clearly stated. The circumstances surrounding the entire Rose Valley School program are somewhat atypical, so making any generalizations are quite limited. Contrasting the results of these upper class SLD persons with the stated hypotheses, the review would indicate that:

Hypothesis #1. (accepted)—Higher IQ, higher SES individuals do complete high levels of education and enter high status occupations, primarily in data and people-oriented categories;

Hypothesis #2. (rejected)—In this Rose Valley population, a reading or spelling disability did not seem to interfere with completing education or achieving a higher occupational status. It should be recalled however, that we do not know how severe the original learning disabilities were;

Hypothesis #3. (accepted)—The Rose Valley subjects clearly had higher attainment levels compared to EMR or hearing impaired subjects in all areas of functioning and outcomes;

Hypothesis #4, is retained in that all subjects were well above fifth grade literacy levels.

Statistical Analysis of Rawson Education and Employment Data

Using a Chi square (X^2) statistic to test the significance between the observed and expected theoretical frequencies for the Rawson education and employment categories, the following results are reported:

High School Completion

The first question asked was, "Is there a difference between expected and observed numbers of subjects in their high school completion rates in comparison to their comparison group?" A nonsignificant result was obtained as there were no dropouts reported for either of Rawson's groups. Recall that both groups were educated in the same private school but divided on degree of language ability.

College Completion

The question, "Is there a difference between expected and observed numbers of subjects completing a four year degree among the two groups?" resulted in the relationship proving not significant at the .05 level ($X^2 = .46$, df = 1). The two groups differed only by a few percentage points in college attainment.

Employment Rate

The question, "Is there a difference between expected and observed number of subjects on employed, versus not employed (actively seeking work) among the two groups?" proved to be nonsignificant as there were no subjects in either group seeking work.

Employment Status Attainment

To analyze this attainment component, the occupational classifications of managerial/sales, professional, and skilled were collapsed as one factor and unskilled/semiskilled were collapsed to form a second factor. Results of this anlaysis for the Rawson subjects indicated that there was no significant difference between the SLDs and the comparison group ($X^2 = 1.76$, df = 1, > .05). Both groups were predominately in primary sector employment.

Combining both the subjective and statistical hypothesis evaluations, it is quite clear that Rawson's SLD population shows little negative residual effects of having a learning disability with reference to educational and occupational attainment.

Gottfredson's Follow-up Review of Gow School SLDs

The Gow Preparatory School for SLD boys, located in a suburb just southeast of Buffalo, New York, enjoined the *Johns Hopkins Center for Social Organization of Schools* to survey their alumni representing the years of 1940-1977. The purpose of the survey was to assess the long-term effects of SLD on occupational outcomes. The adult careers of over 300 Gow alumni were compared to related data of the U.S. Census Bureau and nonhandicapped alumni of Baltimore's Gilman Preparatory School, a prestigous private school for boys. Gilman Preparatory School was selected as a control group sample because it had maintained information for its graduates during the same study period as Gow, and also attracted students with similar intellectual abilities and socio-economic backgrounds (Gottfredson, Finucci, & Childs, 1984).

Similarities between Gow and the previously mentioned Rose Valley programs are numerable despite the fact that Gow is a secondary school designed specifically for SLDs and Rose Valley is not. For example, the mean IQ of Rose Valley moderate to severe SLD students was approximately 123, while Gow's students had a mean IQ of 118. Both Gow and Rose Valley used the Stanford-Binet in their assessments and both administered these tests prior to the students beginning their respective programs. Gow's students, being of adolescent age, were tested at about Grade 9 and Rose Valley's in the earlier grades. Both schools used the *Gray Oral Reading Test* and the *Stanford Achievement Test Batteries* in their testing programs.

Socioeconomic backgrounds of both Gow and Rose Valley students were not exactly similar, with 31 percent of Gow fathers employed in professional and technical careers, while approximately 50 percent of the Rose Valley fathers were in the same career area. The Gilman (Gow's control group) fathers were represented by having 48 percent in the professional and technical fields, thus, being somewhat more similar to the Rose Valley fathers than Gow. Approximately 53 percent of the Gow fathers were in managerial positions, while Rose Valley and Gilman were represented at 35 percent and 40 percent, respectively. Again, the Gilman controls appear to be more similar to the Rose Valley population than to Gow School for SLD students. There were no significant relationship between the educational attainment between Gow fathers and sons.

Unfortunately, Gilman controls did not have comparative Stanford-Binet IQ data. To make such an IQ comparison for Gilman students, it was estimated from Gilman's *SAT* Verbal test scores that Gilman controls would have a mean IQ of about 127, which is 10 points lower than the Rose Valley control group and 9 points higher than Gow's SLD students. Interestingly, all three schools were started in the late 1920s, with both Gilman and Rose Valley starting in 1929, and Gow having begun its program in 1926.

Academic and Occupational Status of Gow Students

At the time Gow men left their school, they were, on the average, two years below grade level in oral reading and three years below in spelling. Mean achievement coefficients for reading and spelling were both 0.75. Only a third of Rose Valley SLDs were at a similar level in reading, but 90 percent of Rawson subjects were at a similar level in spelling.

Professional/Technical Occupations of Gow Men

Gow alumni were found in professional/technical occupations at a rate of just over 17 percent of their population; Rose Valley had 60 percent in the same occupational group. Professional/technical occupations held by Gow men included accountant, architect, computer specialist, lawyer, physician, dentist and college teacher. Rose Valley SLDs also held similar professional positions, such as lawyer, medical doctor and research scientist. A larger number of lawyers, physicians, and college teachers were represented in the Gilman controls, as was occupational attainment data reported by the U.S. Census Bureau in the normal white population (Gottfredson et al., 1984).

Managerial/Sales Occupations of Gow Men

Gow men and their fathers were found to be represented more often in the managerial/sales type occupations (both were about 65%) when compared to the 22.4 percent of U.S. white males in such occupations (using 1980 U.S. employment figures). The Gilman controls had approximately 43 percent of their alumni in managerial/sales, while their fathers were in this category at a 49 percent rate. Rose Valley controls, at 42 percent were nearly equal to Gow's controls in managerial/sales occupations. It appears that Gow SLD alums were, clearly, more participative in management/sales type careers than white males in the general population, or for that matter from Rawson's SLD subjects, but then, so were the Gow fathers.

The Gow men in professional/technical occupations were more likely to be school teachers, technicians, designers or computer specialists rather than lawyers or physicians, who were well represented among Gilman alumni and fathers of both groups. Thus, the Gow men, stated Finucci (1985), in professions were underrepresented in the most reading-intensive jobs. Finucci interpreted this finding as follows:

> Because the Gow men had relatively high levels of SES and IQ, Gottfredson and colleagues predicted that they would have relatively

high-level jobs. This prediction was supported, since well over 80 percent of the subjects were in white collar jobs. The results of a path analysis showed that much of the difference between Gow and Gilman men could be accounted for by differences in educational attainment. Severity of dyslexia restricted occupational attainment to a large extent by placing limitations on educational attainment. But it is important to recognize that most of these subjects were drawn from middle to upper SES levels who had benefitted from special schooling. If dyslexia limits the educational attainment and restricts the occupational attainment of these subjects who had such opportunity, it can hardly fail to place limits on dyslexic people who do not have such advantages.

It is of particular interest to dyslexic individuals, their parents and vocational advisors that many dyslexic people found career success in prestigious positions that were less reading-intensive than other positions having similar pay and responsibility. For instance, Gottfredson and coworkers (1983) found that many dyslexic individuals were engaged in management occupations in which nonacademic competencies such as taking initiative and responsibility or being persuasive were important (p. 115).

Blue Collar Workers of Gow

Both Gow and Rose Valley SLD alumni were less likely to be holding clerical, skilled, semiskilled or unskilled jobs. In all job categories, Gow and Rose Valley men were underrepresented in blue collar jobs, when compared to white men in general. In comparison to Gilman controls, however, Gow alumni were less likely to be in professional jobs, but more likely to be in management and sales, and to hold significantly higher percentages of blue collar jobs. Due to the smaller sample in the Rose Valley group, this type of blue collar comparison is not generalizable. Commenting on the above Gow findings, Gottfredson et al. (1984) stated that:

> Compared to men in general, then, these dyslexic men are quite successful on the whole, because they are equally often represented in professional work and more highly represented in management and sales, but they are much less often employed in the lower levels of work which employ most of the male population (p. 363).

Hypotheses Evaluation for the Gow School Study

Hypothesis #1: There is, again, evidence from these Gow school subjects that higher ability and a higher SES family background can lead to more education completed and higher status occupational attained, although to a somewhat lesser degree than the Rose Valley's SLD subjects. This difference was particularly noticeable with regard to graduate school participation with 70 percent for Rose Valley subjects but only 8 percent for Gow's. Two factors require emphasis here: (a) Gow subjects are similar in IQ level to Rose Valley subjects but are more academically disabled in reading, and spelling; and (b) more Rose Valley fathers were in professional work (50%) than were Gow's (31%). In conjunction to this disparity, it should be noted that Gow men completed less college, 55 percent, to Gilman's 94 percent. From the Jencks et al. (1979) data, we know that completing college over high school is worth approximately 25 points on Duncan's (1961) *SEI* which ranges in point value, as per occupational type, from 0-96. Occupations in the bottom one fifth of the *SEI* are unskilled and lower paying jobs, while the top fifth are the professional, technical and higher level managerial occupations. Based on the status attainment model estimate, (chapter one) as much as 48 percent of the variance in occupational attainment is based on educational attainment, and knowing that Jencks et al. (1979) derived from their data a mean of 40 and a standard deviation of 25 (points) on the Duncan *SEI,* it can be forwarded that completion of college over high school is worth one standard deviation or 25 occupational status points. Further, Jencks et al. also found that men whose test scores differed by fifteen points could expect to work in occupations whose status differed by one third to one half a standard deviation or 8-13 points. Considering the differences in the Gow and Gilman families with respect to the higher occupational status levels of Gilman boys/fathers, it is important to report that when Gow and Gilman subjects were asked if their siblings were affected by specific learning disabilities; 19 percent of the Gow men reported positive cases, while Gilman reported only a 7 percent SLD incidence rate.

Finally, Jencks et al. (1979) have noted that men who fail to convert their ability (Gow men had IQs of 118) advantage into additional schooling (only one half of Gow men participated in college) do not have much of an occupational advantage over men with lower scores. These results, according to Jencks et al. (1983), suggest that "if instruction were changed in school so that the relationship of ability to educational attainment fell, adolescents with differing abilities [SLDs] would have more equal occupational chances as adults. This might occur if low ability students were to learn more, receive more encouragement, have higher aspirations and therefore, attend school longer" (p. 115). This opinion may have even more relevance for the lower SES, SLD subjects that will be discussed later in the analysis.

The outcome for **Hypothesis #1,** in the Jencks et al. (1979; 1983) line of thinking, is that it is not the cognitive ability of the student affecting occupational mobility per se, but one's perspective about who will be selectively encouraged to learn what is necessary for aspiring to certain occupational positions. Right now this seems to be a question of "selective attention;" those children who come from the most favored SES backgrounds will get the most encouragement. It seems that Rawson's subjects got more of this than did the Gow subjects, thus **Hypothesis #1 is accepted** in that Gow men came from less favorable, albeit higher than the U.S. average, SES backgrounds in comparison to both the Gilman controls and the Rawson subjects.

Hypothesis #2: Effect of SLD on Attainment

With regard to the question "is academic disability interfering with educational and/or occupational outcomes of the Gow population?" is, to some extent, answered by Gottfredson, Finucci & Childs (1983):

> Some of this [performance] is due to socio-economic advantage. These men are primarily from advantaged backgrounds and they happened to be above average in intelligence as well, both of which help them proceed into successful careers despite their disability. Another important reason for their success is that they gravitated to high-level jobs that de-emphasize reading skills. The jobs they tend to hold are those in which we found that skills other than reading and writing are important. In business, especially, skills such as persuasiveness, taking initiative, and creative thinking may be critical (p. 13).

However, returning to the fact that Gow school fathers had the highest level of managerial positions, more than their controls and Rose Valley SLDs, leaves some questions as to whether the disability or family background factors inflated the number of Gow subjects in managerial positions. Could it be that Gow fathers had similar learning disabilities, as well, which caused them to enter management careers and then passed along this reportedly familial disease (Duane, 1979b) onto their sons? The **third and fourth hypotheses, as in the Rose Valley study, are also confirmed** to the extent that Gow subjects are operating at higher occupational levels than EMR adults nor are Gow subjects, as a group, functionally illiterate.

Statistical Evaluation of the Gottfredson et al. Study

High School Completion

High school completion rate differences between Gow SLD subjects and their controls from the Gilman School were significantly different ($X^2 = 16.29$, df$= 1$, $<.01$). This ratio was significant as no Gilman subjects dropped out while 4 percent of the Gow men did.

College Completion

Four year college completion percentages between Gow and Gilman subjects were also significantly different ($X^2 = 15.11$, df$= 1$, $<.01$). The percentage difference between Gow and Gilman subjects (40%) was much greater than high school completion rates. This finding is expected if the factors mitigating higher high school dropout rates (higher than Rawson's), among the Gow SLDs is still present for the next higher functioning but still limited Gow group wanting to complete college but unable to do so.

Employment Rate

Both Gow and Gilman subjects were fully employed, and thus, no differences are present on this factor.

Employment Status Attainment

Comparing the differences between combined categories of unskilled/semiskilled as one factor and managerial/sales, professional and skilled occupations as a second factor, Gow SLDs and Gilman controls were shown to differ significantly ($X^2 = 12.30$, df$= 1$, $<.01$). Accounting for most of this difference is the larger percentage of Gilman subjects in professional occupations over Gow subjects (51% versus 17%). A brief discussion on this finding is presented at the end of this section.

Conclusions of Combined Hypotheses Evaluations for Gow Adults

With the exception of employment rate, Gow subjects did significantly less well than their Gilman peers. This is a complete contrast to the somewhat similar but slightly higher SES subjects in Rawson's study. The greater Gow sample size can be one factor accounting for such a difference, but the way in which Gow men are enrolled may also be important. It is stated by Rawson that most Rose Valley subjects began their attendance at this school for reasons other than the school's facility to assist with learning problems. Only a few students actually came to the Rose Valley School specifically with academic remediation as a primary purpose. Gow subjects, on the other hand, attended that school for its advertised ability to educate students with learning disabilities. As such, one would expect a different learning prognosis simply on this selection bias factor alone.

Thus, the subjective evaluation of the Gow School SLDs, which found for Hypothesis #2 that only partial support could be given for the belief that this SLD adult population was affected by childhood learning disabilities, coupled with the above statistical differences on educational and occupational attainment, it can be stated that these Gow School subjects have been significantly affected by the long term effects of having a specific learning disability.

An Aside on Professional Versus Business Management Occupational Attainment

Given the differences found between Gow subjects and their controls with respect to entrance into professional versus business/managerial occupational classifications, a brief discussion is presented on how and why individuals enter these two differing occupational status levels.

According to research by Tinto (1980), the processes of occupational attainment through schooling, which characterize professional and business/managerial occupations, are quite different. Among professional occupations, more than half of the total effect of college origins upon attainment is direct; however, among business/managerial occupations, no direct effect of college origins is observed (Tinto, 1980). For those occupations (business/managerial) it appears to be the case that where one goes to college has little significant impact upon subsequent status attainment. These differences appear not to be related to the social mobility of those entering professions, but, rather, appear attributable to having achieved higher grade point averages in college, possession of higher occupational expectations during college and having completed postbaccalaureate degrees with greater frequency. While where the professionals went to college did have an impact upon subsequent attainments, so did their performance in those colleges; in fact, the performance indicators exceeded those attainment variances attributable to college origins. According to Tinto (1980), "the individual, rather than the institution, appears to be the primary causal force in the process of attainment described in these analyses" (p. 481-482). Coincidence or family background may be associated with one's entrance into the business/managerial occupations, it appears that within the professions, both individual initiative and institutional location are factors of concern regarding attainment; "it is evident from our analysis that being able to be at the right place (i.e., a high quality college) is not a socially random phenomenom. Access to these institutions is, from this data," a function of both social origins and the type of high school attended" (Tinto, p. 482). If Tinto is correct in these assumptions, it would provide further support for the hypothesis confirmed above that concluded that the Gottfredson et al. Gow School subjects, differing in academic ability from their Gilman School counterparts, are not able to achieve the same rates of professional occupation participation because of these differences in individual ability levels; however, this also differs from the Jencks et al. 1979; 1983) view that "selective attention" is the reason individuals fail to achieve these occupational status levels.

Robinson and Smith's University of Chicago Clinic Follow-up

Background of Study

This follow-up study, reported in 1962 by Robinson and Smith, differs from the previous two in that the subjects comprised a population from the University of Chicago Reading Clinic (UCRC), and there was not a comparison group. Opening in 1944, the UCRC was designed to provide diagnostic and remedial service for students in the University's laboratory schools and the greater Chicago community. A total of 44 former SLD clients were randomly selected for the follow-up, from files which included only those who had received both a diagnosis and remedial intervention. The study was actually conducted in 1958 and drew from pupils who first contacted the UCRC in 1948.

Description of UCRC Population

Among the UCRC students, the extent of reading retardation varied from one to several grade levels. There was a range of specific reading problems in this group including word recognition difficulties, vocabulary deficits and poor reading comprehension. Intelligence quotients ranged between 85 and 147, with a mean of 120. Only 8 of the 44 pupils had IQs below 100 (18%). Most all of the subjects completed high school (93%), with about three fourths of those completing college. Another 9 percent went on to master and doctoral level programs. No information was available on the educational attainments or specific socioeconomic levels of the parents.

Occupational Attainment of the UCRC Group

Of the 44 subjects, 15 were still in college or graduate school (34%). Seven subjects (25%) of the employed group were in teaching and social work, and eight (29%) were in business fields. The remaining subjects were distributed over such areas as the Armed Forces (3 = 11%), housewives (4 = 14%), and unskilled/semiskilled and skilled workers (another 6 = 21%). (These figures are combined when reported in the table). Only one subject was unemployed. These figures are quite similar to the previous two studies, particularly the Gow group. As in the Gow SLD alumni, the largest concentration of careers in the UCRC group was clustered around the business careers area.

Also quite noticeable about these two populations (Gow & UCRC) is the similarities in level of IQ and the high percentages of careers in the management fields. A major weakness in identifying the SLD population of the UCRC group, however, is that no pretest or posttest information is provided on academic functioning. SES is only estimated to be middle class or higher. Also remarkable is the fact that the Gow and UCRC subjects are less likely to be in the professional level occupations at the same percentages as their parents, and without a control group, comparisons about their SES and significance of disability are most speculative. However, it appears that Hypothesis #2 is rejected, as most of these subjects have done quite well, with normal distributions of workers. Obviously Hypotheses #3 and #4 are retained.

Kansas SLD Follow-up by Vetter (1983)

Background of Study

A SLD follow-up study was conducted by Vetter (1983) with a population from a middle-to-upper class suburb just outside Kansas City, Kansas. A major purpose of the study was to determine the adult adjustment of a group of 63 school identified SLD students. A comparison group of nonhandicapped students was included in the follow-up. Vetter's SLD sample was drawn from a school district's special education records.

Demographics of Vetter's SLD Population

Age differences were slight between the SLD and comparison groups, with the SLDs being somewhat older. The two groups were not significantly different on the basis of sex, race (mostly white, 92% for SLDs, 98% for controls), number of years out of school, or percentage completing high school (94% for the SLD group, 99% for controls). The SLD students were, however, significantly older when exiting the school system (18.3 mean years for SLDs, 17.5 for controls). SLD subjects, according to Vetter, came from significantly lower socioeconomic backgrounds than their nonhandicapped controls.

Vocational Outcomes of Vetter's SLD Population

SLD subjects in Vetter's population obtained significantly lower status jobs than did the control group subjects. No differences existed, however, on the basis of income their respective jobs generated or whether the jobs were full or part-time. Employment rates did not differ greatly, with SLDs employed at a 95 percent rate, while an 89 percent rate was reported for controls. Obviously, some nonhandicapped subjects in this study are still active in education or training.

Job Satisfaction and Future Planning Attitudes

Vetter's SLD population and controls appeared not to be greatly dissimilar in their degree of job satisfaction (controls reported being happy while SLDs were only slightly happy with their jobs), a finding not entirely consistent with other SLD adult studies (Fafard & Haubrich, 1981). The SLDs did express a strong need for more job security. While Vetter's SLD population did not express significantly different feelings about being satisfied with their jobs, they did place the need for occupational guidance and preparation above daily living skills and personal-social skills, while ranking the need for academic assistance just above career assistance.

Future Perspective and Educational Planning

In the Vetter SLD population, it was found that SLDs were significantly different in terms of amount of educational planning for the future. SLD subjects concerned about job security should be planning about how they would deal with a job change. More specifically, only 55 percent of Vetter's SLD group had plans for the future while 74 percent of the controls had such plans. Combined with this lesser degree of future planning perspective, the SLD group also had significantly lower career aspirations than the control group. Finally, in the area of future goals, approximately half of the SLD group expressed such goals compared to 89 percent for planning and time perspective.

Educational and Vocational Training Participation after High School

With regard to participation in a four year college program, this SLD population was significantly underrepresented (10.8% vs. 69.7% for controls). However, in the areas of vocational schooling and apprenticeship participation, SLD subjects had higher participation rate than their controls. Enrollment in junior college programs was less so, with SLDs participating at a rate of 35 percent compared to 44.7 percent for controls.

Summary of Vetter's SLD Population Characteristics

A limitation of this study is that it is not known to what degree the SLD group and the control group differed on intellectual and achievement levels, which weakens the generalizability of the findings. Secondly, it would be helpful to have identified the specific occupations that SLD and control groups went into, rather than inferring from Duncan's SEI what types of occupations might be represented. Finally, the age range of both groups begins at 19 and extends to 25, thus, the lower age individuals have not really had much opportunity to experience a significant work history. In fact, the largest percentage of adults from both groups had only been out of school for two years. A later follow-up of this same population will provide a much more extended interpretation of the effects of having a specific learning disability with respect to attainment in work adjustment.

Two final observations from Vetter's study that could have a bearing on assisting the futures of SLD adults are: (a) the future educational/training aspirations that SLD persons indicated were clearly identified as being in the area of the vocational trades. This finding may be a clear indication that SLD adults in this follow-up are ready to move out of their lower status jobs and into more skilled (and more secure) kinds of work; and (b) Vetter reported that SLD subjects were holding more full time work than the nonhandicapped group, particularly with regard to their first two jobs. This could mean that nonSLD adults were also concentrating on obtaining more education/training. Implications of this finding would suggest encouraging young SLD adults to be not as concerned about immediate financial gratification but to be equally concerned about developing long term job skills for more permanent and rewarding employment.

Hypotheses Evaluations for Vetter's SLD Follow-up Subjects

Hypothesis #1: SES Effects

In the Vetter SLD population, there was reported to be a 7-18 point difference between SLDs and controls of occupational status using Duncan's (1961) SEI Scale (the SEI ranges from 0-96 points with the bottom fifth of the scores representing unskilled, semiskilled and low-paid workers and the higher fifth of scores representing professionals and government officials, etc.). Using the Jencks et al. (1979) attainment data, which attributes education to account for almost one half of the variance in predicting occupational status, the mean for Duncan's SEI is 40, with a standard deviation of 24. Completion of high school rather than only elementary school, according to the Jencks et al. data, is worth an occupational advantage of almost half a standard deviation (12.5 points), while among men from the same background and ability, the advantage is only a fourth of a standard deviation (6.25 points). Completion of college would result in more than a full standard deviation (25 points) of occupational status, regardless of background or ability. As Vetter's population is only old enough to use high school completion rates (SLDs are 94% to 99% for controls), the SES comparisons will be confined to that level of educational attainment.

First, the mothers and fathers of the SLD group had mean SEI's of 41.43 and 43.31, respectively, while the control mothers and fathers had SEI's of 52.89 and 55.69, respectively, a significant difference, according to Vetter. The occupational difference between the two parent groups (SLD parents versus control parents) is approximately 12 SEI points or one half of a standard deviation or the value of completing high school over only elementary school. It should also be noted here that men whose test scores differ by 15 points can also expect to work in occupations whose occupational status differs by one third to one half of a standard deviation.

Secondly, the SLD population, who were not that different in high school completion rates, had occupational status point differences of 7-15, on the average about the same point differential as between SLD and control parents. Therefore, it might be concluded that occupational status differences between the SLDs and controls were what one would have expected on the basis of socioeconomic status. This negates any assumption that the difference is due to the learning disability per se.

Thirdly, the fact that Vetter found no significant differences in job satisfaction between SLDs and controls is consistent with the above interpretation. This is so because the SLDs are working at occupational status levels (for their age) that are proportionate to their parents SEI occupational status, that is, the SEI point differences between SLDs and controls is about the same as between the SLD parents and control parents.

Fourthly, but in a more speculative prediction, we know from the KGS Study (1985) that SLDs had mean IQs of 109. Given that the Vetter study was taken from a Kansas population included in the KGS, it would not be illogical to use these KGS IQ scores as proxy for the Vetter study, which omitted them. In achievement, also omitted from the Vetter follow-up data, the KGS showed a mean of 82 for SLDs and 97 for nonSLDs. Thus, the 12 point IQ difference between Kansas SLDs and nonSLDs represents a predicted one third to one half of a standard deviation in occupational status (8-12 points), almost exactly the occupational difference SEI found between Vetter's SLDs and controls.

Given these assumptions, Vetter's SLDs are different from their controls not because of their learning disabilities, but because of their lower SES backgrounds. This confirms the original hypothesis that individuals who come from more favorable socioeconomic backgrounds will have completed more schooling and consequently will have achieved a higher occupational status. This is also consistent with the findings of the Rawson and Gottfredson et al. SLD populations. Robinson and Smith's study lacks a control group, thus, it cannot be compared in the same manner. Finally, all other studies reviewed thus far lend support to status attainment model (Blau & Duncan, 1967; Jencks et al., 1972, 1979, 1983) for accounting for the adult occupational success differences between SLDs and their nonSLD controls, of which family background, test scores and years of schooling can explain as much as 51-54 percent of the variance in such success. Adding aspiration, which seems to be associated with being treated differently while in school and being in college, would bring the accounted for variance, including personality traits, to about 55-60 percent of the variance for such adult occupational success. Hypothesis #1 is retained.

Hypothesis #2: Effects of the Learning Disability

It appears that the primary difference between these two groups can be attributed to socioeconomic status rather than to a specific learning disability. Hypothesis #2 is rejected.

Hypothesis #3: EMR Comparisons

The occupations presently held by Vetter's SLD group appear to equate employment levels more characteristic of mildly mentally retarded students except for the rate of employment. Hypothesis #3 is partially rejected.

Hypothesis #4

While specific achievement levels are not stated, it appears that most of these students have achieved at least functioning above the fifth grade level. Hypothesis #4 is retained.

Statistical Evaluation of Vetter's Data

High School Completion

High school completion rate differences between Vetter's SLDs and controls were found to be nonsignificant ($X^2 = 1.87$, df $= 1$, $> .05$).

College Participation

Because of the younger mean age of this population, college participation at follow-up was used rather than BA completion rate as in the previous studies (Rawson, Gottfredson et al., Robinson & Smith). Using this factor, the differences between SLDs was significant on an overall postsecondary (education & training) participation ($X^2 = 13.25$, df $= 1$, $< .01$). The higher SES control group population was much more participative in postsecondary education despite the nonsignificant differences in high school completion rate. Vetter's data reported 60.3 percent (n $= 58$) postsecondary participation for SLDs and 91.23 percent for controls (n $= 57$). (College "only" was 11% versus 70%).

Employment Comparisons

No significant difference between rate of employment was found between SLDs and controls ($X^2 = 1.73$, df $= 1$, $> .05$).

Employment Status Comparisons

This statistical result was taken from Vetter's data (as was the postsecondary) in that she did not report the actual breakdown of subjects into occupational classifications. However, on the basis of comparing occupational status via Duncan's (1961) SEI, Vetter found a significant difference between SLDs and controls for both their first full-time jobs held, and their second full-time jobs. The SLD first job rating on SEI was $\bar{x} = 19.74$, SLD second job SEI rating $\bar{x} = 23.70$. For the control group SEI rating was also significant, first job $\bar{x} = 33.26$, second job $\bar{x} = 40.13$. It is important to note that both groups moved up in SEI, 4 points for SLDs and 7 points for the controls. Recall that the Jencks et al. data (1979) yielded a one standard deviation equivalent of 25 points with a mean of 40 for Duncan's SEI. The Vetter controls reached the mean on Duncan's SEI, the actual mean SEI status point differences between SLDs and controls are within one standard deviation.

California SLD Follow-up by Hartzell and Compton (1984)

A population of Northern Californian identified learning disabled students (SLD) (n = 114) were randomly selected from a larger clinical population pool (n = 223) for the purpose of assessing their academic, social and work histories (Hartzell & Compton, 1984). A control group of nonhandicapped students was included in the study. It is important to note that these students came from upper middle class socioeconomic backgrounds, with 73 percent of fathers having completed college degrees.

This predominantly male SLD group (72% vs. 38% for controls) had original *WISC* full scale scores ranging from 74 to 151 (mean = 107). Verbal scores were just slightly higher than performance subtest scores. At their original evaluations, these SLD students ranged in ages from 5 to 15 and were followed up ten years later. Ninety-one percent of the SLD group was white. Of the SLD families, 80 percent reported a family history of learning disabilities. Severity of learning disability was judged by: (a) number of years below expected reading grade level, (b) number of academic areas affected, and (c) number of learning modalities involved (i.e., visual, auditory, etc.). Using these criteria, 23 percent of the sample were considered mildly disabled, 44 percent as moderately disabled, and 33 percent were categorized as severely disabled.

Treatment provided these SLD students between evaluation and the follow-up date (treatment was not controlled by investigators) ranged from less than two years of special education (30%), special education services for two to six years (37%) and continuous special education over the ten-year period (33%). At the time of follow-up, the average age of the SLD group was 19, but ages ranged from 15 to 27. Within the SLD group, 37 percent were retained for at least one grade, but 91 percent completed high school compared to 99 percent for the controls. Ages and sex of the control group differed somewhat from the SLD group, for the controls, 21.5 was the mean age and only 38 percent were male. Shown in Tables 3 and 3a are comparative findings for education, academic, social and job success. Only limited generalizations about SLD job attainment can be made due to subjects not being old enough to be fully participative in work. In fact, no significant difference was found in the types of entry level jobs that SLDs and their controls had obtained. Rate of employment was not reported. Over one third of the SLD group were still in school.

Summary and Conclusions of the Hartzell and Compton Study

Given the mean age of these SLD students, it would be premature to predict their future academic, social or employment outcomes. Despite the fact that more than twice as many controls were attending four year colleges would not, however, preclude that many controls who were attending two year colleges may go on to a four year program or that those not now in school might also choose to do so at a later date. However, as the SLD mean average for college attainment in all of these control groups included studies is exactly one half of that for the nonSLDs, the outlook for SLDs completing college would appear dim. Over and above these more descriptive observations, Hartzell and Compton did conduct a stepwise regression analysis to ascertain which variables accounted for the most variance for predicting positive outcomes in three areas. They were, according to Hartzell and Compton (1984), as follows: (a) effective family functioning and a high full scale I.Q. accounted for the most variance (35%) for predicting higher academic success, (b) full scale I.Q. and the psychosocial functioning of the child were the best predictions of social success (22% of variance), and (c) job success was best predicted by current age and full scale I.Q. (30% accounted variance). Based on the limited data of this study, no further analysis can be made in order to make hypothesis comparisons.

Bruck's Canadian SLD Follow-up Study

In another research effort to present a comprehensive picture of the specific long term consequences of learning disabilities, Bruck (1985) has conducted an ongoing SLD follow-up research project as part of the McGill-Montreal Children's Hospital Learning Centre, established in the 1960s by Samual Rabinovitch, an early Canadian SLD pioneer. Bruck defined SLD as "a heterogeneous group of children who, along with many intact abilities, show significant deficits in some areas of academic achievement. Although the predominant symptom is usually learning to read, this may be accompanied by other difficulties such as physical awkwardness, directional disorientation and the more familiar problems of spelling, math and written work" (p. 91). Noting that results of previous follow-up studies suggest that SLD persists through adolescence and adulthood, yet the field of SLD lacks a comprehensive picture of the problem, Bruck's study attempted to determine the following: (a) Do children become SLD adults? (b) What are the subsequent consequences of a childhood SLD on academic, occupational, social and emotional adjustment? (c) What is the relationship between childhood remediation and adult measures of academic, social, occupational and personal adjustment? (d) What combination of events best predicts the type of adjustment that children with SLD will make in late adolescence or in young adulthood?

Overall, Bruck reported that in comparison to a group of tested, non-learning disabled peers, and to an untested group of age-matched, non-learning disabled siblings, SLD does persist into late adolescence and young adulthood. However, Bruck cautioned that: "While the majority of LD subjects were considered non-readers when assessed as children, at follow-up there were extremely few who were illiterate. Most had the necessary skills to function adequately in various situations. Second, while learning disabilities did persist, the data suggest that continued exposure to literacy tasks in demanding situations can result in the continuation of skill development in the learning-disabled population" (p. 125). In the academic and occupational domain, Bruck reported that SLD unemployment rates were comparable to controls, and only a few held unskilled jobs. High school completion rates were above average and similar numbers of controls and SLD subjects did go to higher education and were successful. SLDs did take longer to complete their studies and reported mild to moderate difficulties with their academic studies.

Finally, comparisons with the peer control group on measures of social deviance indicated that there was no association between juvenile delinquency, problems of drug and alcohol abuse and childhood learning disabilities. SLDs did show to be at risk in the area of peer relationships and psychological adjustment. Bruck believed that the reason for such positive outcomes for these SLDs is that they were identified at a young age and, with that, benefitted from early intervention for the learning problems. Counseling for the parent and teachers was also part of that intervention in Bruck's population. Another factor accounting for a positive outcome, according to Bruck, was the fact that the SLD sample was carefully defined. All potential subjects with childhood symptoms which, by themselves may have been antecedents of poor adult outcomes, were omitted from the study. As such, Bruck's population is believed to be representative of children with "primary learning disabilities" (p. 127).

Outline of Bruck's SLD Study

The experimental group of SLDs consisted of 101 subjects who had been diagnosed as SLD during their elementary school year at a specialized hospital clinic, and who, at the time of their follow-up, were between the ages of 17-29. The controls consisted of one group of 50 nonlearning disabled subjects matched for age, sex and SES and referred to as the peer control group. Another group of 51 nonlearning disabled subjects of the SLDs were siblings also matched for age, sex and SES and called the sibling control group (the comparison group included in Table 3a). Each of the SLDs and control subjects and at least one of their parents were interviewed to determine the long term consequences and permanence of learning disabilities. The SLD subjects' status at follow-up was compared to that of the tested peer control group and to that of the untested normal sibling control group whose status was determined from the interview data.

Nature and Selection of SLD Subjects and Controls

From a bank of 5,000 children diagnosed as SLD by clinic staff, a list of 259 potential cases were considered. On this list of 259 were subjects who were between the ages of 5 and 10 upon first clinic contact and assessment, with IQ scores of at least 90 (WISC verbal or performance score or the Stanford-Binet score). The population of 259 had no primary behavioral or emotional disturbances, no major neurological abnormalities or other physical disabilities that might explain learning impairments. Assessments at the time of the presenting problem at intake, available in the clinic files, also included a reading score. Subjects were between the ages of 17 and 29 at the time of follow-up and were no longer attending high school. And finally, there was a confirmation of the initial diagnosis of SLD by a staff psychologist who reviewed the patient file information after computer identification. Of the 259, 78 percent of the subjects and their parents were located after an average interval of 13 years between initial clinic assessment and follow-up. Out of this 78 percent, 156 families agreed to participate in the study. A total of 101 families were selected from this sample pool on the basis of age and treatment history (one half had clinic treatment for 1.5 years and one half had no treatment services).

Peer group controls were selected on the basis of recommendations by the SLD subject but screened for absence of learning difficulty. The sibling controls were selected on the basis of the peer controls being highly achievement oriented, therefore to get a more representative estimate of the academic and occupational status of nondisabled persons, siblings of the SLD group were also used. Test instruments included the *Gray Oral Reading Test,* reading portions of the *Stanford Diagnostic Reading Test* and the reading, spelling, and math subtests of the *Wide Range Achievement Test.*

Background Status of Bruck Subjects

Typical of other SLD studies was the finding of a male majority having SLD (79%). Mean IQs at a child's first entry was 103 (SD = 11.22). All subjects were assessed as having primary problems with language (reading and spelling). In addition, Bruck reported that 75 percent of the SLD cases were having difficulty in the area of mathematics. Childhood performance reviews indicated that SLDs were associated with difficulties with visual processing and/or spatial skills for 45 percent of the cases. Another 6 percent had difficulties in auditory processing and/or language skills. Combined poor visual/spatial and poor auditory language skills were present in 48 percent of the subjects. With respect to severity, incidence ranged from 43 percent of the cases (most severe) to 27 percent (least severe) of the respective cases. On the average, each SLD subject received 4.47 years of special assistance for their learning problems, only 4 out of the 101 cases never received any special help.

Persistence of Learning Disabilities into Adulthood

There was a significant difference between SLDs and peer controls at follow-up with respect to reading, spelling and arithmetic. A four grade level difference for reading, a near five grade difference for spelling, and a 3.5 grade level difference for arithmetic were found. For the SLD group, the relationships between years of education and test scores were highly significant, suggesting that skills developed as a function of education experience and not automatically as a function of maturation. An important finding with respect to the correlation between the number of years of schooling and test scores was that after adolescence, continued exposure to literacy tasks in demanding situations were associated with the continuation of literacy skill development in SLD individuals. This finding is at odds with the Deshler et al. (1982) report that claims that SLDs seem to "peak out" academically about the tenth grade. The most commonly reported difficulties of the SLDs were related to spelling and written expression. SLDs rarely read for pleasure. Math deficiencies were related to functional skills such as checkbook balancing and so forth. Between 3 and 16 percent of the SLDs had severe academic problems, as defined by functioning below grade six in all academic areas. The mean IQ of these severe cases was 93.62, all were males, and all but one were rated as having severe childhood disabilities. Of the 43 subjects rated as severe in childhood, 27 had a mean IQ of 95 and had acquired academic faculty above the sixth grade. A small number of subjects felt they were limited by their lower level of skills, but most did not consider their shortcomings as a handicap.

Long Term Consequences of Having a SLD

The peer control group was shown to be above average in academic achievement, a factor which Bruck admitted may have been caused by the SLDs' choice of a control, allowing the selection of their "smartest friends." Average peers may not have perceived the importance of such an experiment and thus declined participation. On the other hand, the SLDs' siblings represented identical family backgrounds and actually received the same mean number years of schooling, including similar drop-out rates. Eight of the eleven who graduated from college went on for advanced degrees, noting however, that they had to work harder and longer to get through school.

SES Differences in Educational Attainment

Pointing out the differences between SLDs who achieved more schooling from those that did not, Bruck noted that the six subjects who came from lower class backgrounds dropped out of high school (n = 2) or completed only high school (n = 4), which prompted Bruck to state that "these data highlight the importance of controlling for, or examining the effects of social class on follow-up measures. One suspects that follow-up studies, which reported poor outcomes for SLD individuals, included a larger proportion of non-middle class subjects than were included in other studies, which reported more positive outcomes. The results of other former studies [Rawson's is presumed] may reflect the effects of social class on follow-up status rather than of a learning disability as such" (p. 116).

Severity as a Function of Attainment

With respect to disability severity, Bruck posited that children with the most severe disabilities were most at risk for not completing high school (6 out of 10 were severe). Of those not continuing their education, 44 percent were severe, while most of those going on to college were of the mild range (77%). But, note that a fourth of the severe did go on to college. Bruck concluded that the academic prognosis for SLDs is positive and they are not at risk for dropping out. And while they will have academic difficulties, it will not impede their careers.

Employment Attainment of SLDs

With respect to those employed, the SLDs had an overall employment rate of 83 percent. The controls' overall unemployment rates were not significantly different. The least employed SLDs were the 15-19 year olds (63%), followed by the 20-24 year olds at 85 percent. The SLDs in the range of 25 years and older had total employment, as did that age ranges of controls, both peer and sibling. Interestingly, for the 15-19 year olds, the peer and sibling controls had employment rates far different from the SLD group, 40 percent and 50 percent, respectively.

Occupational Levels of SLDs

As in the Vetter (1963) study, Bruck used SES equivalents for describing the occupations held by the subjects in her study. Citing employment statistics from Canada, Bruck noted that the peer controls were atypical of the general population in that, for those working, their occupational levels were quite high. Comparing the siblings' occupational outcomes with SLDs', it was reported that there was only a slight SES difference. We are only told that the occupations were exemplified as social workers, radio installers, mechanics, computer analysts, nurses, accountants, shippers, dispatchers and so forth. Bruck stated rather directly that "occupational achievement was not associated with severity of learning disability" (p. 118).

Overall, the SLDs reported satisfaction with their jobs, with most stating that "they would like to eventually change jobs to more responsible or skilled placements" (p. 119), a notable contrast, as will be seen in reviewing Spreen's Canadian subjects, later in this chapter. Further, Bruck found that most of the SLD subjects felt that they had the requisite skills to function competently in their occupation.

Hypotheses Comparisons for Bruck's SLDs

Hypothesis #1: SES

Clearly, SES is a factor in the successful outcomes of these subjects. With the variables of family background controlled via the use of siblings, we found support for the Jencks et al. (1979, 1983) findings that if individuals are able to complete schooling and go on to college, the differences on the basis of achievement/ability will be less than that of family background factors. **Hypothesis #1 is retained.**

Hypothesis #2: Effects of SLD

Bruck has pointed out rather convincing evidence that her subjects have not been adversely affected by having a SLD. **Hypothesis #2 is rejected.**

Hypothesis #3: EMR Comparisons

These Canadian SLDs are performing well above average in all areas. **Hypothesis #3 is retained.**

Hypothesis #4: Literacy Levels

A small percentage of Bruck's subjects were reported to be functioning at or below a sixth grade level, but the predominant group was functioning at an eighth grade level or better, except for math. According to Jencks et al. (1983), the poorer math scores should restrict success, however, it is not ascertainable in this study. **Overall, Hypothesis #4 is retained.**

Statistical Hypotheses Comparisons of Bruck's Education and Employment Data

High School Completion

High school completion rate differences between Bruck's SLDs and the peer control group were not significantly different ($X^2 = 3.09$, df = 1, >.05).

College Participation

College participation differences were not significantly different between SLDs and the peer control group ($X^2 = 2.31$, df = 1, >.05).

Employment Rate

No significant difference between SLDs and peer controls was found ($X^2 = 2.81$, df = 1, >.05).

Employment Status

Bruck reported that only a few of her subjects were in unskilled/ semiskilled occupations. No breakdowns on type or quantity within qualifications were given.

Overall Summary

This population is very different from the other studies, with the exception of Rawson's subjects. All outcomes were positive. As Bruck noted, however, much of this positive outcome can be attributed to the extreme selection bias of the sample and/or the effects of early intervention.

ACLD Follow-up Study of SLD Adults

The Association for Children with Learning Disabilities (ACLD), through its vocational committee, began a survey in 1981 to determine the status and needs of adults who have, or have had during their school careers, a learning disability. In 1982, two ACLD *Newsbrief* articles published the results of the SLD adult survey.

SLD Adult Job Related Findings

In this survey, of which there were 562 completed and valid surveys returned from parents or SLD adults themselves, over 100 (18%) of the

SLD adults were not employed or enrolled in any school or training program. Of the 274 employed (49%), 23.5 percent were employed in unskilled labor positions. The semiskilled group was employed at a 27 percent rate and 24.5 percent were employed in the skilled employment group. The managerial/sales group were employed at a 10 percent rate, and 15 percent were in professional occupations. The age group 25-29 (32.3%) had the highest unemployment. The 18 percent unemployment rate can be compared to a 1981 national unemployment rate of 7.4 for males and 7.9 for females (*Statistical Abstract of the United States,* 1982).

Income levels beneath $10,000 were reported for 61 percent of those responding, and 31 percent were earning between $10,000-$20,000. Poverty level income for 1981 was $4620 for a single household. Responses in the domain of job satisfaction revealed almost half of those responding to be dissatisfied in their current employment. Employment success as a result of vocational training participation has apparently been limited, with only about one half of those who participated in vocational training able to find a job as a result. Of those who did find a job, a significant number could not keep the job for various reasons.

ACLD Respondents Want Career and Social Skill Help

Career development programs, whose curriculums are designed to help students make transitions from school to work, and in which nearly one half (45%) of SLD individuals of the ACLD study have participated, could be a positive indicator of which SLD individuals attained employment success. It is most important to note here that of ten major categories in which SLD individuals reported their needs or desires for assistance, social relationship skills and career counseling were the top two selected. These expressed needs are underscored by the ACLD reported job satisfaction results which indicated that SLD individuals may be selecting career areas incompatible with their aptitudes, interests and values, as well as losing that job because of poor interpersonal communication skills. It is quite obvious that these SLD individuals and their parents have identified realistic and appropriate areas of need that professionals need to address if there is to be an improvement in these employment related statistics.

Hypotheses Evaluations

In this kind of survey where there is no control group and responses are from several states, it is not feasible to attempt generalizations from the data, other than to observe the patterns of employment and education as they relate to U.S. national trends. No statistical comparisons were made due to lack of a control group.

Hypothesis #1: SES as Predictor of Adult Achievement of SLD Individuals

There was no specific mention of SES levels in the survey with the exception that 61 percent of the total reported incomes were below $10,000, while another 31 percent had incomes between $10,000 and $20,000 for the year 1980-81. Thus, 91 percent of the sample were under the $20,000 a year income level. A poverty level income for the year 1981 was considered to be $4620 for a single person, which most of these ACLD study respondents were. In 1981, 20 percent of families nationwide had incomes at or below $10,000, while another 30 percent had incomes between $10,000 and $15,000 (*Statistical Abstract of the United States,* 1982). This comparison indicates that this ACLD population of current/former SLD persons are in the bottom fourth of income level. However, it must be remembered that only 49 percent of the sample were reported to be in competitive employment and, therefore, may have reduced the mean income levels.

Another factor that could aid in estimating the SES of this follow-up population is their level of occupational status. The distribution of occupations is nearly even across unskilled (23.5%), semiskilled (27.0%) and skilled (24.5%). In addition, there were 25 percent participating in professional, managerial and sales positions. Given the differences between income (which is comparatively low) and occupational status of this ACLD sample, it cannot be estimated whether SES is a factor in this ACLD population with regard to their educational and occupational attainment.

In contrast, nationally the percentage of managerial and professional persons in a category of white males with at least one year of college (ACLD respondents had a 19% BA college completion rate) or more is 48 percent, but with high school completion only the rate is only 11 percent. The combined managerial and professional categories in the ACLD sample of employed persons (n = 274) had 17.5 percent participation. In the area of skilled employment, the ACLD group had nearly one fourth of their workers in this category, which compares to a national average of 29 percent for white males with four years of high school.

Occupationally speaking, these ACLD respondents may have had an average SES status, however this occupational status was not matched in income level.

For educational attainment comparisons, the national drop out rates for 1968, 1970, 1975, 1980 and 1981 for white individuals 16-24, were 11.9, 10.8, 10.5, 11.3 and 11.3, respectively. (Statistical Abstract of the United States, 1982). The ACLD overall dropout rate was 12 percent. College enrollment for whites who came from families with incomes up to and including $25,000 in 1981 averaged 42 percent, for those families below $20,000 in income (Statistical Abstract of the United States, 1982) the college enrollment rate was 37 percent. Not calculated in the ACLD group for the overall comparisons (Table 3) were the ACLD participants presently enrolled in college, which these national figures include (not just graduates). By adding the currently enrolled ACLD subjects to the graduates, the college enrollment percentage for the ACLD group jumped to 68 percent. That figure (68%) is closer to the college mean enrollment percentage of 53.1 for those students coming from families with incomes of $25,000 or more.

Given this data, it would appear that these ACLD subjects could be from middle to upper class SES families, and that their educational attainment is commensurate with the national averages for high school completion (in 1950, 1975, 1980 and 1984, the completion rates were 56, 74.3, 71.4 and 73.9%, respectively, and ACLD's was 88%) and college enrollment. It appears that in occupational and educational attainment, these ACLD subjects are performing at a level equivalent to average individuals from middle class backgrounds. Only in income and employment rate do they differ greatly. Thus, the final SES hypothesis conclusion is only partially accepted; income attainment and employment rate are excluded. Remember however, that completing college rather than high school is associated with a full 25 points on Duncan's SEI, with respect to derived economic benefit of the occupational advantage (Jencks et al., 1979). This might mean that the 126 ACLD subjects now in college could, upon graduation and after a reasonable employment period, have quite an effect on the mean income levels now reported for this total sample. It could also represent the increasing opportunities for students with learning disabilities to enter college; thus, if the survey review were followed up again ten or so years later, we could validate that hypothesis.

Finally, Jencks et al. (1979) noted that high school dropouts (ACLD had 18%) are economically disadvantaged largely because they fail to finish school. The apparent advantages enjoyed by high school graduates derived to a significant extent from their prior characteristics, not from their schooling. Unless high school participation is followed by a college degree, its economic value is moderate. Jencks et al. summarized this point by stating that "while the distribution of elementary and secondary education has become considerably more equal, the distribution of higher education has become somewhat less equal" (p. 190). A review of educational statistics over the last 20 years will, in fact, show that national high school dropout rates have improved (1968 = 13.1%; 1981 = 11.8%) while percentages of four year college degrees conferred has declined (1950 = 40 BA degrees per 100 high school graduates; 1980 = 29 BA degrees per 100 high school graduates) (*Statistical Abstract of the United States,* 1982). This point has been presented to offer the theory that lower incomes (over and above inflation) will prevail as long as the above trend continues, but students who have not done well in school but are now getting greater attention (as SLDs are) will and should be reflected in time with respect to higher incomes, even higher than the national averages. Lacking hard data, however, a final hypothesis evaluation cannot be made.

Hypothesis #2: Effects of a Learning Disability

This hypothesis cannot be addressed as no academic achievement information or IQ data was included. The only assumptions that can be made were presented above. These SLD adults have accomplished a great deal, with exception of the higher than average unemployment rate and lower than expected income levels.

Hypothesis #3: EMR Comparisons

Given the ranges of educational and occupational attainment of this population, it cannot be considered approximal to the mildly retarded population.

Hypothesis #4: Literacy Levels

As no information was provided about level of academic ability, no evaluation can be made.

Balow and Blomquist (1965) Minnesota Follow-up Background

The SLD sample consisted of 32 males initially studied at the University of Minnesota Psycho-Educational Clinic during the years 1948-53. Selection of the sample was based on sex, age, clinical diagnostic classification, intelligence and amount of retardation in reading. Initial reading was two to five years below age-grade expectation, two thirds of the pupils were reading at or below second grade level. Subjects were between 7.8 years (2nd grade) and 13.5 years of age at first referral.

Demographics of Minnesota Sample

Of the entire group of 32 slow readers whose median IQ was 100 in childhood, 27 had graduated from high school (84%), and 23 had some postsecondary education. Education attained by the subjects exceeded that of their fathers. Three subjects were in managerial occupations (14%), one was in a professional position (5%), eight were in skilled positions (38%), three were in semiskilled (Armed Forces, actually, 4%), and six were in unskilled positions (28.5%). Ten subjects were in college. Balow and Blomquist intimated that proportionately more men with an early reading handicap would be found in semiskilled and unskilled occupations than would a group of average readers who had made normal progress in school. Most of the men in this study reported that they did not like school and that inadequate reading had hindered their academic efforts. Balow and Blomquist concluded that these middle class males who were severely disabled in reading would attain average adult reading proficiency (approximately 10th grade), graduate from high school, possess mild emotional disorders of a neurotic type and find jobs over a wide range of occupational levels. However, a large proportion of these men, compared to average readers, would have semiskilled and unskilled jobs.

Hypotheses Comparisons

No statistical comparisons were made due to lack of a control group.

Hypothesis #1: SES Status

Considering the fact that many of these subjects came from lower middle SES backgrounds and had average IQs, some lower and some higher, the equal distribution between unskilled/semiskilled employment (43%) and skilled/managerial employment would be about what one might expect with 16 percent of the population not completing high school and just a third going on to college. Clearly SES status in this study ranged from lower to upper middle class subjects. A control group would have helped clarify this hypothesis. As it stands the hypothesis is equivocal.

Hypothesis #2: Effect of SLD

Again without a control group it is difficult to assess if the reading level or SES status predicted drop out and lower status jobs. Thus, this Hypothesis #2 is equivocal.

Hypothesis #3: EMR Comparison

This Minnesota population had a 100 percent population employment rate and an equal number of skilled/managerial jobs and unskilled/semiskilled. This population in no way equates to EMR outcomes. The hypothesis is retained.

Hypothesis #4

This Minnesota sample had a mean reading performance scale of 10.23. Thus, this hypothesis is also retained.

Humes and Brammer's Virginia Rural Community Follow-up Background

In a SLD follow-up survey conducted in a small county school district in southwestern Virginia, Humes and Brammer (1985) reported on 26 graduates of a high school SLD program begun in 1978. Since that SLD high school program began, 33 students had been served who were to graduate between 1978 and 1983. A final participating sample of 26 SLD subjects were evaluated for their postschool status.

Postschool Attainment

In the reporting of this study, there was no mention of the SES of the population, ages nor was a control group utilized. High school was completed by 83 percent of the students served in the program. Ninety percent of the subjects were employed in the following categories: (a) unskilled (6%), (b) semiskilled (63%), (c) skilled (38%), and (d) sales/managerial (11%). None of the subjects would have had time to complete enough education to participate in a professional level of employment.

College participation was limited to one student in a vocational-technical school and one student in a community college program. One of the subjects, who also had cerebral palsy, was working in a sheltered workshop and was being served in a local rehabilitation program.

Hypotheses Evaluation

Due to the limited information included in this study, very few, if any, generalizations can be made about their relationship to the four hypotheses being used in this review. However, in this population, and compared to the seven previously discussed SLD follow-up populations, there are fewer numbers of high school completions and employed workers.

Frauenheim and Heckerl's SLD Study

Defining reading disability as a "disorder in which the capacity to learn to read is impaired despite adequate intelligence, appropriate educational and socio-cultural opportunities, and basic intactness of those sensory functions associated with 'normal' learning" (p. 339), Frauenheim and Heckerl (1983) examined the psychological and educational test performance patterns in a group of adults diagnosed as reading disabled in childhood. No control group was included. Included in the follow-up data were occupational achievement data.

The study had a total sample of 11 males, with a mean age of 27. As children, all were from predominately middle class families in the Detroit, Michigan, area. Nine of the eleven subjects were married. All of the subjects as children experienced academic difficulties from the onset of their schooling. Mean IQ level of the group was 92. The subjects had mean reading, spelling and arithmetic scores in childhood of 1.9, 1.4 and 3.1, respectively. Retest academic achievement scores at the mean age of 27 were 2.6, 2.1 and 4.6, respectively.

Educational and occupational attainment of the 11 subjects is reported: 80 percent completed high school; 72 percent were employed, 9 percent in unskilled work, 27 percent in semiskilled positions and the remaining 54 percent in skilled positions.

Hypotheses Evaluation

Again due to the lack of a control group, any generalizations about SES effects of a learning disability, and so forth, are limited. Some general comments are made about each hypothesis but recognize the limitations in making such comments.

Hypothesis #1: SES

The authors of this study stated quite specifically that these 11 subjects came from "predominately" middle class families and communities in the Detroit metropolitan area. IQs of the sample ranged from 82-104, but their performance scores on the *WAIS-R* ranged from 92-121, and the verbal score range was 78-94. Like many reported SLD cases, digit span and digit symbol/coding were the lowest subtest scores, which are indicative of poor word decoding ability. The fact that these subjects came from middle class backgrounds with high IQs in the performance scale of the *WAIS-R*, makes their 54 percent participation in skilled employment understandable. With the high *WAIS-R* performance scores, one might expect more of this population to fall in unskilled/semiskilled than there are (0% in unskilled and 45% in semiskilled). It is also important to note that of the 28 percent unemployed, all were no doubt related to Detroit's auto industry labor cycle. These middle class adults are characterized by working in semiskilled and skilled occupations but none in unskilled work. Given that the subjects have had and continue to have severe reading deficits, their occupational achievement levels are consistent with the hypothesis that higher SES individuals will participate in higher status occupations. Based on this above perspective **Hypothesis #1 is retained.**

Hypothesis #2: Effects of a Learning Disability

Of the studies reviewed thus far, the data presented by Frauenheim and Heckerl on IQ, performance, achievement and specific occupational outcomes, presents the most compelling case for a specific learning ability disadvantage effecting adult occupational outcome. The verbal ability of these subjects is significantly lower than their performance scores which explains why none of these subjects have participated in college and, subsequently, lacked participation in white collar occupations. It must also be kept in mind that these subjects not only were reading underachievers but also had arithmetic achievement scores ranging as low as 3.8-6.3 as adults, a point which Jencks et al. (1983) noted is most critical (math ability) for male success. It seems apparent that given the middle class SES of these subjects, they are functioning quite well.

Finally, it is noted here that the authors did a rather extensive evaluation of test performance patterns and literature review comparison with respect to their subjects. As such, Frauenheim and Heckerl stated in conclusion of their findings about why these subjects do so poorly academically is that "the skill deficits implied in the definition of dyslexia and further exemplified by the dyslexic adults in this study seem to reflect basic difficulty in symbolization processes. These include both auditory and visual memory for symbols and visuals and auditory association skills along with sequencing, etc." [visual and discrimination skills did not present a problem] (p. 341). Virtually no significant academic improvement occurred over the 17 year period between diagnosis and follow-up of these subjects, despite specific attempts at remediation. It appears that the learning abilities of these 11 adults are such that they were not able to obtain occupational positions any higher than skilled, despite the fact that their middle class backgrounds would have allowed some of the sample to obtain such a level. Perhaps with a larger sample this would have occurred. Clearly, **Hypothesis #2 is retained.**

Hypothesis #3: EMR Comparisons

The mean performance IQ and even the mean verbal IQ of these subjects, along with the fact that none were in unskilled jobs, would indicate that the 11 were more unlike EMR adults than like them, despite the fact that their employment rates were equal to those reported for EMR populations. Again, the Detroit auto industry, from which the unemployed were laid off is a cyclical one which may account for their particular rate of unemployment. As such, **Hypothesis #3 is also retained.**

Hypothesis #4: Degree of Literacy

All 11 of these subjects were operating at a functionally illiterate level, that is, below fifth grade in all subjects, reading, spelling and mathematics. Only three of the subjects met or exceeded this literacy level and that was in the area of arithmetic. Of the studies reviewed to date, these SLDs are the most severely disabled, particularly when their SES and performance IQs are taken into account. Despite this, most of them appeared to be functioning occupationally quite well. **Hypothesis #4, for this population, is rejected.**

Cove School Follow-up by Rogan and Hartman

In 1947 Alfred Strauss and one of the authors of this Cove School review (Laura Lehtinen-Rogan) wrote and published *Psychopathology and Education of the Brain-Injured Child,* long considered a classic in the field of learning disabilities. In this text and others, Strauss and his associates defined a new category of exceptional children, which they referred to as the brain-injured child; heretofore a group of children who had previously been classified as mentally retarded, emotionally disturbed, autistic or aphasic. Strauss, a physician who received his training in Germany, joined in 1937 the staff of the Wayne County Training School to study mentally retarded adolescents with severe learning problems. Later, in the states of Wisconsin and Illinois, Strauss and associates established the Cove Schools for brain-injured children. Seeking a medical cause for the behavioral characteristics of these children with learning problems, Strauss observed that the behavior and learning patterns of these children were manifestations of brain insult (Lerner, 1981) in that their behavior was similar to adults who had suffered an observable brain injury. In Strauss' thinking, however, a child could be diagnosed as brain injured without hard evidence of any of the accepted major biological signs, that is, (a) slight (soft signs) neurological signs, for instance, awkwardness in gait, inability to perform five motor skills; (b) history of neurological impairment in which there was a medical history of brain injury (hard signs) before, during or after birth; and (c) unexplained causes of learning problems where there is no history of mental retardation (ruled out genetic abnormalities of the brain). Definitions for these children and their learning problems proved to be confusing in that not all children with brain injuries have a severe learning problem. For example, many children with cerebral palsy may or may not have learning disorders, so it was suggested instead that the label "Strauss Syndrome" be used to describe this category of problem learners. The "Strauss Syndrome" cases have been described according to Lerner (1981, p. 34) as follows:

1. Erratic and inappropriate behavior on mild provocation.
2. Increased motor activity disproportionate to the stimulus.
3. Poor organization of behavior.
4. Distractability or more than ordinary degree under ordinary conditions.
5. Persistent hyperactivity.
6. Persistent faulty perceptions.
7. Awkwardness and consistently poor motor performance.

Strauss hypothesized that children who exhibited characteristics similar to those of the children in his studies at the Wayne Training School had also experienced an injury to the brain that produced the abnormal behavioral symptoms reported above (Lerner 1981; Kavale & Forness, 1985).

Thus, considering the above concerns with the brain-injury hypothesis, generalizations about the Cove School population must be tempered, and, for that matter, all studies that derive their theoretical assumptions about learning problems of presumed brain injury(s). These biologically and neurologically based categories explaining learning disorders (soft signs, hard signs and unexplained) identified by Strauss, are, despite their questioned validity, still used today and represent the definitional categories for a long term follow-up study in progress by Spreen and associates (1983) in Canada, reported upon here as one of the follow-up studies for review.

Etiological and Behavioral Characteristics of the Rogan and Hartman Cove School Population

Inheritor of the above classification system formulated by Strauss, the Cove School accepted a broad range of disabilities with learning disorders being paramount. The etiologies of the Cove School subjects' learning disabilities ranged from unknown (36%), to difficult delivery (24%), trauma (16.5%), premature delivery (7.7%), and pregnancy complications (6.6%). The remaining etiologies were spread over such incidences as cyanosis, arrested hydrocephalus, Caesarian births and jaundice. Of the 91 final follow-up subjects, 55 percent had additional physical or developmental handicaps, which either complicated the student's learning problems or constituted an identifiable symptom to the problem. In the area of language skills, 53 percent of the subjects had a speech and/or language difficulty of some kind. Another 53 percent were afflicted with cerebral palsy. Significant numbers of these subjects had emotional problems (64%), but the emotional problems were considered secondary to the learning disability(s). Poor behavior control was exhibited by another 31 percent and 19 percent were reported as having a significantly lowered sense of self-esteem. Large percentages of referrals to the Cove School were made by psychologists (34%) and psychiatrists (14%).

Intelligence measures of the Cove follow-up population ranged from approximately 69 to 130, with the means for verbal IQ being eight points higher than performance; in the groups with IQs of 80 or higher, the overall IQ mean was reported at 98. Rogan and Hartman (1976) noted that, over and above the subjects earlier IQ scores on the *WISC*, "the consistency and, in fact, the slight increase in IQ on adult testing suggests that education, intellectual stimulation, and supportive family environment may maintain and enhance intellectual growth and development in children with learning disabilities" (p. 91).

Educational and Occupational Attainment of the Cove School Students

Follow-up achievement tests were given, as were follow-up IQ tests, with the adult levels reported in Tables 4 and 4a. As can be seen, the reading and spelling attainments are not much different from Gottfredson's Gow School subjects. Arithmetic was the lowest of the three academic areas. Of the 49 subjects (65%) who were employed at the time of the follow-up interview, 39 (52%) reported satisfaction with the job, 7 (9%) had negative feelings and 3 (4%) were ambivalent. Much of the discussion around job satisfaction concerned the people with whom the subject was associated in the work situation. Frequently, the employment situation appeared to offer these subjects social contacts (friendship) and recreational activities related to work. Overall, Rogan and Hartman emphasized IQ as a mediating factor in successful adjustment, as noted by the belief that, in general, those subjects who have been

TABLE 4

CHARACTERISTICS OF COVE SCHOOL SUBJECTS LISTED AS MARGINALLY EMPLOYABLE

Sex	Adult Age	WAIS VIQ	PIQ	FIQ	Highest Education Completed	WRAT Readg Grade	Readg Comp.	Additional Problems in Childhood
F	34	92	80	86	High School Program for EMH	7.7	5.0	Emotional Problems
M	25	95	72	84	High School	9.6	9.8	Left Hemiplegia Emotional Problems
M	24	96	100	99	High School Basic Level	11.6	7.0	Emotional Problems
M	23	82	89	84	Non-graded Special Ed. Schools	4.4	4.5	Speech, Language Poor beh. cont. Emotional Problems
M	23	71	80	73	2 yrs. High School in EMH and Emotional Disturbed Programs	6.3	4.2	Emotional Problems

The marginally employable group consisted of four males and one female, ranging in age from 23-34. Two had completed high school, either in the regular program or in a basic track.

TABLE 4a
**CHARACTERISTICS OF COVE SCHOOL SUBJECTS ON
SHELTERED WORKSHOP SETTINGS**

Sex	Adult Age	WAIS			Highest Education Completed	WRAT Readg Grade	Readg Comp.	Additional Problems in Childhood
		VIQ	PIQ	FIQ				
M	28	128	99	116	High School Adjusted	16.8	14.1	Aphasia, Emotional Problems, Bizarre beh.
M	28	79	52	66	Non-graded Spec. Ed.	8.5	3.2	Cerebral Palsy (Athetoid), Seizures, Emotional Problems
M	25	87	94	90	Non-graded Spec. Ed.	8.7	4.5	Poor behavior, Control, Emotional Problems
F	23	83	76	79	High School Program for EMH	5.6	4.2	Vision, Speech, Mild High Freq. Hearing Loss
M	23	-	-	-	High School Program for EMH	-	-	Cerebral Palsy (Rt. hemiplegia) Seizures, Emotional Problems

The five former students, four males and one female, who were in sheltered workshops shared several characteristics. All were living with their families. Three had multiple physical problems of which two were handicapped neurologically by cerebral palsy and seizures. One of the two had deteriorated physically and mentally from the time he was in attendance at Cove School (specifically experiencing a progressive increase in seizures).

academically successful expressed goals and aspirations of self-improvement, additional knowledge and movement toward professional attainment. Those less successful academically still desired mastery of those basic skills in which they were still not truly competent (Rogan & Hartman, 1976); more specifically, Rogan and Hartman noted that: "If one subdivides the group on the basis of obvious physical handicaps, such as cerebral palsy, visual and hearing defects, and then further divides these subgroups according to intellectual levels, it appears that the ability to compensate may be related to intellectual abilities. Those who are able intellectually do attain professional and managerial status" (p. 84).

Observing the statistics shown in Tables 3 and 3a, it is clear that a decrease in percent of high school completions correlates with a lower rate of competitive employment. In the previous three studies reviewed, all were above the 90 percent high school completion rate and almost all were employed. It is also quite apparent in this Cove School group that there is a significant drop in managerial and professional involvement. In fact 63 percent are in unskilled and semi-skilled occupations, and 69 percent of the 91 subjects in the study were associated with primarily "things" oriented occupations.

Cove School Comparison on the Four Review Hypotheses

Hypothesis #1

Students who attended the Cove school represented a SES cross sectional stratum of middle to upper class. As IQ scores of this population ranged from 69 to 130, the overall mean IQ falls out of the "above one standard deviation in IQ points" range. Their mean IQ is reflective of the range exclusive of those Cove School subjects with IQs below 80 to be consistent with the more current definitional IQ range for SLD. In most all respects, including employment and education, the Cove School adult population seems to be functioning more similar to other SLD groups within the one standard deviation IQ range. However, the Cove School population is not functioning academically or occupationally in concordance with their reported middle to high socioeconomic backgrounds. **Hypothesis #1, therefore, is not supported.**

Hypothesis #2

Overall academic levels of the Cove School subjects were not much different from the Gow School's SLDs, yet their educational and vocational outcomes were considerably less favorable than Gow's. It might be concluded, therefore, that other factors besides academic skill level are contributing to lowered educational and vocational outcomes. The "other factors" may be that of not quite as high a socioeconomic level as Gow or Rose Valley subjects and having more "related" physical and emotional disabilities. Academic inability cannot necessarily be considered the primary correlate of less favorable educational and vocational outcomes in the Cove School population. **Therefore, Hypothesis #2 is rejected.**

Hypothesis #3

The Cove School subjects, as a group, did not show to be function-ing, in educational attainment and occupational status, much higher than some of the reported outcomes for the educably mentally retarded. **This hypothesis is rejected for the Cove population.**

Hypothesis #4

The Cove School subjects are far from being functionally illiterate and, in fact, had one of the highest overall group reading levels of the studies reviewed. **This hypothesis is retained.**

A final comment about this study needs to be made. By the time offi-cial legislation was adopted for SLD student recognition, the idea of emotional problems being a characteristic of the SLD condition had somehow been struck from the definition. Recall comments from the first chapter that presented Kirk's (1962) first SLD definition, which in-cluded emotional disturbance as a possible cause of the learning disabil-ity. The reader will realize that the emotional problems associated with the Cove School population are the same ones that first led Kirk to in-clude them as a cause. However, somehow this notion lost favor despite no empirical justification to excise it as a cause or correlate of SLD. Mental and/or emotional problems, which many of these Cove School clients had, present the most difficult kinds of problems in the employ-ment environment. As such, it is the opinion here that the unexplained variable for lack of more occupational success for these Cove School peo-ple is contained in the associated mental and emotional overlay asso-ciated with their original learning disabilities. Due to the lack of a control group, no statistical analysis was attempted.

Howden's (1967) Nineteen Year Follow-up of Good, Average and Poor Readers

A follow-up study, originally begun in 1942, conducted in a small logging community (Springfield, Oregon) and completed as a nineteen year follow-up of students identified on the basis of reading ability, was reported in a doctoral dissertation by M.E. Howden in 1967. The groups investigated consisted of: (a) an original group of 9 fifth and sixth graders whose reading level on the *Gates Reading Survey* was at least 1 SD above the class mean (4 females, 5 males); (b) an original group of 22 children whose reading performance approximated their class mean (115 males, 7 females); and (c) an original reading group consisting of

22 children whose childhood reading performance was 1 SD or more below the class mean (17 males, 5 females). Thirty-two percent of the 22 below average readers had Binet IQs below 79. The follow-up questions administered by Howden consisted of current adult reading habits, SES and social participation. All subjects were white with socioeconomic backgrounds approximating the middle and lower class levels.

Attainment of Howden's Follow-up Population

Ability levels of the average group, as measured by the use of the *Stanford Binet Intelligence Test,* was expressed as a mean of 106.5, while the below average reader group mean was 88 (Tables 3 & 3a reflect the average of these two IQ figures). IQ scores were not available for the above average readers. All graduated from high school, six had additional schooling beyond high school (1 B.A. degree and 1 M.A. degree). In the average reading group, 20 out of 22 had high school diplomas or the equivalent, 2 of the subjects had B.A. degrees. In the below average reading group 15 out of 22 had a high school diploma or the equivalent, none had college degrees.

Occupational status of the average readers consisted of a 100 percent employment rate, 23 percent of which were in unskilled jobs, 23 percent were in semiskilled jobs, and 27 percent were in skilled and managerial and sales positions. None were reported in professional occupations. The occupational status of the poor reading group consisted of a 95 percent employment rate. Twenty-six percent were employed in unskilled jobs, 37 percent were in semiskilled jobs, 26 percent were employed in skilled positions and 10 percent were in managerial or sales positions. Data was not available for the above average readers.

The age range for the average readers was 29-35, while the age range for the below average readers was 19-35. Mean IQ levels for the below average readers, when the subjects with average IQ scores were omitted, was 97.

Hypotheses Comparisons for Howden's Study

Hypothesis #1: SES Factors

In formulating a response to Hypothesis #1, it can be seen that within the Howden SLD group the high school completion rates were quite different (68% for below average readers versus 91% for the average.) This compares to a 96 percent and 100 percent completion rate for Gow SLDs and their controls, respectively. The Gow SLD group showed a higher high school completion rate than the Howden controls, thereby showing a quite notable SES difference. As might be expected, the lower SES population of Howden's study paid a higher price for their below average reading ability than did the high SES Gow subjects, that is, the difference between high school completion rates for the Gow men versus their controls was only 4 percent, while the high school completion rate difference for Howden SLDs and controls was 23 percent.

The IQ differences between the Howden SLDs and controls was 10 points, while the IQ differences between Gow men and their controls was 9 points. Recalling what Jencks et al. (1972, 1979) found in their attainment research, that is, the direct effects of grades, intelligence, and aptitude on occupational success are virtually zero among persons of equivalent schooling, we can see why the attainment gaps between the Howden groups are larger than those of the Gow SLDs and their controls. Based on the Jencks et al. attainment perspective about what factors do or do not predict occupational success, it should follow that the occupational attainment of Howden SLDs should be comparitively less than their controls because Howden's SLD educational attainment differs by so much more (23%). Conversely, the occupational differences between Gow SLDs should not be nearly as variant from their controls, given the small high school education completion gap. However, in the Gow study the occupational statistics are much higher and college completion rates are the bench marks for entering higher status occupations. It is here that Gow SLD men fell behind their controls. The Gow SLD men had a college undergraduate completion rate mean of 55 percent and 8 percent for graduate work, while their controls has 94 and 58 percent, respectively. Reviewing the occupational status of both Gow SLDs and their controls, we see that there is a considerably smaller percentage of professional occupational participation (18% for Gow SLDs and 53% for the controls). Clearly, this is a result of a lack of undergraduate and graduate school participation. It would appear that reading and spelling disabilities do intervene in occupational attainment, but they do so by preventing the equal participation in undergraduate and graduate programs.

Returning to the Howden occupation comparisons, it is seen that neither average nor below average subjects entered professional positions, perhaps due to the lower SES. However, 27 percent of the average readers were employed in managerial and sales, compared with only 10 percent of the below average readers. In this category, white collar jobs for these below average readers were nonexistent. In sum, it can be seen that SES plays a role in occupational attainment, particularly with respect to how much education one attains. **Based on this data Hypothesis #1 is retained.**

Hypothesis #2: Effects of Learning Disability

The impact of having a below average reading ability, in comparison to average readers, appears to be associated with a rather significant difference in high school completion rate. However, both groups had fairly equal employment rates (95% for below average readers and 100% for average readers) and were equally represented in unskilled, semiskilled and skilled employment. Only in the white collar division (managerial & sales) were there employment differences (10% of the below average readers were in such occupations while 27% of the average readers were). On the basis of employment attainment, it would not appear that below average reading ability significantly impaired occupational attainment. **Hypothesis #2 is partially rejected but only for educational attainment.**

Hypothesis #3: EMR Comparisons

Below average readers in this study comprised a population with a mean IQ of 97, and a 36 percent participation in skilled and managerial/sales employment positions. The employment rate of the below average readers was 95 percent. Overall, these subjects appeared to be more unlike mildly mentally retarded adults than like them, with respect to IQ and occupational attainment outcomes. **Therefore, Hypothesis #3 is retained.**

Hypothesis #4: Functional Literacy

The below average readers surveyed by Howden had reading grade levels of 6.3, thus, classifying them above the functionally illiterate level of 5.0. Grade level scores were not available in other academic areas such as spelling and arithmetic. **It follows that this hypothesis is also retained.**

A variable that must also be considered in analyzing the Howden population is that of availability of high paying jobs in the Oregon lumber industry, where most of the jobs that pay high salaries are based more on physical ability than academic ability. These employment figures could also change drastically depending on the time of the year a survey was taken, as the lumber industry has very cyclical employment patterns, with winter months often bringing high rates of unemployment to the industry. Hypothesis #4 is retained.

Statistical Comparisons for Howden's Data

High School Completion

The differences between Howden's SLDs and controls were significantly different ($X^2 = 5.62$, df $= 1$, $< .05$) with respect to high school completion rate.

College Participation

The college attainment levels of the Howden SLDs was significantly less than the control group ($X^2 = 6.07$, df $= 1$, $< .05$).

Employment Rate

Employment rates between these SLDs and controls did not differ significantly ($X^2 = 1.18$, df $= 1$, $> .05$).

Employment Classifications

The Howden SLDs did not differ significantly with respect to occupational status classifications ($X^2 = 1.06$, df $= 1$, $> .05$).

Overall Summary

The Howden population, when compared statistically, does not fare nearly as well educationally, but employment outcomes are positive. Thus, it appears that learning disabilities did affect academics but with this lower SES environment it has less of a negative effect.

Rehabilitation Service Administration (RSA) Sponsored SLD Adult Survey as Reported by Steidle et al., 1985

As part of the RSA effort to support regulations concerning the rehabilitation services offered to adults identified as having specific learning disabilities, a research and development grant was given to the Woodrow Wilson Rehabilitation Center in Fisherville, Virginia, to identify, (a) the vocational rehabilitation (VR) needs of adults with specific learning disabilities (SLD), (b) existing and potential barriers to provision of

VR services to adults with SLD, and (c) factors leading to successful job placement and job maintenance in adults with SLD. Reported here are only those data that relate to education and employment attainment levels. Also included in this review are some demographic highlights of the population studied by the Woodrow Wilson Rehabilitation Center staff.

Populations and Size Represented in Study

Potential SLD clients for VR service, SLD clients and cases closed as ineligible, consisted of 490 (53%), 381 (41%), and 59 (6%), respectively, for a total of 930 subjects. Service providers were divided on the basis of vocational professionals, psychologists, SLD teachers and others, totaling 414, 221 and 143, respectively. Consumers, family members, represented 212. The fourth and final sample consisted of 326 employers.

Mean Ages of Client Populations

The mean ages of the client populations were as follows: eligible clients, 23.2; clients in evaluation, 21.3; and ineligible clients, 23.8; compared to 20.3 for the 196 SLD adults in VR in Pennsylvania, Virginia and West Virginia reported by Rehabilitation Services Administration in 1983.

Sex Ratio and Race and Geographic Origin

Males outnumbered females 7:3 (in all these groups), which compares to the RSA (1983) finding of 8:2. This figure compares to the ACLD (1982) study sex ratio of 6.5:3.5 with a general adult SLD population and also to a similar finding by Stocking (1984) where 66 percent of the 126 SLD high school students were males. Another study by Cato and Rice (1982) reported a ratio of 5:1 male to female. It is possible that fewer females seek Vocational Rehabilitation Services. Nearly 86 percent of all their populations were white, 13 percent were black. Similar racial proportions were reported by VR in Pennsylvania, Virginia and West Virginia, and also in Stocking's (1984) study of adolescents was the majority of SLD white, but only 64 percent. Again, this would indicate that females and blacks are not getting VR services at the same rate as white male SLDs. Most eligible SLDs came from the states of Pennsylvania and Virginia.

Education

Eligible SLDs had high school completion rates of 63 percent, those in evaluation, 53 percent and ineligibles, 54 percent. College participation of the eligibles was 12 percent with at least one year of attendance, the in evaluation group, 18 percent and ineligibles had a 12 percent college participation of one year or more. Two year college degrees held by both eligible SLDs and in evaluation were 67 percent and 73 percent, respectively, while four year attainment represented 22 percent and 20 percent, respectively. There were only two ineligibles getting college degrees, one a B.A., the other a M.A.

Special Education

Of the total special education categories, 75 percent had been labeled SLD, of which only 10 percent had reported not receiving special education services. Significantly fewer ineligibles had been labeled SLD previously.

Employment Status

The percentages employed for the eligible, ineligible and in evaluation were 36, 49 and 35, respectively.

Family Support and Marriage Figures

Parents supporting SLD unemployed were 62 percent for eligibles, 76 percent for in evaluation and 43 percent for ineligibles. Marriage for the eligible SLDs represented only 17 percent, while clients in evaluation were married only 12 percent of the time. Ineligibles had marriage rates of 24 percent.

Summary of Statistics

According to Steidle et al. (1985), the following summation is made:

In this study the typical subject in the total group of 930 adults referred for VR because of suspected LD can be described as an unemployed, unmarried 22 year old white male from Pennsylvania, Virginia or West Virginia who had graduated from high school, had received some form of specialized education, had been previously labelled LD and was being supported by his parents. The typical subject in the group of 381 subjects found eligible for VR services as LD can be characterized as an unemployed, unmarried 23 year old white male from Pennsylvania, West Virginia or Virginia who had graduated from high school, had received some form of specialized education, had been previously labelled LD and was being supported by his parents (p. 81).

Hypotheses Comparisons

No comparisons will be made with this study because of the obvious lack of data relevant to the nature of this review. It has been included to illustrate of what the demographics of a population of SLDs seeking Vocational Rehabilitation might consist. The Woodrow Wilson Rehabilitation Center researchers will no doubt continue to analyze this population and report on their relevant outcomes.

Spreen's Canadian Longitudinal Study

Recently reported by Spreen (1983) are the results of a second phase follow-up of his longitudinal study of learning disabled adolescents and young adults. Spreen and his colleagues initially identified and evaluated over 200 children aged 8 to 12 in Vancouver, B.C. Using neurological examination procedures, Spreen divided these subjects according to three types of learning disabilities. These types were (a) learning handicapped due to observable brain damage (i.e., manifesting "hard neurological signs"); (b) learning handicapped due to "soft neurological signs," often referred to as minimal brain dysfunction; and (c) learning handicapped without observable evidence of neurological deficit. Also included as part of the study was a matched control group of 52 nondisabled subjects. (Only Category C and controls are included in this review).

Job Status of Spreen's Subjects at Age 18

In the first follow-up at age 18, Spreen noted that the academic prognosis of this group of learning disabled was poor, with the exception of high socioeconomic level subjects, a finding consistent with Rawson's (1968) follow-up reports. Spreen (1983) stated that "LD children were found to be more likely to drop out of school, and unlikely to obtain jobs requiring high school completion" (p. 11). More specifically, Peter and Spreen (1979) had noted that clinic-referred subjects of the study, whether neurologically impaired or not, demonstrated significant deviate behavior and greater maladjustment than their normal peers as adolescents and young adults. Further, Peter and Spreen stated that these findings were consistent with other LD follow-ups by Balow and Blomquist (1965), Masterson (1967) and Silver and Hagin (1964).

Finally, within this initial follow-up sample, Peter and Spreen noted that subjects with learning difficulties without any neurological signs showed poor adjustment patterns in comparison to the other referred groups, as well as a tendency to present acting out and antisocial behaviors. In this group, IQ level proved to be a significant prognostic indicator of behavioral and adjustment outcome. However, in females, there was a higher frequency of maladaptive behaviors, but level of intelligence was not a factor in predicting female behavior. Spreen (1982) summarized the Phase I data as follows: "Not only do these youngsters suffer through a miserable usually foreshortened school career, live a discouraging social life, full of disappointments and failures; they also have a relatively poor concern for advanced training and skilled employment. The need for early educational intervention and appropriate job counseling and training is obvious" (p. 490).

Age 25 Follow-up of Spreen's Learning Disabled Subjects

According to Spreen (1983), former clients aged 13 to 25, as time elapsed, tended to have firmer plans for the future and better occupational adjustment. With an increasing degree of neurological impairment, these clients had more difficulty in finding a job, finding more than temporary employment and had less earnings. Academically, mathematics was still a problem for all three groups with a large percentage noting these problems as severe and interfering with their choice of jobs.

At the time of Spreen's first follow-up, 69.3 percent of the subjects were employed and at Phase II, 70.7 percent were employed. In the control group, 88.2 percent were employed compared to 60, 73, and 54 percent; respectively, in Group 1 (brain damaged), 2 (minimal brain dysfunction) and 3 (no brain dysfunction). Most interesting is the finding that, in comparison to the Phase I interview results, the employment rate of the two brain dysfunction groups remained stable while employment for the SLD group without neurological impairment decreased from 80 to 54 percent. Spreen noted that a large number of the SLD subjects without positive neurological signs were engaged in seasonal type occupations which could account for the drastic drop in employment for this group. A significant difference between groups was found for the types of jobs held with more skilled and advanced training jobs occurring in the control group. Spreen further reported that when asked what type of job the SLD groups would really like to obtain, they responded by making a less ambitious selection. A number of the brain-damaged subjects appeared to be expecting no more than their present type of employment.

Hypotheses Comparisons

Hypothesis #1: SES Effects on Adult Attainment

A number of these Canadian SLD adults were employed in the Canadian lumber industry and represented a typical lower middle class group. As these SLD individuals were also part of a clinical group, there is a strong selection bias in the profile. Given the lower average IQ (92) and a high school completion rate of only 36 percent, it would appear that SES has not aided this group in the way that it has the other (with higher IQs) reviewed studies. Even the employment rate is extremely low; however, Spreen noted this is related to the cyclical lumber industry much like the Detroit auto industry layoff cycles. It is obvious that the Spreen SLDs are only one point lower in IQ than the Frauenheim and Heckerl (1983) SLDs, and both are from similar SES backgrounds, except for literary level, yet there are major differences in attainment. The advantage that we see in the Spreen controls reflects higher IQs and significantly higher high school completion rates with commensurate college participation. Clearly, if these SLD subjects are of a similar SES background as their control group, then SES has not exerted its influence over the SLDs as has some other factor, that is, the group's learning disabilities. Thus, **Hypothesis #1 is rejected**; if these SLDs are in fact lower middle class.

Hypothesis #2: Effects of Learning Disability on Adult Achievement

The academic levels of these SLD adults at follow-up were reported by Spreen to be at the seventh grade level for reading and spelling and middle eighth grade for arithmetic. These academic grade levels are three times as high in reading and twice as high in arithmetic as the levels for Frauenheim and Heckerl's population. In fact, they are just a year or so lower than Gottfredson's Gow school population. Beyond the advantages the control has with respect to completed education, there are 41 percent unskilled and semiskilled occupations compared to almost 60 percent for the SLD group; therefore, both groups seem to be above average in this category. Remembering the advantages for higher IQ, the controls have a 16 point advantage which may, according to Jencks et al. (1979), confer an occupational status difference of one third to one half a standard deviation of occupational status (8-13 points). Note that Jencks et al. (1979) also found that part of the association between test performance and occupational status derives from the fact that they both depend on family background.

Given the IQ level of this SLD group and the academic achievement level, it may be that these Canadian identified SLDs are achieving closer to their academic potential than might be expected for a person labeled as SLD. The occupational status does not seem as variant as might be expected, given the opportunity these men have of making higher wages in the forest industry, when in season. The final hypothesis evaluation is that while it appears that other variables are also affecting the educational and occupational attainment levels, the academic functioning at a seventh to eighth grade level for a population with an IQ mean of 91, which is low but in the average range, is certainly indicative of learning disability. If these SLDs are in fact from middle class background, the SLD is affecting performance. **Hypothesis #2 is retained but with some questions.**

Hypothesis #3: Comparisons to EMR Attainment

Given the high school completion rates, unemployment rates and occupational status levels, these SLDs appear to function more like mildly retarded young adults than unlike them. **Hypothesis #3 is rejected.**

Hypothesis #4: Functional Literacy

All of these SLD subjects are reading, spelling and computing above basic illiteracy levels. **Hypothesis #4 is retained.**

Some Final Comments on Comparing Spreen's SLDs and the Jencks et al. (1979) Findings

It was reported by Jencks et al. (1979) in the previous chapter, that arithmetic was the major academic predictor of later success for males. In that regard, it is mentioned here that a primary objective of Spreen's (1983) research was prognostic in nature, that is, "to take each individual test and check it's predictive value for a number of variables in a given adult outcome area" (p. 424). For example, Spreen examined 15 research questions relating to job and employment as one adult adjustment area and attempted to assess how well this area of outcome was predicted by IQ tests, achievement tests and so forth (recall that Jencks et al. [1983] also found that achievement is a better predictor [as early as sixth grade] of adult attainment than is ability). The methods of statistical analysis used by Spreen to ascertain the wanted prognosis was a Stepwise multiple regression procedure in which certain variables, that is, IQ test scores, are entered into a regression prediction formula to determine which variable accounts for the most variance in explaining an adult outcome. Spreen (1984) reported that "of the various tests used in the initial assessment of the participants at age 10, achievement in arithmetic [6.9] and in spelling, the *Stereognosis Test* for the right and left hand, reading achievement and IQ test results [.43] provided the best prediction in that order" (p. 424). This is an important confirmation of the Jencks et al. findings, particularly because of the thoroughness of the Spreen research design overall. Spreen's detailed findings allow the research findings by Jencks et al. to have meaning with respect to a special population (SLDs) not actually identified in the many general population studies Jencks et al. used in obtaining their findings.

Some other important findings by Spreen included results obtained using a discriminate function analysis which generated, from predictor variables, a classification system for correctly catagorizing the groups in a specific study, that is, Spreen's SLDs with brain damage, SLDs with minimal brain damage, SLDs without brain damage and controls. When using the previously mentioned test scores along with outcome variables such as: having had a previous learning disability, difficulty finding a job and rated manner of relating to a job interviewer, and so forth, the overall correct classification rate for all three SLD groups contrasted with the control group, was 95 percent. When using just the outcome variables, a correct classification rate for the four groups was 75 percent, with previous learning disability and rated manner of relating to the interviewer being the most significant predictors in this category. Also interesting is the finding by Spreen that the best rate for classifying the three SLD groups (after the controls, 90.4) was obtained for the SLD group without neurological associations. This can be interpreted as meaning that of all the variables brought into the statistical analysis model, it works best for the SLD without neurological findings.

Finally, and in the vein of Jencks et al., (1979) status attainment research by using canonical analysis rather than path analysis, Spreen undertook the task of using all the major test variables at age 10 as predictors of the major outcome variables at age 19. As a result, Spreen obtained a R^2 of .71 for his efforts. Spreen's analysis of all predictors, test scores, young adult outcomes and so forth, therefore resulted in a SLD adult attainment model that predicted 50.3 percent of the variance attributable to such adult attainment for the SLD population at age 19. The same analysis for the age 25 follow-up is currently under investigation by Spreen and is not yet published. Such as the Jencks et al. findings for the general population, there is still as much unexplained about SLD adult achievement as there is explained by Spreen's model.

Statistical Comparison of Spreen's Data

High School Completion

A significant difference was found between Spreen's SLDs and controls ($x^2 = 14.66$, df = 1, < .01).

College Participation

Consistent with the high school differences, Spreen's SLDs also completed less college than the controls ($x^2 = 11.64$, df = 1, < .01).

Employment Rate

Differing from most of the other studies was the significant difference from controls on employment rate. Again, Spreen attributed this to the cyclical Canadian lumber industry in which many of these SLDs were employed ($x^2 = 8.74$, df = 1, < .01).

Employment Classification

This was the only area where no significant differences were found with respect to the Spreen population ($x^2 = 2.36$, df = 1, > .05).

Overall Summation

Spreen's SLD sample does poorly on every economic and employment marker except occupational status. The type of industry, with high paid forest products, could have a bearing on this result.

Carter's (1964) Indianapolis, Indiana SLD Study

The purpose of Carter's (1964) study was to provide descriptive information regarding the postschool functioning of adults who were previously identified as being disabled in reading and secondly, to determine the nature of their adult vocational and social adjustment.

The sample population for this study was derived from a list of students who had been referred to a local high school reading clinic in Indianapolis, Indiana. Sixty-one students met initial criteria for inclusion in the study and 35 were available for follow-up interview. The Carter data also show that of the total surveyed students, 23 were retarded in reading (SLD) during high school. Of the 21 SLDs currently employed, 14 were in semiskilled positions (clerical and sales were put in this category), 4 were in skilled and 3 were in unskilled positions. Of the remaining 12 students who were not retarded in reading in high school, 3 immediately entered college, 3 entered unskilled occupations, 3 entered semiskilled jobs, 2 entered skilled occupations and 1 entered a clerical job (classed as semiskilled). As adults, the SLD group was rated by their housing conditions as being in the category of lower class, whereas the control group was rated in lower middle class housing (Carter, 1964).

Reading Difficulty and Employment Selection

To determine whether SLD subjects sought jobs with their weak abilities in mind, the question was asked, "Was your ability in reading a factor of consideration when choosing your first job?" Sixty-five percent (15) of the SLD group responded negatively. Sixty percent (14) responded similarly regarding their present occupation. According to Carter, this would imply that reading ability was not a conscious factor of job type consideration. The majority of jobs held by these persons, however, required little or no reading. Perhaps the reading disability did affect career selection in that the SLD individual considered only those jobs which required minimal communication skills. The adults in the control group responded similarly to this question in that 83 percent (10) felt that reading ability was not a factor of consideration when choosing their first or present job.

Considering current employment levels of the SLD group, these data would then indicate, according to Carter, that the occupational mobility of the disabled reader is more horizontal than vertical. Examination of the SLD job classifications revealed that their mobility involved primarily kindred occupations, which suggests that even the horizontal movement of Carter's SLD population was somewhat restricted. Occupational mobility of the control group is of a vertical nature as evidenced by the comparison between the entry occupations and current occupational status of the control group members.

Although the SLD group and the control group are of unequal size, the control group shows a proportionally larger number of persons who are currently employed in skilled occupations and significantly fewer persons (SLD) who are in semiskilled or unskilled jobs. It is also significant to note that there were no SLDs attending college, while 25 percent of the controls were. In terms of job stability, the average number of occupational moves for SLDs was 1.47, with 10 persons maintaining their original occupational status. Controls had an average of .66 in terms of occupational changes.

Career aspirations, as with the case of job mobility, was horizontally oriented for the SLD group. Only three SLD adults indicated a desire to move vertically within their present occupations, eight were undecided as to their career goals, five anticipated maintaining their same job, and seven expressed interest in vocations quite different from their present jobs but on the same job status level. Eight controls gave as their career goal positions which were above their present occupations, three were undecided, and one planned to remain in his father's business.

Educational Attainment

The curriculum pursued by the SLD student can hold, according to Carter, particular career significance in terms of the reading instruction provided. A reading program often neglects the individual needs of a student while in school as well as the reading needs after terminating education (Carter, 1964). While in school, it has been shown (Deshler, et al., 1982) that the SLD student engages in fewer extracurricular activities and participates in fewer social events than a nonhandicapped person. All of the SLD subjects pursued either a vocational (22%) or a general (78%) curriculum. It was reported for SLD subjects that, due to the low verbal scores obtained on standardized achievement tests administered in the seventh and eighth grades, a vocational course was often recommended by school staff.

The curriculums and number of extracurricular activities of the controls are quite different from those of the SLD group. Five persons (42%) pursued college preparatory courses and graduated with high school diplomas, six (50%) pursued a strictly vocational course, and one student followed a general course of study and dropped out of high school during his tenth year. There seemed to be greater persistance on the part of the control group, as significantly more of them completed a program of study which had immediate use in terms of future employment.

Proportionately greater numbers of extracurricular activities of the control group would suggest that these persons were more socially able.

High School Completion Rates

A comparison of the two groups regarding high school completion shows the SLDs with only a 30 percent completion rate, whereas only 17 percent of the controls dropped out. Considering those students who were behind in reading and had dropped out of school, 13 reported that their reading ability was a causal factor, one person could not respond either yes or no, one attributed his termination to serious illness and one felt that his reading ability had no effect whatsoever.

Postschool Attainment

Of the 18 persons who dropped out of school, only two (both SLDs) obtained any additional education or training. Sixteen subjects (14 from the SLD group and 2 controls) had made no effort to complete their high school work or to receive training in a vocational area. Data from control students who graduated from high school show that of the 17 who completed a sequenced course of study in high school, 12 went on to obtain additional education or training. Viewing the two groups separately, only 7 of the 23 (30%) SLDs secured additional training beyond high school, whereas 7 of the 12 (58%) of the controls pursued such training.

The Nonwork Adjusted SLD

The responses of SLDs who were vocationally nonadjusted, but who had graduated from high school, were also analyzed. The question was asked: "What significance has the reading disability in job dissatisfaction?" Four of the five adults in this category stated that they had advanced as far as they were able with their present skills. They explained that the "next step up" would require an exam and they would need a great deal more reading proficiency than they now possessed. Overall, their job dissatisfaction seemed to emanate largely from the inability to progress to a more advanced, more demanding job. In order to change jobs, they would have to move horizontally to another company. One person, as a result of this situation, was giving serious thought to applying for entrance to college. He had already begun advanced educational training through night school. The career aspirations of the school completors are vastly different from those persons who had dropped out of high school. Three expressed a desire to own their own business, one desired advanced training in electronics, and one was undecided but had several possibilities in mind, all of which were above his present job. Those SLDs who were considered to have good work adjustment (83%) were in business with their family.

The next category to be considered is those persons who were not disabled in reading, but who were vocationally nonadjusted. Three of the five persons in this category had graduated from high school but were in jobs which they described as "dull, boring" and "unexciting." As they were not disabled in reading, this did not seem to contribute to their job dissatisfaction. They felt that in time they could change to an occupation which was more to their satisfaction. The remaining two persons had dropped out of school and were not specifically trained for a particular occupation. Without the diploma, they were handicapped regarding their vocational opportunities. The two occupations represented by these two persons are welding and service station attendant.

An examination of the data revealed that of those seven persons who were not disabled in reading and were vocationally adjusted, all had graduated from high school. Five were presently attending college, and anticipating various professional jobs. Another person was self-employed as a painter, while the remaining person anticipated owning what is now his father's retail store. These persons had all overcome the initial reading deficiency and engaged in extracurricular reading activities to a considerable extent (Carter, 1964).

Hypotheses Comparisons for Carter Study

Hypothesis #1: SES

Using a SES rating system based on the type of housing a family lives in, the SLD group was ranked by Carter as lower class and the controls were ranked as lower middle class. This factor is a major piece of evidence for understanding why the SLDs and controls may have differed in high school attainment but not in employment rate. Further, evidence of the educational attainment affecting occupation is shown in the occupational status differences, particularly in semiskilled and skilled positions. Interestingly, IQs were about the same, thus they cannot be considered a factor in the educational and occupational status differences. In fact, Jencks et al. (1972, 1979) have shown from their research that individuals with equal family backgrounds and IQs should differ in occupational status, by only about 2.5 SEI occupational status points (a 16 point difference in IQ is worth about 8-13 points). Given that these SLDs differed on the basis of lower class versus lower middle class one could expect the not-so-major differences in occupational status between the two groups. **Hypothesis #1 is retained.**

Hypothesis #2: Effects of SLD

We only know that the SLD group was one or more grades below, academically, while the controls were average. In their own responses to the question: "Did reading inability affect your choice of a job?" 65 percent answered no. Carter stated that the jobs these SLDs held required little or no reading, however. The SLD high school graduates who were employed did state, however, that their reading inabilities were preventing them from taking exams that would lead to higher job classifications and, as such, restricted their occupational vertical mobility. It could be concluded, therefore, that reading inability does not restrict employability, but it does restrict educational attainment and occupational mobility of the vertical nature. **Hypothesis #2 is retained.**

Hypothesis #3: EMR Comparisons

The educational attainment of these SLDs is more like a population of mildly handicapped individuals, however, the employment rate is not. Over 80 percent of the SLDs are in unskilled and semiskilled jobs which makes them more equal to mildly retarded adults than unlike them. **Hypothesis #3 is partially rejected.**

SES Differences Between SLDs and Controls

Class rankings given by the authors in each of the reviews was, for the most part, a very subjective matter and thus cannot be given great credance. Generally, the rankings in the studies can be divided according to seven levels: (a) upper class, (b) upper middle, (c) middle, (d) lower middle, (e) upper lower class, (f) lower and (g) lower lower. In the SLD total sample, 54 percent came from middle class and above, while in the control group, 86 percent were in the upper, upper middle and middle SES range. The remaining SLDs (46%) came from lower middle, upper lower and lower classes. In only one study was the control group identified with this lower group of categories. Clearly, SLDs and controls reviewed in this chapter were not matched well for making assumptions about the attributable learning disability factors associated with the educational and occupational differences.

IQ Differences Between SLDs and Controls

The overall mean IQ for the total SLD sample was 104.23 (SD = 10.24), compared to the control mean of 115.83 (SD = 10.76), which is not a statistically significant difference (t = 2.11, df = 5, > .05).

Academic Grade Level Differences

This is another extremely weak data collection category. For example, only 6 of the 15 SLD studies reported specific grade level or standard score data for the populations of the follow-up data. Only two of the eight control groups reported this data in a form that could be compared to other data. Due to this limited data, it is only reported that, of the academic scores that were reported the SLD's mean scores were highest in reading (8.0 grade level), spelling (6.94) and the least highest in arithmetic (6.58). Controls also scored highest in reading (11.85 grade level), next highest in spelling (11.5) and lowest in arithmetic (10.75). Rawson's data only stipulated that 35 percent of her subjects were one half of a grade level or more below expected levels. For spelling, it was 90 percent of her group that was 35 percent below or more, while in arithmetic, 50 percent of the group was one half grade level or more below. Interestingly, Rawson's controls did poorer in arithmetic than the SLDs, 50 percent below one third or more below compared to 55 percent for the controls. Considering the importance Jencks et al. (1983) put on arithmetic for male success, this slight difference might account, in part, for the fact that there are more Rawson's SLDs in professional careers than the controls.

High School and College Participation

In the status attainment model presented in the previous chapter, it was advanced that the social status of one's parents affects the level of schooling achieved, which in turn affects the occupational levels that one achieves. In this perspective schooling is seen as an intervening variable between parental status and one's own occupational status. Preceding educational attainment are important social-psychological process influences such as aspirations, parental, teacher and peer encouragement to attend school, which lead to the making of career plans. Effects of academic achievement tend to operate through a similar sequence of influences.

In these 15 SLD studies, high school completion rates ranged from 10 percent to 100 percent. Interestingly, and consistent with an earlier quote from Vanfossen (1979), IQ is only moderately correlated to these high school completion rates (r = .39, df = 11, > .05). Insufficient data preclude a similar analysis using achievement comparisons. SES of the SLD families appears to be a much better correlate of high school completion, although objective proof of this hypothesis is lacking. Rates of high school completion for SLDs versus controls, overall, was statistically significant ($X^2 = 36.95$, df = 1, < .01). Because of the control groups being illmatched on SES, it is difficult to ascertain if the significant difference is due to learning disabilities or a lower SES background, the latter seems to be the most plausible with the data that is presently available.

Overall, college participation differences between the SLDs and controls was also statistically significant. Also noteable, however, was the finding that the higher SES group of Rawson SLD subjects and Bruck's selectively biased SLD sample, were the only studies that were not significantly different in their college attainment.

Using national high school completion rates for 1984 and reported high school figures for the deaf, SLD statistics on this factor are quite similar. Figure 2 data illustrates the possibility that once a SLD student completes college, they are as likely to complete graduate work as the American population at large but not near the rate of their higher SES control groups.

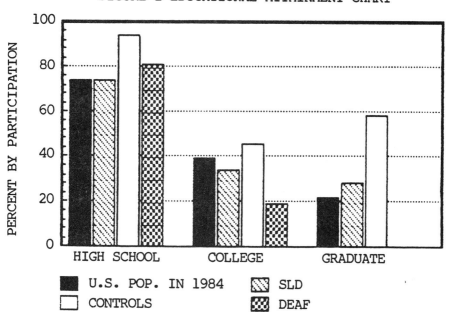

FIGURE 2 EDUCATIONAL ATTAINMENT CHART

Employment Rates and Classifications

The only SLD study that proved to be significantly different from controls, with respect to rate of employment, was Spreen's Canadian subjects, which were noted to be employed in the cyclical but high paying lumber industry. The lure of high paying salaries for working in the physically demanding jobs of choker setter, green chain puller and so forth, may also account for the poorer high school completion rate as well. In figure 3 it is shown that SLD employment rates are almost equal to 1982 national employment data for 20-24 year olds with a high school diploma. In the same table, the 1982 national employment data for 20-24 year olds shows that high school graduates with 1-3 years of college have employment rates of 90 percent, a figure comparable to the controls listed in this review, as well as to the rate for deaf adults who have completed rehabilitation.

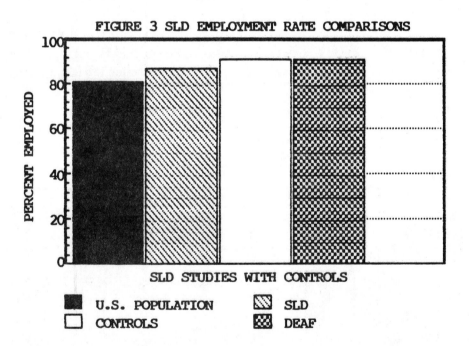

FIGURE 3 SLD EMPLOYMENT RATE COMPARISONS

Occupational Classification

When the occupational groups of unskilled and semiskilled are combined and compared to the combination of skilled, managerial/sales and professional, there is a significant difference between SLDs and controls ($X^2 = 9.1$, df = 1, < .001). Figure 4 data illustrates this difference but also compares the SLD occupational attainment with U.S. employment data for 1974 (this year was selected as a median year to the follow-up studies completed in the middle 1960s as well as the 1980s) and rehabilitated deaf persons.

FIGURE 4 SLD OCCUPATIONAL GROUP VARIANCE

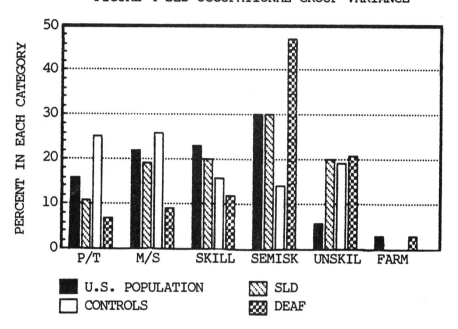

When viewing the occupational classification attainment of the total SLD groups which reported such classification detail (n = 12) (see figure 5), the inverse relationship between greater high school completion percentage versus lower (recall that in this follow-up review all SLD rankings, A-P, are listed in order of most high school completed to least) can be easily seen with respect to professional and managerial/sales being most prevalent in the greater high school completion and unskilled/ semiskilled being the most prevalent for less high school completion. Looking at the same kind of data for controls only in figure 6 (n = 5 studies), the same inverse relationship for SLDs is observed with regard to professional and managerial/sales, skilled versus unskilled and semiskilled. The effects of high school attainment on future occupational attainment, as the status attainment model stipulates, is clearly in operation for both nonSLDs and SLDs. Remember also that family background is the major contributor to educational attainment and that it was the control groups that had the highest percentage of families in higher SES levels.

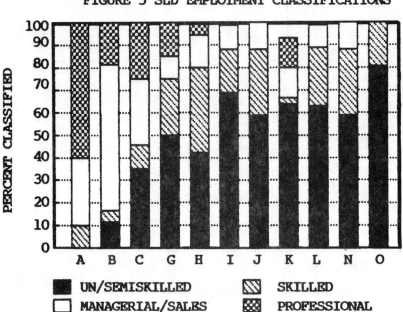

FIGURE 5 SLD EMPLOYMENT CLASSIFICATIONS

FIGURE 6 SLD CONTROLS JOB PROPORTIONS

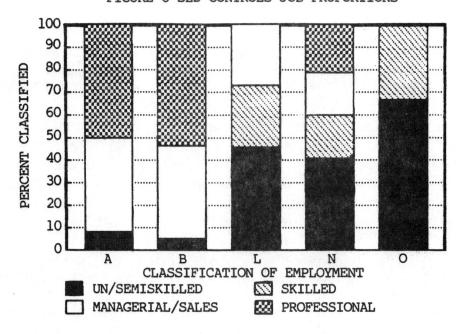

Summary of Subjective and Statistical Hypotheses Evaluation

There were four major hypotheses to be subjectively and statistically evaluated with reference to these currently reviewed SLD studies (eight of which [50%] had control groups):

1. Individuals who come from more favorable SES backgrounds will have been more successful in school, completed more of it and consequently will have achieved a higher occupational status.
2. Having a specific learning disability (SLD) would have a negative impact on one's educational attainment and subsequently on occupational outcomes over and above differences attributed to SES differences.
3. Adults who have or had a learning disability should have attained more educational and occupational achievement than other handicapped individuals, such as the educable mentally retarded or the hearing impaired.
4. Adult populations affected now or at some point in their school careers with learning disabilities are not functionally illiterate, that is, academic skills in reading, writing and arithmetic are above a fifth grade level.

Hypothesis #1 Summary

In the subjective analysis of Hypothesis #1, only two follow-up studies (Rogan & Hartman, 1976; Spreen, 1982) appear to refute this hypothesis. Both of these SLD populations were reported to be from middle to middle upper SES backgrounds, yet as a group their educational and occupational attainment was less than expected for such backgrounds. In the case of Rogan and Hartman's population, their reported academic grade levels in reading and spelling were as good or better than Gottfredson's similar SES level Gow School subjects. Both populations, Rogan and Hartman's and Gottfredson's, came from private schools. Intelligence levels differed by more than one standard deviation and thus, may account for part of the reason for not achieving commensurate to their SES backgrounds. A final explanation for Rogan and Hartman's population not achieving commensurate to their reported SES backgrounds, given that Gottfredson's population was at least equivalent in academic achievement, is that many of the Rogan and Hartman SLD population also had associated medical and psychological problems. Recall that Bruck's SLD population was finely screened to eliminate such associated problems and thus, may account for their

(Bruck's) similar SES backgrounds but more successful adult attainment over the Rogan and Hartman SLDs.

Spreen's SLD population was rated as a lower middle to middle SES population, yet had poor success in educational and occupational attainment, but since their intelligence level had a mean of 92 (dull normal), it may account for part of the lower achievement. Also contributing to the lower adult success may be, as stated by Spreen, that these men were forest products workers making high wages in an occupation that does not require academic skill but rather strong physical ability. This industry is also subject to very cyclical employment periods. Also notable is the fact that Spreen's Canadian controls who were rated as middle SES, only completed high school at an 80 percent level, the lowest percentage for any of the eight control groups included in this review. Academic achievement of the Spreen controls, while at least three grades higher in reading, spelling and arithmetic than the SLDs, was nearly equal to the Gottfredson, Bruck, and Rogan and Hartman SLDs in reading, but not spelling or arithmetic. The point being that this total Spreen population appears suppressed for a reported generally lower middle to middle population and, as such, may be an artifact of their region's economic environment.

In sum, the status attainment model appears to be supported for the vast majority of these SLD follow-up studies. That is, higher SES background subjects achieve more education and obtain higher status occupations than do those subjects from lower SES backgrounds. This appears to be true for both SLDs and their respective control groups.

Hypothesis #2 Summary

This hypothesis evaluation was much less decisive in its final outcome. Fifty percent of the SLD studies were evaluated as rejecting the belief that a specific learning disability, per se, interfered with educational and/or occupational attainment. Those studies were done by Rawson, Gottfredson (partially rejected), Robinson, Vetter, Bruck and Howden. Of the 15 total studies, 4 did not have enough data to evaluate this hypothesis or the previous one. Those studies where the evaluation supported the belief that SLD restricts educational and/or occupational attainment were those of Frauenheim and Heckerl, Rogan and Hartman, Spreen, Carter and Hardy. It should be noted that within these two groups, the group in which the hypothesis was rejected and the group in which it was not, represent nearly opposite ends of the high school completion continuum, except for Howden. Howden's population was rejected on this hypothesis because their SES level was so different that a SLD may not have been the primary cause for lack of attainment. Obviously, and consistent with the status attainment model, those SLD populations that do not complete high school are going to be at higher risk for not attaining the occupational status of their nonhandicapped peers. Academic achievement is obviously one of the intervening variables that will influence such attainment. In another perspective on support/nonsupport for the actual effects of a specific learning disability on attainment, it would be helpful to know if any of these reviewed studies would meet any of the various SLD discrepancy criterions. In the Kansas SLD Study (KGS, 1985), it was found that when using either a Full Regression Discrepancy Model or Estimated Regression Model, the mean differences between IQ and achievement (in standard scores) were 20 and 21 points, respectively. Shown in Table 5 are the seven follow-up studies that reported both IQ and grade level achievement for reading. Converting the grade level score to a *Wide Range Achievement Test* (Jastak & Jastak, 1965) Scale Score, averaged for the respective mean ages of the seven studies, it can be roughly estimated which follow-up study populations would be considered to have a discrepancy large enough between ability and achievement. Only the subjects in Frauenheim and Heckerl's follow-up population (–25) and possibly Howden's population (–14), would meet the Kansas approximate point

TABLE 5

APPROXIMATE ESTIMATE OF IQ/ACHIEVEMENT DISCREPANCY USING 1965 WRAT STANDARD SCORES AND MEAN AGES OF SLD FOLLOW-UP STUDIES

SLD Study	IQ Mean	Reading Grade Level	Standard Score Age/Conversion	Difference
Gottfredson	118	9.6	108	–10
Bruck	103	9.7	99	–4
Balow and Bloomquist	100	10.2	100	–0
Frauenheim & Heckerl	92	2.6	67	–25
Rogan & Hartman	98	10.4	104	+6
Howden	97	6.3	83	–14
Spreen	92	7.0	84	–8

difference of 21 points or more between ability and achievement, criteria for receiving special education. Of course, the grade point averages reported in these seven studies are "at follow-up" scores and, as such, represent "after treatment" effects which may have greatly differed among the study populations. However, we do know that Frauenheim and Heckerl's (1983) clinical population has been extensively studied over their life span and the treatment records are fairly complete (see also Frauenheim, 1978). It is known that this population has had extensive special education, yet are still the most severely disabled academically but not necessarily occupationally. Students in the KGS Study (Chapter One) referred for SLD special education but found not to meet the discrepancy criterion were approximately equal in IQ and achievement scores. After the Frauenheim and Heckerl and Howden studies, Gottfredson's SLD population (-10) would be the third most severe with respect to an academic discrepancy, at least of the seven studies that have data available.

In the previously discussed and individually evaluated follow-up studies, it was partially rejected that a learning disability would negatively affect adult attainment in the Gottfredson SLD population. The estimate shown in Table 5 that these Gow school SLD alumni had only (mean) moderate academic/achievement discrepancies offers further support for only making a partial rejection. Similarly, Hypothesis #2 was totally rejected for Bruck's SLD population, and the small discrepancy (-4) between that population's ability and achievement scores supports the rejection. In the Balow and Blomquist study, only partial acceptance was given for the second hypothesis. As can be seen in Table 5, there was no discrepancy between their overall ability and achievement, which fully supports the only partial acceptance given Hypothesis #2.

The Frauenheim and Heckerl study was given full acceptance on the belief that a learning disability negatively affects educational and occupational attainment, and well it should, as this population exhibits a very significant discrepancy (almost two standard deviations, -25) between ability and achievement. In complete reversal of the trends noted in the previous four follow-ups, Rogan and Hartman's population shows to be academically achieving above their ability, a tribute to the Cove School program. Despite the middle class backgrounds of the subjects, their academic achievement and their near average intellectual ability, only 70 percent graduated from high school, and two thirds of those employed are in unskilled and semiskilled occupations. It appears that accepting the belief that having a learning disability negatively affects educational and occupational outcome was appropriate. It also appears that improving one's reading ability (as noted in the higher than expected achievement) does not necessarily lead to success in other areas of attainment.

Because we do know that this SLD population had a number of physical and mental difficulties along with their academic disabilities, and we also know that in Bruck's positive outcome SLD population that there were no such related problems, it seems quite logical to attribute the poorer prognosis of the Rogan and Hartman population to those related problems and not to the ability to read well, per se, assuming, of course, that the discrepancy estimates in Table 5 are accurate.

In the Howden population, the second hypothesis was partially rejected on the basis that the population was at a disadvantage in educational and occupational attainment, not because of a learning disability but because of their lower SES backgrounds (lower than their control group). Given what is shown in Table 5 with respect to a -14 point discrepancy. The partial rejection is warranted with part of the difference due to SES differences between SLDs and controls and part due to reading inability.

Finally, Spreen's population, like Howden's, heavily involved in the high paying occupations associated with logging, the former in British Columbia and the later in Springfield, Oregon, was evaluated to have been negatively affected by a learning disability. Having come from lower middle class backgrounds, one would not expect such a poor rate of high school completion. Yet, when considering the peer and parent group influences (significant others) that probably encourage youth in lumber communities to seek such high paying jobs, the hypothesis evaluation may be in error. Perhaps Spreen's next follow-up study, or the planned additional analysis of the vocational data will shed more light on this controversial question.

Hypothesis #3

Achieving higher levels of education and holding higher status occupations than those adults who are mentally retarded or hearing impaired, seems to be a reasonable expectation for a population of adults whose otherwise normal backgrounds and disabilities are normally distributed. Sixty-two percent of the follow-up studies (8) did in fact show this. Among the higher rates of high school completion where this hypothesis was partially rejected (Vetter), the mean age was quite low (19-25) and the SLD group was from a reportedly lower class family background. Data about occupational attainment was limited to the comparison that the SLD group was holding significantly lower status levels of occupations. More time will assess if Vetter's SLDs will achieve higher attainment levels than the mentally retarded and hearing impaired. The remaining four studies that were rejected on this hypothesis were Rogan and Hartman, Spreen, Carter and Hardy. Because all of these groups represented the lowest spectrum on the high school completion rate continuum, it is suggested that lower SES backgrounds, poorer academic ability and commensurate but lower levels of academic achievement, all add up to placing these four groups in the same economical occupational environment that less cognitively able and language impaired deaf adults are remitted to.

Hypothesis #4

Only one study had a mean achievement level that placed them in a class of adults referred to as functionally illiterate. It seems, however, that, even though these SLD adults are functioning below the fifth grade level in reading and spelling, most of them (72%) are doing quite well given their severe academic limitations.

Summary of Statistical Comparisons of High School, College and Occupational Attainment of SLD Studies with Control Groups

High School

Of the eight studies with control groups, 62.5 percent (5/8) yielded significant differences in high school completion rates ($X^2 = 36.95$, df = 1, <.05). Those studies not differing from their control groups were Rawson, Vetter and Bruck (see figure 7).

College Attainment

In this total population of SLDs versus controls, 75 percent (6/8) of the SLD groups were significantly less accomplished with respect to college attainment ($X^2 = 196.1$, df = 1, <.001). Those SLD studies not differing from their controls were Rawson and Bruck (see figure 8).

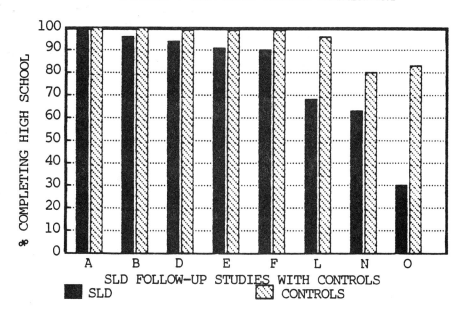

FIGURE 7 SLD HIGH SCHOOL ATTAINMENT

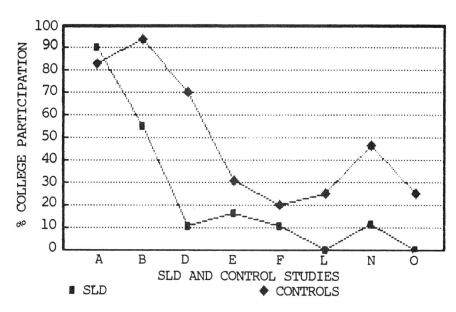

FIGURE 8 SLD COLLEGE COMPARISONS

Occupational Attainment: Employment Rate

A reverse of the above findings was found as only one out of the eight studies differed significantly from their controls with respect to percentage of population working who were actually seeking work (see figure 9).

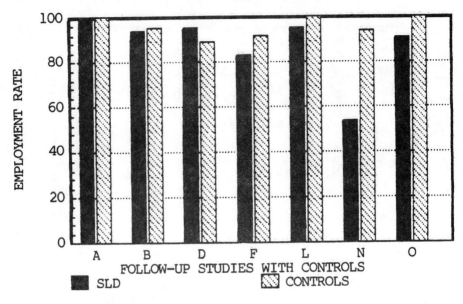

FIGURE 9 SLD/CONTROL RATE OF EMPLOYMENT

Occupational Attainment: Classification of Occupations Held

To analyze this attainment factor, the unskilled/semiskilled classifications were combined, and the skilled, managerial/sales and professional classification were joined to divide them into a primary versus secondary sector occupational dichotomy. Only one of the five studies (Gottfredson, Finucci, & Childs, 1984) useable for such an analysis yielded a significant difference between their respective control group.

Summary of Statistical Evaluation

Putting all of the subjective remarks made throughout this chapter aside, it would appear that adults who once had or still have a mild to moderate or severe learning disability can be most noted by their differences in attaining education, both high school and college. With respect to Schonhaut and Satz's (1983) unanswered question about what occupations these people will enter, the answer is simply: "The same as other nonhandicapped groups with similar family backgrounds, and ability and achievement levels." There appears to be one exception as raised by the Gottfredson data. The explanation for Gottfredson's occupational difference may be as simple as admitting that perhaps the only truly learning disabled populations were Frauenheim and Heckerl's severely learning disabled and Gottfredson's Gow School mildly learning disabled but high SES subjects who have but followed their fathers' leads into the business world. The Howden group, who might be considered SLD under current guidelines, were also operating under a disadvantage with respect to family background.

Overall Conclusions of SLD Follow-up Studies

Firstly, it should be restated that only one of the 15 studies had subjects who had been identified as having a specific learning disability according to a consistently applied SLD identification formula. As such, making any generalizations about the academic and occupational behavior of the adults studied in these 15 studies is extremely limited, particularly when recommending programmatic and curricular improvements for the currently identified SLD student or adult. Secondly, it seems most obvious that a national longitudinal study is needed with regard to SLD populations now being identified in schools and rehabilitation agencies but with rigorous matching requirements for comparison groups. Such a study may in fact reveal that occupational attainment levels are more a function of the socioeconomic backgrounds in which these students are reared. Thirdly, it must be decided if it is necessary or even ethical to designate so many children as handicapped when that handicap may not differentiate them from their adult peers, when a label of handicap was determined on minor discrepancies between academic ability and achievement, or on the basis that lower ability students should be automatically expected to achieve at desired level of competence based on a test score. Fourthly, the most significant change that could be made based on the limited generalizability of these findings is an overall improvement in not only graduating students from high school but making that high school experience meet the needs of all students, not just the strictly college bound or the purely vocationally bound, but also for those students in the middle spectrum who have not yet decided where their future careers will be.

Finally, it is known that in higher SES environments such factors as peers and parental encouragement to do well in school and to persist in staying in school are common. This attitude must be transmitted to youth through channels that may not be otherwise available to them, for example, school developed "Encouragement Centers" where teachers, administrators and other school staff have a responsibility not only to deliver their "product" but to help shape and enhance the attitudes of all students, not just those that approximate their own respective values. Sixth, special education programs that operate in addition to the mainstreamed SLD students should be reserved only for the most severely disabled subjects and should not be holding tanks as they sometimes are. Included in these special programs should be intensive academic, career, and socialization projects designed to allow the students to benefit from high school and also to make a smooth transition from there to independent and productive life styles.

PART THREE

CAREER ASSESSMENT AND
DECISION-MAKING PRACTICE

CHAPTER 5

ASSESSMENT OF CAREER DEVELOPMENT AND DECISION MAKING

Assess (ə-sĕs´): "To evaluate; appraise"

Goals, Objectives and Definitions for Career Assessment

AS PART OF an overall decision-making model to guide adolescents and young adults with specific learning disabilities during the ongoing career selection process, a basic model for assessing the present status of one's career development, as well as readiness and degree of importance for making a career decision is presented. The career assessment model presented in this chapter is adapted from Biller (1985b) but now includes an interrelated decision-making assessment system known as the *Assessment of Career Decision Making* (ACDM) model (Buck & Daniels, 1985) originally developed by Harren (1979). Also included is a new section on conducting functional assessments.

Career Assessment Goals

Counselors, teachers, and other professionals responsible for assisting the adolescent with specific learning disabilities in career and educational planning have to be concerned with at least three directives: (a) to determine where the student is in his or her career development; (b) to identify the readiness of the student to select among the available curricular and occupational choices; and (c) to determine how the unprepared student can be helped (Thompson, Lindeman, Super, Jordaan and Meyers, 1981). In accepting the premise that the career assessment process can help adolescents to better understand themselves, not only in terms of one's interests, values and personality characteristics, Herr and Cramer (1979) have stated the importance for the above career assessment directives:

> The greater the degree of accurate self-understanding an individual has, it is assumed, the more likely that person is to make realistic, satisfying educational and career choices. While accurate self-understanding does not guarantee good decision making, good decisions probably cannot be made without a realistic picture of one's abilities and interests (p. 329).

Herr and Cramer further noted, however, that the career assessment process for most students has consisted primarily of a brief "test 'em and tell 'em" session. Further, for many adolescents with specific learning disabilities there has never been a career planning session. Follow-up studies have shown that there has been little, if any, career-related counseling for the SLD student (Fafard & Haubrich, 1981) despite a high priority that adults with specific learning disabilities have given to the need for such school-related career assistance (ACLD, 1982).

Career Assessment Objectives

With regard to conducting comprehensive career assessment and planning as more than just a "test 'em and tell 'em" experience, Prediger (1974) has forwarded three major career assessment objectives:

> It is essential to differentiate between assessments of human attributes and square peg uses of the assessments . . . the role of tests in career guidance is three fold: first, to stimulate, broaden, and provide focus to career exploration; second, to stimulate exploration of self in relation to career; and third, to provide "what if" information with respect to various career choice options (p. 21).

Career Assessment Definition and Purpose

While a number of definitions for career assessment have been forwarded over the last two decades (*Vocational Evaluation Project Final Report*, 1975), a more recent perspective was presented by Frey (1984) as follows:

> To assess means "to sit beside" or "to assess the judge." Appropriately assessment concerns the collection of data and the presentation of data in useful forms. Decisions about courses of action are made on the basis of data gathered and the interpretation of their meaning (Anderson et al., 1975). Assessment is a broader term than either measurement or

testing. It usually refers to multiple methods of gathering pertinent data (information) on variables that are relevant to a particular decision-making process. The variety of techniques that are employed in assessments may include tests, questionnaires, naturalistic observations, ratings and interviews (pp. 13-14).

Further explaining this definition, Frey noted that in serving special populations, assessment refers to a dynamic process of determining the quantitative and qualitative needs of clients. This would include an appraisal of the individual's physical, mental, social and vocational abilities and related work behaviors. From these observations come descriptions of the client and are used with the client to make decisions about a career plan. This assessment information becomes additionally useful in establishing the baseline information required for evaluating client progress and service delivery effectiveness (Frey, 1985).

Functional Assessment

An often used but rarely defined term in discussions on assessment is the concept of functional assessment. The most recent definitional clarification of functional assessment has been offered by Halpern and Fuhrer (1984), "functional assessment is the measurement of purposeful behavior in interaction with the environment, which is interpreted according to the assessment's intended uses" (p. 3). Where **measurement** means both the method and level of detail that are incorporated into the process of gathering assessment information, such as interviews, self-reports, rating scales, tests and **purposeful** means that the behavior being measured has been emitted by a person with a goal or objective, that is, a behavior is analyzed primarily in terms of its consequences, although its antecedents may also be examined. For example, in measuring a person's reading ability in the assessment task of deciphering a passage of a vocational-technical manual, we are not concerned primarily with documenting the effect of reading disability (antecedent), but rather with ascertaining the residual function available for performing useful skills (consequences), for example, reading rate may be well below average for the required work, with some word misidentification, while reading comprehension is average. **Behavior** means the object of assessment, the entity being measured. Typically, these entities have been noted as one's physical, emotional or mental capacities, performance of useful tasks or skills and performance of social roles. These three areas are also commonly discussed under the labels of impairment, disability and handicap. Before completing the example of a functional assessment for an individual's reading disability, brief definitions for **impairment, disability** and **handicap** are given.

Impairment

Impairment, as defined here, is a functional consequence of pathology, disease or injury and is a restriction of some physical, emotional or mental capacity. Halpern and Fuhrer (1983) described impairment as "behavior" because of its operational role within the context of functional assessment. In other words, when impairment is assessed **functionally,** one is interested in its **impact** upon disability and handicap, in addition to merely documenting the **consequences** of disease or injury. This relates to the "purposeful" component of our definition of functional assessment. Due to its location in the chain of events, impairment serves as an interface between the medical care system, which attempts to **cure** (i.e., eliminate impairments and therefore their consequences of disability or handicap), and the rehabilitation system, which attempts to **ameliorate** the consequences of chronic disease or injury. For example, we measure visual acuity in order to document and, it is hoped, ameliorate its impact upon mobility. The measurement of visual acuity also documents one consequence of glaucoma. In a client with specific learning disabilities, we measure reading rate in order to document and improve, if necessary, its behavioral impact upon school success, leisure or work performance. The measurement of reading rate documents, in some cases, one consequence of an academic learning disability.

Disability

Disability refers to the skills (or lack thereof) that a person exhibits in his or her interaction with the environment. Measurement of skills has been one of the most prolific areas of activity in the field of functional assessment, particularly as represented by the many ADL (activities of daily living) scales that have emerged. For learning disabled adolescents and adults, the *Crites Maturity Inventory (CMI)* and *Career Development Inventory (CDI)* assess functional aspects of a client's readiness to deal with the career choice process (Biller, 1983, 1985a; Bingham, 1978, 1980) and is an area reported to be in need by SLD adults.

Handicap

Handicap refers to any disadvantage or shortcoming that a person experiences while attempting to perform any of the major social roles that are generally available to other people. This includes a wide array of activities and opportunities such as work, recreation, residential environment and family relationships. Amelioration of handicap is the ultimate goal of rehabilitation.

Applying Impairment, Disability and Handicap in a Functional Assessment

Of immediate concern for the individual identified as having a specific learning disability, for example, would be the degree to which a documented reading **impairment,** that is, reading rate, accuracy or comprehension is sub-average, has restricted the individual to the extent that he or she cannot perform at an average rate the tasks or the prerequisite tasks of an occupation that he or she is otherwise qualified for. For example, the SLD client who wants to be an aircraft maintenance technician and has the physical attributes, interests and mechanical aptitudes, but, because of the prerequisite tasks (classes that require reading and understanding of technical manuals as evaluated in timed test situations), and perhaps because of the tasks of the job itself (required to be able to, in a specified amount of time, look up, read and comprehend a section of a FAA Manual to repair or replace a mechanical dysfunction), is not able to meet the entry level performance standard, is an example of **behavior** as the object of assessment. If the reading rate of the SLD client precludes him or her from repairing or maintaining a specific component of an aircraft in the time standards generally allotted to such maintenance/repair procedures, and an employer or technical school denies access to that job or training on the basis of the slower reading rate, then the **impairment** (below average reading rate) that has **disabled** the client's speed in performing a task at a required rate, would, therefore, constitute an employment **handicap.** Noting especially that it was previously determined that, in all other respects, that is, interests, aptitudes and physical ability, the SLD client was qualified. It should be strongly emphasized that unmeasurable behaviors such as those traditionally associated with underlying causes (antecedents) or reading disability, that is, faulty psychological processes, minimal brain dysfunction, and/or visual/auditory imperception, are currently of little practical use when determining functional behavior within the context of the above definitions, although they may be required evaluation criteria, by some states, to ascertain if the client is servable in respective state vocational rehabilitation agencies.

Of more habilitative value than the above mentioned, nonmeasurable behaviors would be modifications of the work environment. Such a modification might entail having the more technical parts of the Federal Aviation Agency (FAA) manuals taped and catalogued for easy access. If such adaptation were not feasible, the next step would be to have the SLD person consider a career objective not requiring such a high level of technical reading skill, for example, an aircraft technician's helper. Of course, this would constitute placing the client in a "more restrictive" work situation or environment. Similar scenarios could be outlined for the SLD client who has severe social skill behaviors. For example, a SLD person who cannot work with co-workers for more than an hour without criticizing someone and/or instigating an argument which results in lost productivity on the job site, would also constitute an employment handicap, with social skill being the **impaired** function, and the inability to get along with others in the work place being the **disability** condition.

Environment means the various places where purposeful behavior occurs such as the home, the community and the work place, all of which are thought to shape an individual's behavior. For example, an SLD student who has been passed along in school with reading demands being minimized often finds that his/her reading skills are not adequate for the career objective they have had in mind. In fact, disparities do exist between work and school reading demands (Sticht, 1985). In the social skills area, SLD persons have always had a friend(s) and family members to understand them, but their social skills shaped for this accepting environment are not generalized or workable in work settings that include people who have no special reason to accept their variant behavior(s). Thus, assessments for such behaviors are optimally conducted within the environment in which the client(s) will eventually be expected to perform.

Interaction refers to the dynamic relationship that exists between behavior and environment in a functional assessment. The concern here is not only with the behavioral resources of the person but also with implicit or explicit demands or behavioral expectations of the environment. The need for change in either the person or the environment can only be determined after completion of an assessment of both and then evaluating the significance of any gap that may exist between them. **Interpretation** refers to the process of determining the meaning of assessment within its **intended use** (eligibility for services, developing an IWRP or building a national profile).

In summary, a current trend in career assessment is the development of functional assessment systems to augment traditional assessment strategies. This trend stems from a major shift in assessment philosophy and practice that accurred in the early 1940s. Now, functional assessment methods are aimed toward classifying and evaluating client's abilities to perform in their environment, and away from delineating diagnostic labels, traits and aptitudes which characterized the traditional approach. Yet, the traditional assessment approaches are going to be a part of the process and if used properly can be an important part of the assessment. All of what we do in assisting SLD persons depends on our abilities to make appropriate, reliable and valid assessments of those variables that facilitate the educational/career development process. These assessments serve as the basis for all professional service activity, including (a) determining eligibility, (b) setting individualized goals and treatment strategies, (c) evaluating service outputs (such as a SLD's change or exit criteria), and (d) facilitating agency administration and personnel planning.

Career Assessment Model for Adolescents and Young Adults with Specific Learning Disabilities

Congruent with the developmentally based career development theory outlined in Chapter 2, a career assessment model based on Super's (1983) updated developmental career assessment framework (see Figure 10) is suggested for specific application with learning disabled adolescents. As noted earlier, adaptations of the Harren and Krumboltz decision-making models are also incorporated. Prior to the introduction of the assessment and decision-making model, precautions specifically relevant for evaluating the learning disabled are given.

Precautions for Assessing SLD Populations

Because of the broad range and types of aptitudes and skills learning disabled students possess, it is especially critical to evaluate each student as an individual who, like all other students, has many different academic strengths and weaknesses and learning styles. Thus, prior to beginning the formal assessment process, reading level, as expressed in comprehension level, decoding skill and vocabulary level should be carefully examined to ascertain which evaluation tools will need to be modified, rejected or exchanged for alternative measures. As Harnden,

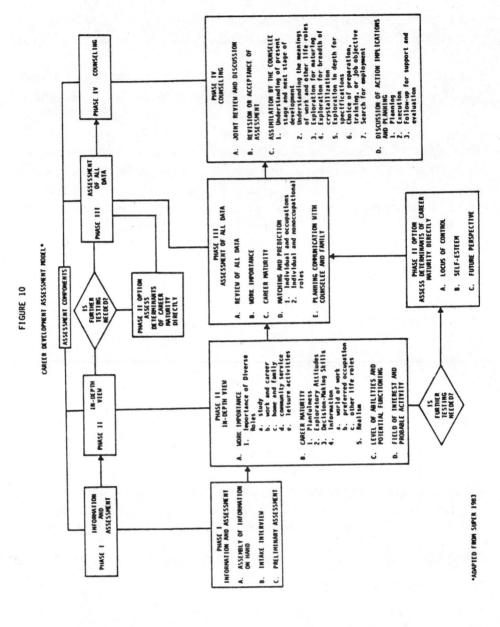

FIGURE 10

CAREER DEVELOPMENT ASSESSMENT MODEL*

Meyer, Alley and Deshler (1980) cautioned, "the LD students' poor performance . . . may be more indicative of deficient reading skills than of poor vocational potential" (p. 8). Also important is the need for collection of data from both home and community sources in developing a preliminary career assessment profile. Learning disabled students, when outside of the academic environment, may demonstrate traits and behaviors not seen in the traditional school milieu. In order to get an accurate and complete initial career behavior profile of the learning disabled student, both student and environmental factors must be reviewed.

Career Assessment and Decision-Making Model for the Learning Disabled

Phase I: Information and Assessment

Phase I of the Career Development Assessment model (CDAM) (Figure 10) has the teacher, counselor or vocational evaluator responsible for conducting the assessment and gathering relevant quantitative and qualitative data already on file. Objectives of this initial intake interview should include (a) establishment of rapport with the student; (b) gathering of specific biographical data pertaining to family, medical, social, psychological, educational and economic factors; and (c) determining the student's present needs and career goals. At the completion of this preliminary assessment phase, the student, parent and appropriate staff members determine if and what additional types of assessment are needed. Involvement of the student and parents in the decision-making process is critical to the success of the assessment. If the student and parents have not fully participated in the development of the assessment plan, they cannot be expected to be fully supportive of it.

Prior to beginning the discussion of the in-depth assessment of Phase II, a departure from typical career assessment practice is required. It has been suggested by Super (1983) that the initial question to be asked about the need for more in-depth testing is not that of what level of occupation or what field of work should be considered, rather "that of readiness to assess [one's] abilities and interests, of readiness to make self and occupational matching decisions" (p. 559). This type of readiness differs from the career assessment models whose references to career readiness often denote readiness to function within a job setting. The theoretical assumptions and research results presented by Biller (1983, 1985a, b) show that many learning disabled adolescents are not ready (career mature) to cope with career decision making tasks required in the adolescent life stage.

Phase II In-Depth View: Work Importance and Career Maturity

Work Importance

In Phase II of the assessment model is incorporated the constructs of work importance and career maturity. Work importance consists of five diverse life roles: (a) study, (b) work and career, (c) home and family, (d) community service, and (e) leisure activities. Each of these roles, the combination of which are played by an individual during the course of a lifetime, also represents a developmental definition of career. As such, how motivated and how efficiently one copes or manages the tasks of each role represents one's degree of commitment and maturity in and through the career development life process. To assess this aspect of career development, Super (1983) has developed criteria as part of the *International Work Importance Study,* which, through measures of work salience, assesses the relative importance of each major life role. The instrument used by Super to assess work importance is the Values Scale and the Salience Inventory (Super & Nevill, 1984).

Super (1983) noted "that to people to whom work does not seem important, the attitudes and information that constitute career maturity must seem irrelevant" (p. 558). Ruling out socioeconomic status and sex as correlates of one's career maturity, Super also advanced that for some people, work and careers do not appear as a personal reality. Subsequently, readiness for career decision making encompasses more than what is encompassed in the construct of career maturity. It is posited here that adolescents must also be motivated to want to attain a certain career level. Spreen's (1983) reported data on job-related aspirations of learning disabled subjects suggest that motivation for higher SES occupations may be lacking. For example, an adolescent's readiness (career maturity) to cope with the developmental career tasks of **crystallization, specification,** and **implementation** has been shown to be significantly related to one's degree of participation in and commitment to work, particularly with regard to the attitudinal components of career maturity, that is, planning and exploration. As SLD adolescents have shown to be less career mature than their nondisabled peers (Biller, 1985a) and to have lower career aspirations, and, given the known association between work salience and career maturity, knowing how motivated SLD students are to pursue the work role, and why they want to pursue it if so motivated, is basic to planning a career decision-making program relevant to SLD students' needs.

It has also been suggested that the relative importance of study, home-making, work, leisure, and community service to an individual is an important determinant of the time and energy that will be devoted to each major career life role. According to Super (1980, 1982), life is a changing constellation of roles, the amount of time given to each, and the amount of affect attached to each varies with changes in maturity and in the environment. In order to understand a person's readiness to make career decisions, one needs to know the relative importance of study, work and homemaking and of leisure and community service too, to that person. In order to interpret scores on a vocational interest inventory, one must know how important work is to the student or adult in question, as well as the nature and degree of exposure to work and occupations.

For high school students, leisure and work tend to be rated most important, studying and community activities least and home and family in the middle. That leisure tends to be important to high school students is not surprising, but that work appeared more important than studying was somewhat unexpected. Perhaps high school students in general are not involved in their school work, and view it as a means to getting a job or becoming an adult, and as something "one does what one has to." The moderate importance of home and family is expected at an age in which the main focus is on peer relationships, and so is the low ranking by the high school population of community activities. By the college years, participation in leisure activities appears important, but the maturing of role values might be seen in the greater affect given to work and home and family, with only moderate emphasis on leisure. Participation in studying tends also to be high, as would be expected. The more serious students go on to college from high school (Super & Nevill, 1984). With specific reference to the importance of the work and career role (shown as [B] in Figure 10), Super (1983) further posited this type of career readiness: "those who are not yet ready for this need to be helped to identify the types of experiences that they need in order to be equipped to make the educational and occupational decisions required by their own psychological and social development and structure and content of our educational and occupational systems" (p. 559).

Career Maturity

The five career maturity dimensions listed in Figure 10 Phase II, as developed by Super (1983), can have extensive implications for enhancing the learning disabled's level of career maturity. For example, these dimensions can provide points of reference from which the desired attitudes and competencies related to effective career growth can be diagnosed, assessed and enhanced. A delineation of desired attitudes and competencies within each dimension allows the specification of objectives for instructional and counseling projects designed to promote mature development.

Assessment of these dimensions and their variations can be accomplished through the use of several career maturity assessment devices: Crites' (1978) *Career Maturity Inventory* Westbrook's (1973) *Cognitive Vocational Maturity Inventory* and Super et al.'s (1981) *Career Development Inventory (CDI)*. Career maturity assessment inventories are primarily measures of individual career development. The *CDI* is the model consistent with the theoretical framework of this assessment model (CDAM), and is the only career maturity instrument discussed in this text. An overview of the *CDI* is presented below.

The Career Development Inventory

The *CDI* is based on longitudinal research begun in 1951 that documented the lack of readiness for career decisions of students in the ninth grade. The *CDI* was developed by Donald E. Super and others of Columbia University, Teachers College. The *CDI* originated from a pool of indices thought to be representative of vocational maturity. From this original pool of vocational maturity indices, five were considered especially pertinent for grades 9-12: (a) concern with choice, (b) acceptance of responsibility for choice and planning, (c) specificity of information about the preferred occupations, (d) specificity and extent of planning, and (e) use of resources in orientation (Thompson & Lindeman, 1981).

Attitudinal Scales

The *CDI* is comprised of two attitudinal scales, the Career Planning (CP) scale and the Career Exploration (CE) scale. Comprised of 20 items, the CP scale requires a student to indicate the type and degree of career planning he or she has engaged in. This planning activity would include discussing career plans with an adult friend, obtaining part-time employment and getting a job after the completion of school or training. In addition, students judge their own knowledge of the kind of work they would like to do, including what workers actually do on the job, abilities and training needed.

The CE scale contains a bank of 20 self-report items also. The initial 10 questions require the student to rate relatives, friends, persons in the occupation or college being considered, as well as other adults, printed materials and the media as sources of career information. The final 10 questions ask the student for ratings of the usefulness of the information received from each of those sources.

The *CDI* also includes three cognitive scales, Decision-Making (DM), World-of-Work Information (WWI) and Knowledge of the Preferred Occupational Groups (PO). Represented in the DM scale are 20 short sketches of individuals making career decisions, with the sketches spanning a range of grade and occupational levels. The DM scale measures the ability to apply knowledge and insight to career planning and decision making. The assumption made with the DM scale is that students who can understand and solve the career problems in the sketches can also apply the process to their decision making. This scale loads heavily on the cognitive abilities associated with problem solving, an area consistently weak in learning disabled children and adolescents.

The WWI scale assesses student knowledge of the career development tasks. The scale also addresses a student's knowledge of the occupational structure, of sample occupations ranging from semiskilled to professional and of job-seeking and keeping skills. Overall, the WWI scale assesses the career awareness and occupational knowledge that contributes to positive career planning behaviors.

The PO scale is the fifth dimension of the *CDI*. An objective of the PO is to help students identify the occupational group that interests them most, and therefore is structured to test acquaintance with the classification of work that students indicate is of most interest to them.

Career Development-Attitudes (CDA), Career Development-Knowledge and Skills (CDK) and Career Orientation Total (COT) represent three combinations of the five previously described *CDI* scales. The CDA represents a combination of the CP and CE scales and assesses the career attitude dimensions. The CDK scale combines DM and WWI and assesses the highly correlated knowledge of how to make career decisions with knowledge of the world of work. Finally, the combination of CP, CE, DM, and WWI is used as a composite measure of the most important aspects of career maturity. PO is not included in the COT composite.

CDI Testing with Learning Disabled Adolescents

As the *CDI* has a reading vocabulary of approximately a 10th-grade level, it will be unusable with many LD students. One adaptive alternative would be to select words from the *CDI* and include them in regular vocabulary instruction. Further, the *CDI* was not normed on a LD population, and therefore, interpretations and generalizations must be made cautiously. However, in at least one study (Brown, 1982), the *CDI* attitude dimensions were shown to have adequate coefficients of reliability for specific LD populations. Other adaptations of the *CDI* for LD students could include reading the test to the students as well as allowing them to look at it, and in the CP and CE section where the student must remember one major question and then make several responses based on that question, the question could be written on the board to eliminate testing for memory abilities.

Summary: Career Maturity and Work Salience

Research conducted by Super and Nevill (1984) using the Salience Inventory with high school students, including the disadvantaged, has led to these findings: (a) work salience is related to career planning and exploration attitudes, as measured by the *Career Development Inventory (CDI)* but not to career information held; (b) girls who are career committed tend to be more career mature, including career information, than are other girls and than boys; (c) for all students, commitment to work is positively correlated with career maturity; (d) socioeconomic status is not directly related to career maturity; and (e) for high school students, leisure and work tend to be rated most important, studying and community activities least and home and family in the middle.

Career Maturity and Related Life Roles

Another area to be discussed with reference to career maturity, as shown in Phase II of the model, is "other life roles." As part of the developmental perspective of the CDAM, it is important for adolescents to see themselves as individuals coping with the specific developmental tasks of the life-stage they are in. In contrast to traditional career education programs, which primarily define awareness as knowing about self and occupations, Super's type of awareness or recognition of need encompasses the need to be concerned about not only career planning and exploration, but also the need to recognize the implications of one's role as a son or daughter and a student. After all, how well one copes with the tasks of being a student may directly affect how one will function as a worker. The interpersonal relationships developed within the family as a child will also affect how well one copes with the social roles encompassed in being either a spouse or worker. Readiness or recognition of the need to cope with career development tasks has been termed career maturity. This readiness to deal with all the life roles (spouse, work associate or citizen) can, in the developmental sense, be considered dimensions of career maturity.

Realism: The Final Determinant of Career Maturity

While realism, due to its complexity, is not a measurable construct in the *CDI* assessment, it is important to review its basic definition. Explaining realism in the perspective of career readiness, Super (1983) offered the following definition of career realism: "It consists of self-knowledge, realism in self and situational assessment, consistency of career-role preferences, crystallization of self-concepts and of career goals, and of stabilization in major life roles such as those of worker, homemaker, citizen and leisurite" (p. 558). As such, realism represents a combination of all the previously listed dimensions of adolescent career maturity.

Assessing Abilities, Interests and Potential Functioning

Traditional career assessment activities have primarily relied on a limited sample of student behavior for the purpose of making predictions about an individual's work potential. Unfortunately, the emphasis of those using career assessment instruments has primarily been directed toward identification of static student characteristics rather than toward a better understanding of the dynamic exchange between student behavior and environmental conditions. However, if used appropriately and the data considered in proper perspective, traditional career assessment methods should yield useful information for planning a school's career development program. This career information will be even more valuable if it is strengthened by alternative assessment data that includes information on student performance over time and under varying environmental conditions.

Aptitude Assessment Formats: Traditional and Nontraditional

Interest and aptitude testing, psychological testing, work samples, community or situational assessments, and on-the-job tryouts represent the basic assessment formats used in traditional evaluation of abilities and interests as well as levels of occupational functioning. Career assessment has long been considered an essential part in the career developmental process. The importance lies in its potential contribution toward achieving the ultimate goal of successful work adjustment. Following is an overview of the instruments used to conduct career assessment with respect to abilities and interests.

Psychological Tests

Psychological tests are usually included as part of a comprehensive career assessment. The tests typically involve paper and pencil assessments of cognitive, attitudinal and affective traits that are reported to be important in job performance. Frequently used psychological tests include the WAIS, the Strong-Campbell Interest Inventory, the Iowa Test of Basic Skills, the General Aptitude Test Battery, and the Differential Aptitude Test Battery.

Work Samples

Work samples have been defined by Neff (1968) as a "mock-up, a close simulation of an industrial (actual) operation, not different in its essentials from the kind of work a potential employee would be required to perform on an ordinary job" (p. 178). Their most unique feature, when compared to other assessment methods, is that they are intended to approximate real life situations. A number of work samples have been developed and used in the vocational assessment of handicapped persons; the reader is referred to Botterbusch (1980), in which such systems are described and comparatively analyzed.

Situational Assessment

The situational assessment refers to the practice of conducting a 20- to 30-day evaluation of a student's performance in a structured vocational setting. In these assessment situations, the student is given an actual job to perform and information is collected on work skills and other work-related behaviors. Work skills include the time required to learn new tasks, speed of performance and accuracy. Examples of work-related behaviors are direction following, frustration tolerance, safety, motivation, punctuality, dependability, perseverance and social-interpersonal skills. At the completion of the situational assessment period, a staffing is usually held, and the student's vocational education program is modified according to individual needs.

On-the-Job Tryout

Of all the traditional methods for conducting vocational evaluation information, the on-the-job tryout provides the most realistic setting in which to assess vocationally-relevant behaviors. This method of evaluation gives the teacher/evaluator an opportunity to determine students' ability to work in different settings. Further, this method allows for the exposure of students to a variety of occupations. In an on-the-job tryout, students can be evaluated by the actual supervisory staff and by school personnel. From the students' exposure to a series of community employment experiences, school personnel are provided with assessment data from which they can further develop the relevance and quality of their vocational education program.

Alternative Career Evaluation Techniques

Environmental Assessment

Since career evaluation needs to be more sensitive to the interaction of student behavior and environmental conditions, alternatives are needed to traditionally used methods. These alternatives should be dynamic as opposed to static. Furthermore, these assessment techniques need to include repeated measurements across an extended period of time. As a first step in developing more appropriate career assessment techniques, a detailed analysis of employment situations in the community should be conducted. This assessment can be used to identify the criteria for successful vocational performance across a variety of occupational areas.

Labor Market Influences

Vocational preparation programs in the public schools must be responsive to an ever-changing job market. The content of these programs should reflect those occupations that are presently in demand and those that are projected to be available on the local, regional and national levels. For handicapped students, vocational mobility beyond the local community may be limited, consequently, vocational programs for handicapped students need to be closely aligned with those specific occupations that are realistically available in the home community. Local job availability must be continually assessed by school personnel. Included in this career assessment activity, there should also be the opportunity for students to participate, where possible, in industrial tours, visits to community job sites and exposure to the many activities and courses offered in the secondary school environment.

Computerized Career Assessment: A Motivational Tool

Traditional testing procedures, other than environmental procedures, are very familiar to the LD students as they have been, in most cases, tested much of their school lives. As their learning problems continue to present adjustment difficulties, the LD's confidence and motivation to do well on those tests are diminished. Computerized assessment approaches are a promising, in-school career assessment method for learning about one's aptitudes, interests and work values. A computer guided career assessment model known as *DISCOVER* has been found by Biller (1985a) to be highly motivating for one high school LD group. A brief description of the *DISCOVER* career assessment system is given below.

In keeping with one of the major objectives of the CDAM for LD adolescents, *DISCOVER* promotes an increase in self-understanding by helping students to assess their interests, rate their aptitudes and prioritize their values commensurate with their own needs. The *DISCOVER* career assessment system is able to combine these student needs with occupational characteristics selected by the student. The computer provides occupations that are consistent with the student's individual interests and needs, thus allowing the student to explore occupations in detail without using voluminous (and unreadable) career guidance materials and manuals. In addition to allowing students to gain increased awareness of career options, *DISCOVER* permits students to consider and explore as many alternatives as they like. The students are free to change their minds about any response, with the occupational results of those changes seen immediately. As with all visually presented reading material, LD students are going to have some difficulties with the processing of information presented on the computer screen. In addition, much of the computer career information is geared to a high school vocabulary level. As the computer generates so many different pieces of information, it is unrealistic to preteach this vocabulary. A better suggestion is for the teacher/evaluator to be available for questions while the student is using the computer, or have the student print out (via the computer) any information not understood and present it for interpretation when time permits.

Phase II: OPTION: Assessing Determinants of Career Maturity

For some LD students, the assessment results yielded in Phase II may indicate abnormally low maturity and/or motivation, thus requiring further testing (Phase II: OPTION) to determine if those personality determinants are impeding the career development process. Locus of control, self-esteem, future perspective and cognitive complexity are considered the major determinants of career maturity. Each is briefly discussed below.

Locus of Control

Locus of control or autonomy is identified as a determinant of the career maturity dimension, planfulness. The rationale for using autonomy or locus of control in career maturity is that planning can take place only if people believe they have control over their career direction. The most widely known measure of locus of control is Rotter's (1966) adult *Internal-External Locus of Control I-E Scale.*

Self-Esteem

Self-esteem is also a determinant or component of planfulness. According to Super (1983), self-esteem "has been found in numerous studies to be essential to autonomy; and, anticipating the future, those who consider themselves of dubious worth are not likely to believe that they can control their careers by looking ahead and planning" (p. 557). Those adolescents who view themselves as having dubious worth will not feel enough control of their lives to want to plan for a career. Thus, the occupational self-clarifications that occur through completion of activities similar to those outlined in the Phase II assessment process will likely be cloudy or nonexistent due to the lack of motivation to want to participate in the career development process. Thus, self-esteem becomes the thread that links the manifest academic and career development problems of learning disabled individuals. In support of this hypothesis, Bingham (1974) has validated a correlation between low self-esteem and career immaturity in a learning disabled population. Three measures of self-esteem are the Coopersmith's (1967) *Self-Esteem Inventory,* Rosenberg's (1965) *Self-Esteem Scale* and the *Self-Esteem Questionnaire* by the Test Analysis and Development Corporation of Boulder, Colorado.

Future Perspective

As future or time perspective pertains to the crystallization, specifying and implementing of career preferences, which is dependent on the ability to conceptualize the immediate and distant future, the interview process, as well as the findings of the previously discussed quantitative assessments will reveal a student's adequacy for having a future perspective for career planning. Expressing the importance of time perspective, Gonzalez and Zimbardo (1985) stated "without a time perspective in which the past blends into the present, how could we establish a sense of personality — a sense of self that is stable through time" (p. 21). And without this sense of self, it is difficult for adolescents to "picture" (crystallize) their occupational identities. In a follow-up study of young adults school identified as learning disabled, Vetter (1983) found a significant difference between the learning disabled and a nonhandicapped comparison group in future perspective and goal setting. The future perspective that individuals develop early in life can depend greatly on their socioeconomic class and their personal experiences with its values, influences and institutions. A child with parents in unskilled and semiskilled occupations is usually socialized in a way that promotes present-oriented perspectives, while children of parents who are managers or professionals learn future-oriented values and strategies designed to promote achievement (Gonzalez & Zimbardo, 1985).

Cognitive Complexity

Learning disabled students with cognitive deficits may have their weaknesses identified prior to conducting the career assessment. As Brown's (1982) study on LD career maturity demonstrated, the more cognitively impaired the student, the greater the career immaturity. In Brown's results, arithmetic deficits were a better indicator of career immaturity than reading or spelling skills. Arithmetic deficits, as such, can be associated with enhanced cognitive deficits. The discussion by Winer, Cesari and Haase (1979) emphasized the importance of cognitive capacity to make fine discriminations with respect to clarifying one's self-concept for the purpose of identifying an occupational environment suited to one's personality. Problem solving skills, as part of the decision making process, are also consistent weaknesses in individuals with cognitive learning disabilities.

Activity Involvement

The importance of being involved in school and community activities has been associated with positive attitudes towards career exploratory attitudes. In order to better understand one's abilities, interests and values, it is necessary to experience situations that test performance in a variety of environments. Unfortunately, the observation of a student's degree of involvement in career-related activities must be subjective in nature. The study by Alley, Deshler, Clark, Schumaker and Warner (1983) clearly showed that LD students may be the least likely of all adolescent subgroups to participate in these activities.

Phases III and IV of the CDAM

In the remaining two phases, the career assessment information is reviewed, and the steps are carried out as shown in the flowchart (Figure 10), particularly in the traditional one-on-one counseling framework. During this process, it is ascertained, between client, family and counselor, what the next steps of action are to be. This may include psychological counseling, more career exploration, vocational training, college instruction or, of course, direct job placement.

Assessment of Career Decision-Making Strategies

Once all of the needed career related behaviors have been assessed and their results validated, the SLD adolescent/adult, teacher/counselor and parent/spouse must unite in the process of making the necessary career related decisions. As the principal decider should be the SLD clients, it is of concern that their decision-making strategies, and their subsequent programs designed to operationalize the decisions they have made, are the most optimal ones possible. The steps for making a decision have been outlined previously in a specific career curriculum adapted for use with adolescents and young adults with specific learning disabilities (Biller, 1985b). Therefore, only the specific steps of that decision-making framework are included here, as the immediate concern is on strategical approach(es) used by the SLD person to cope with the steps in the decision-making process. Following the presentation of this strategical model of decision-making, programmatic objectives will be outlined for carrying out the decisions the subject has made.

Decision-Making Skills

Systematic efforts to teach decision-making skills within the schools is a recent trend in American schooling. Currently, there is a lack of information about how students learn the strategies of career decision making, how to teach decision making, what components make up decision-making competence or how this competence can be measured. The need to develop programs in decision making may originate from two sources: (1) "data from recent work (Super, 1974) on the construct of vocational maturity that indicate that decision-making skill is a significant component of vocational maturity, and (2) the increasing ground swell for implementing career education, whose curriculum often included objectives and content related to decision-making" (Super & Harris-Bowlsbey, 1979, p. 42).

Steps for Making Career Decisions

A nine-step process of decision making, detailed in Super and Harris-Bowlsbey's (1979) curriculum, is a restatement of the process and direction that appear in decision-making-related career, decision-making literature (Super, 1979). These processes have been translated into the models used in the Guided Career Exploration program by Super and Harris-Bowlsbey and are outlined below.

Step 1. Becoming Aware of the Need to Decide. This initial step of the decision-making process requires that the decider be consciously aware that there is a need or problem. Obviously, if the SLD client has fully participated in the previous assessment process, then he or she will have attained this degree of awareness.

Step 2. Setting Goals. Here the decider sets a goal which he or she believes will meet the need or solve the problem that was identified in Step 1. Goal setting was discussed as being associated with time and/or a future perspective. If this was an area of concern in the assessment, then extra time may be spent in this step process.

Step 3. Find or Make Alternatives. If there are barriers to reaching the desired goals set in Step 2, then alternatives must be made to achieving those goals.

Step 4. Imagine Alternatives, Consequences and Collect Information. At this step the decider attempts to imagine as clearly as possible what it would be like to follow each of the alternatives selected in the previous step. This may require getting additional information on the topic of concern.

Step 5. Weigh the Value of Each Alternative. The decider carefully weighs each alternative and places the alternatives in order of their desirability.

Step 6. Choose Alternative with Highest Value. Decider selects the most favorable alternative as the tentatively planned course of action to solve the problem.

Step 7. Re-evaluate Choice. Here the decider analyses the choices made just to confirm that it makes sense and will actually assist in solving the problem.

Step 8. Implement Choice. This is an action step taken by the decider to carry out the choices made.

Step 9. Experience Outcomes. Feedback from positive or negative reactions of the decision will further permit evaluation of whether the goal is likely to be met.

Teachers/counselors wishing to teach these steps in a role play situation should consult the curriculum activities guide in Super and Harris-Bowlsbey's (1979) *Guide to Career Exploration.* Types of discussions to be carried out are outlined in the guide, including case examples of different age subjects emitting decision-making behaviors. However, it may be helpful to know ahead of time what kinds of decision-making strategies respective students are using. To that end, an evolving model of career decision making known as the *Assessment of Career Decision Making (ACDM),* originally developed by Harren (1979) and published in test form by Buck and Daniels (1985), is presented below in more detail.

Decision-Making Strategies

In addition to the introduction to the *ACDM* given in Chapter 3, a graphic conceptualization of Harren's model is also presented. Shown in Figure 11 are the basic components of Harren's model. According to Harren (1979) "decision-making models are conceptual frameworks for understanding how decision makers process information and arrive at conclusions. When these models are applied to vocational behavior, they can be regarded as models of career decision making" (p. 119). Furthermore, Jepsen and Dilley (1974) have characterized a decision-making model as follows:

A decision-making conceptual framework assumes that presence of a **decision-maker,** a **decision situation** (social expectation) and

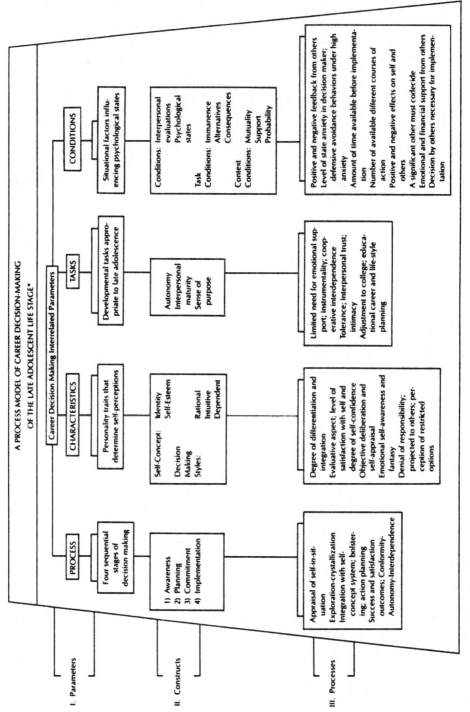

A PROCESS MODEL OF CAREER DECISION-MAKING OF THE LATE ADOLESCENT LIFE STAGE*

Career Decision Making Interrelated Parameters

PROCESS

Four sequential stages of decision making

1) Awareness
2) Planning
3) Commitment
4) Implementation

Appraisal of self-in-situation
Exploration-crystallization
Integration with self-concept system; bolstering; action planning
Success and satisfaction outcomes; Conformity-Autonomy-Interdependence

CHARACTERISTICS

Personality traits that determine self-perceptions

Self-Concept: Identity
               Self-Esteem

Decision
Making
Styles: Rational
           Intuitive
           Dependent

Degree of differentiation and integration
Evaluative aspect; level of satisfaction with self and degree of self-confidence
Objective deliberation and self-appraisal
Emotional self-awareness and fantasy
Denial of responsibility; projected to others; perception of restricted options

TASKS

Developmental tasks appropriate to late adolescence

Autonomy
Interpersonal maturity
Sense of purpose

Limited need for emotional support; instrumentality; cooperative interdependence
Tolerance; interpersonal trust; intimacy
Adjustment to college; educational career and life-style planning

CONDITIONS

Situational factors influencing psychological states

Conditions: Interpersonal evaluations
             Psychological states

Task
Conditions: Immanence
             Alternatives
             Consequences

Context
Conditions: Mutuality
             Support
             Probability

Positive and negative feedback from others
Level of state anxiety in decision maker; defensive avoidance behaviors under high anxiety
Amount of time available before implementation
Number of available different courses of action
Positive and negative effects on self and others
A significant other must codecide
Emotional and financial support from others
Decision by others necessary for implementation

I. Parameters

II. Constructs

III. Processes

*Adapted from Harren (1979)

relevant **information** both from within and outside the person. The information is arranged into decision-making concepts according to the functions it serves. Two or more **alternative actions** are considered and several **outcomes** or consequences are anticipated from each action. Each outcome has two characteristics, **probability** or likelihood of occurrence in the future, and **value,** or relative importance to the decision-maker. The information is arranged according to a strategy so that the decision maker can readily recognize an advantageous course of action and make a **commitment** to this action. (p. 332).

A decision-making model, Harren therefore concludes, "is a description of a psychological process in which one organizes information, deliberates among alternatives, and makes a commitment to a course of action" (p. 119). Career decision making, stated Harren, needs to be viewed in the larger framework of career development, but with particular focus on a particular life stage, for example, college freshmen and sophomores in the process of deciding a college major or career goal. Adaptations of the Harren's *ACDM* are now also being utilized at the earlier adolescent (high school) stage as well (Jepsen & Grove, 1981). Finally, Harren has noted that his model of decision making also specifies how the decision-making process varies according to the characteristics of the decision maker, the decision-making context and the type of decision involved.

Description of the Decision-Making Model

Viewing Harren's (1979) Career Decision-Making Model (CDM) at the upper left-hand corner of Figure 11 is Roman numeral I denoted as Parameters. Harren identifies the CDM as having four interrelated parameters: (a) process, (b) characteristics, (c) tasks, and (d) conditions. These four parameters are listed across the top row of the CDM model in Figure 11. Within each parameter Harren has postulated a number of constructs and processes. The base or core of the CDM, according to Harren, is the **Process,** a four stage, sequential decision-making process through which the person progresses in making and carrying out decisions. Those four stages under Process are identified in Figure 11, to the right of Roman numeral II (constructs) as: (a) awareness, (b) planning, (c) commitment, and (d) implementation. At each of these four stages (within a specified time period, for example, high school senior), the student/adolescent is preoccupied with different concerns or issues and is engaged in different covert and overt behaviors to resolve these concerns.

Decision-maker **Characteristics** (the second parameter parallel to Roman numeral I) refer to somewhat stable personality traits which determine the person's perception of the **Tasks** and **Conditions** and which affect the client's progress in the four stages of decision making. For example, the **Constructs** (Roman numeral II) associated with permitting progression through the **Process** stages are one's self-concept, that is, identity and self-esteem and the style or strategy one employs as part of coping with the decision-making tasks throughout the four stages of **Awareness, Planning, Commitment** and **Implementation.**

The third parameter, **Tasks,** refers to career relevant developmental tasks of adolescents and their related decision-making tasks. These tasks are exemplified (see Constructs, Roman numeral II under Tasks) as gaining independence (autonomy) or internal locus of control, limited need for outside emotional support (interpersonal maturity) and developing a sense of goal directness (sense of purpose).

Finally, the **Conditions** (the fourth parameter) refer to the immediate and anticipated situational factors influencing the person and to the person's present psychological state. The applicable **Constructs** of **Conditions** are: Interpersonal Evaluations and Psychological States; and under **Task Conditions** are: **Imminence** (amount of time available before a decision needs to be made), **Alternatives** (different courses of action one perceives) and **Consequences** (positive and negative consequences to self and others at each stage in the process with respect to each task). **Context Conditions,** the last of the situational factors influencing psychological states are: **Mutuality** (the degree that significant others are affected by a decision made, such that codecisions are needed), **Support** (the conditions that refer to the significant others who provide emotional or financial support for the decision maker in order to implement the decision), and **Probability** (the condition that has to do with whether or not a decision can be implemented).

Interrelatedness of the Four Parameters and Their Constructs

According to Harren (1979), the basic hypothesis of his ACDM is that progress through the stages of the decision-making process depends upon the characteristics of the decision maker, the type of decision to be made, and the context in which the decision is to be made. More specifically, Harren posited that, in general, an effective decision maker is one who can be characterized as follows:

The person has a moderate to high level of self-esteem which is based upon accurate incorporation of the interpersonal evaluations from others. The self-concept system is realistic (i.e., consistent with other's perceptions), yet flexible and open to new experiences. The person's self-concept is highly differentiated (i.e., the individual has a clear awareness of her or his interests, values, skills and other self-attributed traits and is confident in this self-knowledge). At the same time, the self-concept is integrated (i.e., the individual has a relatively stable identity, which results in consistent and purposive behavior). The person takes responsibility for decision making and relies primarily on a rational style of decision making. Finally, the person has made considerable progress in accomplishing the three developmental tasks: he or she is both emotionally and instrumentally autonomous, has mature interpersonal relationships and has developed a sense of purpose (p. 128).

Examples of Interactions in the Stages of Awareness, Planning, Commitment, and Implementation

Awareness: Stage One of the ACDM

Explaining this ideal decision maker in more detail, Harren posited that at the first stage of the **Process**, the construct **Awareness** can be denoted as the individual's capacity to utilize evaluations of others in the appraisal of the self-in-situation and is related to one's level of self-esteem and to the extent of realism and flexability of the self-concept. A case example depicting **Awareness** is offered below:

> For example, a student majoring in premedicine who is receiving failing grades in anatomy and physiology will initially distort these evaluations until the evidence mounts and the student can no longer maintain the distortions. Eventually, the student will consider the significance of the feedback relative to his or her present course of action (i.e., continuing to major in premedicine). As Task Imminence increases (the deadline for applying to medical school), there is greater press to evaluate the feedback. If this student is primarily rational in decision-making style, this deadline will be anticipated in sufficient time to reconsider and possibly revoke the decision and begin recycling through the Process. Assuming the negative evaluations have reached consciousness and their consequences have begun to be incorporated into the self-concept during the person's appraisal of self-in-situation, then the individual, without completely abandoning the present course of action, will begin to recognize the need for alternatives, which signals the transition into the Planning stage (Harren, 1979, p. 129).

Planning: Stage Two of the ACDM

The decision-maker characteristics most important during **Planning,** according to Harren, are **Style** of decision making and **Identity.** For example, the way in which **Planning** is conducted is a manifestation of one's decision-making **Style,** while successful resolution of the **Planning** stage is a function of **Identity.** Harren (1979) summarized the implications for this stage as follows:

> The expanding-narrowing process of exploration-crystallization during Planning requires a clear sense of Identity. The data search in exploration cannot be processed in crystallization without some degree of identity formation. Contained in the concept of Identity is a sense of "who I am;" of "what my need-value priorities are;" of "what I am good at;" of "where I am heading;" and of "what general life goals are important to me now." Identity also assumes that there has been considerable progress with respect to the three student development tasks of Autonomy, Interpersonal Maturity and Sense of Purpose. If Commitment and Implementation proceeds without Identity, setbacks and eventual revoking of the decision are likely (pp. 129-130).

Commitment: Stage Three of the ACDM

For the decision maker, **Commitment** requires that the alternative(s) selected and its career self-concept ramifications be enjoined and integrated with one's overall self-concept system. For this to occur, one must have a "flexible" and integrated (crystallized) self-concept system. More specifically, this can be summarized by stating that:

> As one announces one's commitment, the evaluative feedback from others (their reaction to one's intention) also needs to be incorporated. Upon incorporation of the commitment and reintegration of the self-concept system, action steps can be planned. The amount of action planning engaged in is determined by the available time (i.e., Task Imminence and the person's decision-making style). Finally, the amount of postcommitment dissonance reduction or bolstering, is a functional of degree of Identity, level of Self-Esteem, the anticipated Probability and Mutuality Conditions and the anticipated Success and Satisfaction Outcomes (Harren, 1979, p. 130).

Implementation: Stage Four of the ACDM

Decision-making style or strategy is a critical component of the **Implementation** stage. For the externally controlled or dependent personality, the **Conformity** solution to decision-making concerns of the **Implementation** stage is relatively comfortable for the decision-maker. Stability may be attained in this conformity mode and may continue in it indefinitely. This may not always be in the best interest of the decision maker as Harren (1979) explained:

> To the extent that the individual's needs-values-goals are frustrated, however, the person moves into Autonomy. Here, Identity and Self-Esteem are involved in the person's willingness to assert self in an implementation context that is not conducive to self-actualization. Integration will be accomplished according to: the level of Identity the person possesses, the degree of progress in the developmental tasks, the degree of flexibility in the self-concept system and the degree of flexibility in the implementation context. The effective decision maker recognizes that no implementation context will perfectly match the individual, and he or she appraises those aspects of the person-situation that are negotiable and achieves some level of Interdependence, at least temporarily. As changes in one's Sense of Purpose, especially regarding life-style and changes in one's Mutuality conditions occur, different solutions within the implementation context will be attempted. To the extent that such solutions are unsuccessful, the person may revoke the decision and recycle through the process (p. 130).

How various decision-making styles form, requires looking at some of the research on family interaction patterns.

Family Influence on Career Development and Decision-Making Styles

Focusing on Harren's (1979) three career types of decision-making styles as correlates of behavior in the career decision-making process as influenced by family interactions, Hesser (1981) outlined a number of adolescent career development associations based on his research in family adaptability and cohesion:

1. Rational decision-making style used by adolescents (Harren, 1979) had families which held higher career expectations for them; held greater satisfaction with their career plans; had clear, stable family roles; maintained flexible family rules; exhibited greater sharing of family interests and recreation; and parents viewed their adolescents more as young adults or adults, a perception representative of family transition or adaptability.

2. Intuitive decision-making style used by adolescents has been equated with impulsiveness in families where high family cohesion exists. By equating impulsiveness with the intuitive style, Hesser noted that the opposite was found in his rural subgroup, indicating that lower cohesion scores were associated with greater levels on the intuitive style measure. Additional findings demonstrated that higher intuitive style levels were associated with lower educational-occupational levels for parents, parental dissatisfaction with adolescent career plans, lower parental career expectations for their adolescent offspring and family tendencies toward rapid change or adaptability, particularly the white, female and rural subgroups. Within the rural subgroup, higher intuitive measures were also associated with passive or aggressive family members and high rates of family negotiating.

3. Dependent decision-making style data suggested that most adolescents have a similar degree of decision-making dependency regardless of their measured strength levels on the previous two decision-making styles. According to Hesser, this finding indicated a normative adolescent preoccupation with autonomy formation which might lead to collective underestimation of dependency associated with career decision making.

Summarizing the major findings of this study, Hesser noted several key points, some of which are listed as follows:

1. High family cohesion is associated with favorable outcomes on rational decision-making styles, development of positive career planning and exploration attitudes and acquisition of adequate levels of decision making and world-of-work knowledge.
2. Rational decision-making styles are generally highest in families characterized by: sharing of family interest and recreation, clear and stable family roles, flexible family rules, and adolescents who perceive they are viewed as being mature.
3. Intuitive decision-making styles have higher association with families where there exists rapid change patterns, above normal family negotiation, assertive behaviors reflecting chaotic home situations, loose family affiliation and lower parental educational-occupational levels.
4. Positive attitudes towards the career planning process are associated with closer family cohesion, sharing of recreational activities and family interests, flexible family leadership and assertive behaviors demonstrated in stable home settings. Also noted with favorable planning attitudes are higher socioeconomic status, fewer siblings at home, higher parental career aspiration for the adolescent and congruence between the family and adolescent on future career plans.

5. An adolescent's predisposition to use career resources were also associated with the similar factors listed above, except for the absence of family coalitions.

6. Higher socioeconomic status and higher parental expectations and involvement were directly associated with higher career choice levels.

This sociological perspective to career development advances the idea that the family serves to influence the individual's personal development, which in turn affects career choice events. An appropriate career decision, then, would be one in which the best pairing between environment and personality type occurs (Holland, 1973). It has been suggested that the family's influence upon adolescent career development is multidimensional, that is, sociological, psychological and economic in nature. Finally, according to Harren's (1979) interactive decision-making model, as described by Hesser (1981), the family represents the environment in which a member's autonomy, interpersonal maturity and sense of purpose are developed, and will, therefore, affect that member's career decision-making maturity. With the noted adult career adjustment problems of the learning disabled, these findings should be valuable in planning a parent training component in the school program for the newly identified learning disabled child.

Application of Harren's ACDM to Special Populations

The essential benefit to comparing the optimal strategies for decision making to those of the SLD adolescents and young adults is that knowing one's level of commitment or salience towards work and the level of readiness for making career decisions, is not completely sufficient cause for predicting that SLD persons will make the qualitative decisions one would hope they would. In other words, if all of the assessment requirements are met as outlined in the initial part of this chapter, the adolescent/young adult may still implement a less than optimal style (strategy) for deciding on the information gained. There is, however, a safety factor built into the career assessment model discussed prior to Harren's model. That safety factor is the "optimal phase" of the assessment. If a SLD client scores low enough on the measures of career maturity, the client automatically is given further testing on the variables of self-esteem and locus of control. Recall that each of these two personality factors are part of Harren's ACDM Parameters known as **Characteristics**. The construct of the Characteristics parameter includes self-esteem, while the Tasks parameter includes autonomy (locus of control).

If one's self-esteem is less than positive and acceptance of Tasks are external, a faulty decision-making style may be corrected with the treatment during the career assessment phase (before final decisions are being made).

A more logical approach would be to incorporate the recently published assessment instrument (*Assessment of Career Decision Making*, Buck & Daniels, 1985) into Phase II, the in-depth portion of the career assessment model. If the SLD individual is found to be a dependent decision maker (student shows a lack of willingness or capability to take responsibility for decision making) then counseling/treatment can begin at that point, rather than after a possible series of frustrations with the decision-making process.

Support for the Use of the ACDM

Even though the *ACDM* Test Instrument in the present form is fairly new, there have been a number of field tests and validity studies conducted on it. An early summary of those validity studies was stated as follows:

> Perhaps the overall conclusion to be drawn from these results is that the theoretical propositions generated from the Tiedeman and O'Hara model, with respect to the other variables in the study, have been borne out. . . . Secondly, the data presented on the reliability and validity of the *ACDM* suggest that the instrument is an effective measure of the Tiedeman and O'Hara model and that the decision-style scales, added to the instrument based on later revisions of the model by Miller and Tiedeman (1972), have considerable promise as a mediating variable in influencing the career decision-making process (Harren & Kass, 1972, pp. 14-15).

More recent research on the *ACDM* prototype instrument (Phillips, Friedlander, Pazienza & Kost, 1985) indicated general support for the vaility of the *ACDM*, as did Jepsen and Prediger (1981). The *ACDM* manual by Buck and Daniels (1985) includes information regarding reliability (internal consistency and temporal stability) and validity (content, criterion and construct) indicating favorable results.

In one of the few examples that paired the *ACDM* with the *CDI*, academic and performance with reference to a college age handicapped population as well as a sample of disadvantaged, Phillips et al. (1983) found that scholastic aptitude, background influences, and decision-making style appear to be more effective in predicting career maturity of disabled students than of disadvantaged students.

Use and Description of the ACDM Test Scales

The *ACDM* is intended for use with adolescents and adults, particularly those considering postsecondary training. The scales of the *ACDM* known as Decision-Making Styles, School Adjustment and Occupation are considered appropriate for use with high school students. The major scale can provide useful information for those high school students who have definite plans to obtain some form of postsecondary training. Listed in Table 6 below are the nine scales of the *ACDM*. In sum, the *ACDM* is a 94-item, self-report measure that assesses a student's career decision-making style and progress on three career decision-making tasks. Students respond in a true or false format. Also shown in Table 7 are brief descriptions of each of the nine scales. Students with a beginning middle school level vocabulary should be able to comprehend the questions of ACDM. While there are no known

TABLE 6

COMPARISON OF THE ACDM SCALES TO THE HARREN MODEL OF CAREER DECISION MAKING

Harren 1979 Model	1985 ACDM Scales	ACDM Abbreviation	No. of Items
Decision-Making Process			
Awareness	Not included*		
Planning	Major, Occupation[a]	DMT-O	20
Commitment	Not included[b]	DM-M	20
Implementation			
Decision-Making Characteristics			
Self-Concept	Not included*		
	(assessed in career assmt model)		
Decision-Making Styles			
Rational	Rational	DMS-R	10
Intuitive	Intuitive	DMS-I	10
Dependent	Dependent	DM-D	10
Developmental Tasks	School Adjustment	DMT-SA	24
Autonomy	Satisfaction with School	SWS	8
Impersonal Maturity	Involvement with Peers	IWP	8
Sense of Purpose	Interaction with Instructors	IWI	8
Decision-Making Situation	Not included*		

* Parts of the Harren model that are not represented by any ACDM scale are indicated by "not included".

[a] Explanation and crystallization activities as defined by the model take place at the Planning end of the bipolar continuum.

[b] Choice and clarification activities as defined by the model take place at the Commitment end of the bipolar continuum.

studies with SLD populations, it appears that the instrument would be valuable for the increasing number of SLD students going on to post-secondary education programs and who will be in need of such assistance with career decision making.

TABLE 7

ASSESSMENT OF CAREER DECISION MAKING: SCALE DESCRIPTIONS

Decision Making Style Scales	Decision Making Tasks Scales	
"Strategies"	**"School Adjustment"**	**"Occupational/School Major Commitment"**
The **Decision-Making Styles** scales assess the strategy or combination of strategies a student uses in making decisions.	The **Decision-Making Task: School Adjustment** (DMT-SA) scale measures the student's degree of satisfaction with school attended, level of peer involvement, and degree of interaction with instructors.	The **Decision-Making Task: Occupation** (DMT-O) measures the degree of commitment and certainty the student feels towards his or her choice of a future occupation. This scale is constructed as a single, bipolar continuum. The negative pole emphasizes awareness of the need for career information, recognition of the need to make an occupational choice, and awareness of uncertainty about one's own personality style and personal preference. The Positive pole is characterized by positive feelings and a sense of certainty about occupational choices and career plans.
The **Decision-Making Styles: Rational** (DMS-R) scale assesses the degree to which the student makes a realistic appraisal of self and the situation when making decisions. The Rational high scorer makes decisions deliberately and logically, based on the information available.	The **Satisfaction with School** (SWS) subscale measures the student's sense of belonging, acceptance, respect, and satisfaction with school. The student with a high score feels that his or her expectations are being experienced.	
The **Decision-Making Styles: Intuitive** (DMS-I) scale assesses the student's attention to present feelings and emotional self-awareness in making decisions. Those who score high on the Intuitive scale use fantasy feelings, and imagination as the basis for decision making rather than a logical evaluation of available information.	The **Involvement with Peers** (IWP) subscale is of the degree of interaction the student is experiencing with instructors as well as the positive or negative quality of those interactions. This subscale assesses instructor recognition (through respect and performance feedback) of the student as an individual.	The **Decision-Making Task: Major** (DMT-M) scale assesses the degree of commitment and certainty the student feels toward his or her choice of a major or field of study. This scale represents a single, bipolar continuum. The negative pole is characterized by awareness of the need to decide on a major recognition of the need to take exploratory courses, concern about one's lack of ability, awareness that one's interests are changing and undifferentiated, and failure to develop a systematic strategy for choosing a major. The positive pole is characterized by commitment, feelings of relief, involvement, sense of direction, certainty, and unswerving attitude toward carrying out the chosen courses of action.
The **Decision-Making Styles: Dependent** (DMS-D) scale assesses the student's lack of willingness or capability to take responsibility for decision making. The scorer on this scale is heavily influenced by the expectations and desires of authorities and peers. This type of decision-maker actively seeks out others (e.g., parents, academic advisors, or career counselors) to make decisions for him or her.	The **Interaction with Instructors** (IWI) measures the degree of interaction the student is experiencing with instructors as well as the positive or negative quality of those interactions. This subscale assesses instructor recognition (through respect and performance feedback) of the student as an individual.	

Data adapted from Buck & Daniel's, 1985 Assessment of Career Decision Making: Western Psychological Services, Los Angeles.

CHAPTER 6

TEACHING CAREER DECISION-MAKING SKILLS TO SLD ADOLESCENTS AND YOUNG ADULTS

Skill (skĭl): Proficiency, Ability or Dexterity; expertness

A Social Learning and Strategies Approach to Career Decision Making

THE ACDM criteria, developed to assess career decision-making styles is an important tool for determining where a student may need assistance in his or her approach to making career decisions. Once it has been established that there is a need for assistance in making career decision, a behavior change model relevant to improving decision making is necessary. The model selected for this purpose is Krumboltz's (1979) Social Learning Theory of Career Decision Making. Presented first are several criteria that Krumboltz, Becker-Haven and Burnett (1979) ascertained are the foundations for achieving qualitative career decision-making behaviors. The criteria used to judge positive career decision-making attainment are as follows: (a) improvement in the skills for making career decisions, (b) increases in one's level of career maturity, (c) changes in the nature or quality of the client's choices, (d) improvement in one's employment seeking skills, and (e) improvement in one's job performance and satisfaction. Each of these five areas are discussed below in more detail.

Skills in Acquired Career Decision-Making Ability

According to Krumboltz et al. (1979), individuals who have accomplished decision-making skills did so by having developed the ability to

169

learn about oneself and about career options, having considered a number of alternatives, had sought career related information, clarified their values, made plans, were more internal in their sense of locus, engaged in exploratory activities with positive reactions and overcame indecisiveness and its resultant anxiety. In short, Krumboltz et al. stated that:

> Measures of career decision-making skill presuppose that those possessing the skill have learned more about occupations, have congruent vocational aspirations, have developed various strategies for coping with decision problems and can see connections between present actions and future choices (p. 278).

Further, Krumboltz et al. (1979) noted that students who are less specific in their vocational choices tend to have lower academic achievement, be more anxiety prone and have lower self-esteem, although not all undecided need the same type of career decision-making assistance. For example, in Biller's (1983) comparison of career decision making of SLD and normal college students, undecided and career specific students were not significantly different from controls in their career maturity attitudes; however, SLD career decided, but nonspecific SLD's were less career mature than the career nonspecific controls and also had the lowest overall grade point averages of all groups. It is this career nonspecific group that will most likely need the most immediate and individual career decision-making assistance.

Career Maturity

Career maturity, discussed in Chapters 2 and 3 is a measure of readiness for career decision making. Measures of career maturity are in most instances substantially interrelated, and are positively associated with age, intrinsic work values, higher aspirations and expectations, and internal locus of control, mastery of psychological stage crisis, congruency and social class (Krumboltz et al., 1979). An analysis of these above variables with respect to SLD populations has shown that SLD populations are at high risk for attaining average levels of career maturity (Biller, 1985a, b). In a field test by this author of Super and Harris-Bowlsbey's *Guided Career Explorations* curriculum with SLD adolescents, significant increases in career exploration attitudes on the *CDI* were found, but not in planning attitudes. Only the two *CDI* attitude scales (planning and exploration) were used in evaluating this adolescent SLD and control group in a separate but older group of high school SLD students (12th graders) who were pre- and posttested with the *CDI* attitude scales after completing the interest, aptitude and values portions of the *Discover* computerized career assessment system. SLDs had no significant change in planning scores but did on exploration; however, not in the expected positive direction. It was hypothesized that on the *CDI* pretesting, SLD students overestimated their exploration attitudes and, after completing the initial portion of *Discover*, they become more realistic in their self-evaluation. The SLD control group (those that did not have *Discover* but were given an overview about career) did not significantly change in their posttest scores as did the SLD treatment group.

Nature and Quality of Career Choices

Listing interpretations of "good decision making skills," Krumboltz et al. (1979) stated that good decision makers are those clients who chose occupations inconsistent with conventional sex-role stereotypes, valued a career attainment or orientation for the future, were realistic in their decisions and who demonstrated stability in their choices over time: they were the most reflective individuals who engage in qualitative decision making.

To assess this domain of "quality decision making," Krumboltz, Scherba, Hamel, and Mitchell (1982) developed the *Career Decision Simulation (CDS)* to provide a means of evaluating decisions by comparing the match between the stated values of the decider and the attributes of the chosen occupation. Examples of the simulation were questions such as: "Are 'good' decisions arrived at through different steps than 'poor' decisions?" or "Should one persist in investigating alternatives consistent with one's own highest levels?" The overall scope, therefore, of the *CDS* was to learn more about the relative value of various decision-making procedures in generating "good" outcomes.

Using a population of California community college students, Krumboltz et al. (1982) found that the "good" decision makers were those whose simulated occupational choice yielded consequences most consistent with their own previously stated values. "Good" decision makers were also those who persisted in immediately continuing to explore an occupation that they had just found to be consistent with one of their highest values. This later finding suggests the likely "effectiveness of an analogous strategy in actual career decision making. The strategy would be first to sample occupations for congruence with one's most important value(s) and then to conduct more indepth investigations of occupations on the basis of their initial fulfillment of these primary values" (Krumboltz et al., 1979).

Employment Seeking

This is an area that will be addressed fully in an upcoming text by this author for SLD persons. However, it may be noted here that there are useful training programs for clients to learn job interviewing and job finding such as *The Job Club* approach (Azrin, Flores and Kaplan, 1977).

Occupational Adaptation/Satisfaction

This is another topic that was discussed in greater detail for SLDs in Biller (1985b). In their analysis, Krumboltz et al. (1979) indicated that interest inventories provide counselors with useful but imperfect predictors of occupational satisfaction, however no experimental evidence has been revealed in the last four years to show that counselors can improve occupational success or satisfaction.

Social Learning Theory and Career Decision Making

Derivation of the Approach

Social learning theory (SLT) has some of its roots in reinforcement theory as well as stimulus response behaviorism but is most well-known for the explanations given it by Bandura (1971, 1974, 1977). When applying social learning theory to career decision making, the assumption is that individuals are a thinking, planful organism but who are **not always passively** controlled by the environmental forces that surround him or her, and can actively engage in interpreting those forces and arranging them for his or her own purposes (Unruh, 1979). In other words, "it [social learning theory] assumes that the individual personalities and behavioral repertoires that persons possess arise primarily from their unique learning experiences rather than from innate developmental or psychic processes. These learning experiences consist of contact with and cognitive analysis of positively and negatively reinforcing events" (Mitchell & Krumboltz, 1984, p. 235).

Constructs of Social Learning Theory

Social learning theory is built on three fundamental constructs: (a) instrumental learning experiences (individuals studying for a math exam receive a high letter grade; therefore, they will repeat that behavior to the point that the activity becomes, in fact, enjoyable), (b) associative learning experience (a person's friend is surgically saved from death, therefore, believes in the role of medicine as an altruistic career), and (c) vicarious learning experiences (individuals are able to learn new behaviors and skills simply by observing the behaviors of others or through exposure to various types of media). Putting these theoretical underpinnings of social learning theory into their most up-to-date perspective on career decision-making theory, Mitchell and Krumboltz (1984) stated that:

> The social learning theory of career decision making is designed to address the question of why people enter particular educational programs or occupations, why they may change educational programs or occupations at selected points in their lives, and why they may express various preferences for different occupational activities at selected points in their lives. In addressing these questions, the theory examines the impact on the career decision-making process of such factors as genetic predisposition, environmental conditions and events, learning experiences and cognitive, emotional and performance responses and skills. It is posited that each of these factors plays a part in all career decisions that are made, but the different combinations of interactions of the factors produce the multitude of different career choices that different individuals make. It is further posited that there are four categories of factors that influence the career decision-making path for any individual (p. 238).

These above mentioned four categories and their related factors are identified as: (a) genetic endowment, (b) special abilities and skills, (c) planned and unplanned environmental conditions or events, and (d) tasks or problems. In addition to these four categories there are three factors which may be viewed in a matrix format (with the four categories): (a) antecedents, (b) behaviors, and (c) consequences. Shown in Table 8 are each of the four categories (top to bottom) and each of the three factors (left to right) of William, a high school student. A more complete case example of the SLT decision-making model exemplifying a SLD person's career path will also be presented at the end of this chapter. The example in Table 8 illustrates how the antecedent of behavior acts on William's environment in such a way to produce certain consequences. The behavioral responses of instrumental learning experiences include both cognitive and emotional responses as well as observable behaviors. Consequences of the behavior include immediate or delayed influences on other persons, as well as cognitive and emotional responses persons experience when they are the receiver of these consequences (Mitchell & Krumboltz, 1984).

TABLE 8

**SOCIAL LEARNING THEORY MODEL OF CAREER DECISION MAKING USING
AN INSTRUMENTAL LEARNING EXPERIENCE**

Categories/ Factors	(a) Antecedents	(b) Behaviors	(c) Consequences
1. **Factor:**	**Genetic Predisposition:**		Directly Observable **Result of actions:**
Example:	William S. Age 17 Good muscular coordination Speech is average.		William is all-state Halfback. Coaches, Principals, peers congratulate him.
2. **Factor:**	**Special Abilities/Skills:**		Directly Observable **Results of action:**
Example:	Three grades below in reading, friendly, high spatial, clerical, and reasoning aptitudes.		William fails semester exams in English and History, but in career testing scores high in spatial and abstract reasoning.
3. **Factor:**	Planned/Unplanned **Conditions or Events:**	**Covert and Overt Actions:**	**Covert Reactions to Consequences** (cognitive and emotional responses):
Example:	Medium size high school where being in sport is primary basis for prestige.	William accepts principal's request to enter career counseling if he can stay on football team despite failing in classes. Cooperates fully with school counselors.	William thinks "I'm good at football but poor in English, history and foreign languages. If I could just find career area using my good spatial and abstract reasoning, I'll bet I could be successful."
4. **Factor:**	**Task or Problem:**		**Impact on Significant others:**
Example:	Principal likes William but knows he is failing classes, and because this is William's senior year, a career objective must be formulated quickly.		Girl on whom William has crush turns down date with him to go out with William's brother who is an "A" student and is on the basketball team.

In William's case, he is likely to want to continue playing football, despite doing poorly in school; however, he must cooperate with the principal's demand that academic assistance and career counseling be undertaken if he is to be allowed to stay on the team. The likelihood that William will continue in both football and counseling is contingent on the consequences of his behavior, that is, does well during the game and receives positive feedback about his academic progress and vocational aptitudes. This reinforcement should result in desired continuation of both activities. Because each activity is contingent on the other, a repetitive negative experience in either could result in discontinuance of involvement in both activities. Participating in academic assistance or career counseling may also open William's eyes to a career objective that requires certain educational prerequisites, that is, completing high school in order to enter junior college, where he can play football and also learn more about drawing, one of his current interests. Subsequently William may also become more motivated to improve his grades and by doing so, graduate.

An example of an **associated learning experience** would be as follows: William found out that his brother (an "A" student) dated the girl he wanted to ask out and, therefore, William perceives getting good grades with getting girlfriends. His special abilities (i.e., slow rate of reading) may improve by getting academic help; **behavior** which would, in turn, lead to getting his girlfriend back (consequence). Another example of an associative learning experience for William could be a situation in which William sees a movie in which the sports hero wins the leading lady and the studious brother does not, thus, reinforces his football player behavior while ignoring school work.

Such unrealistic assumptions are related to one dimension of career maturity, realism. Such decision-making behavior as reacting to a movie for guiding behavior may be appropriate for a seventh grader but not for a senior in high school, which is why career maturity measures are age normed. In a more behavioral description, William's associated learning experience can be described as follows: (a) going to a movie with a friend is the circumstance under which the organism is exposed to a paired stimuli or to a real or fictitious model, and (b) the formerly neutral stimulus or model (William sees the star halfback performing in the film); at the end of the film the star halfback marries the prettiest cheerleader (consequence). Thus, the formerly neutral stimulus or model acquires the affective characteristics of the positive stimulus through the process of stimulus pairing, and subsequently William adopts this type of thinking via an associative learning experience in a vicarious situation. Part of a career decision making correction procedure with William would be to point out the fantasy inherent in the movie.

Task Approach Skills: Results of Interactions

According to Mitchell and Krumboltz (1984), interactions among associative learning experiences, that is, antecedents, including one's genetic background, special inabilities, disabilities and environmental influences result in certain kinds of task approach skills. These skills would include "performance standards and values, work habits, perceptual and cognitive processes (symbolic rehearsal, attention and retentions), mental sets and emotional responses. For example, William's reading skill level may have been good enough to get through junior high, however the high school upper division English and science courses are taxing his limited ability. If he desires continuing a football career as well as dating a significant other (girlfriend), he will need to modify his task approach skills. If William neither wants to continue playing football nor seek the favor of his significant other, it is doubtful William will want to modify his task approach skills in reading. The greater the desire for these items (reinforcers) the greater will be the motivation to change his behavior.

Self-Observation: Environmental Feedback of Event

Similar to Tiedeman's (1979) concept of "successive reintegrations of one's identity," Mitchell and Krumboltz (1984) posited that individuals are continually observing themselves and assessing their own performances according to their standards in reference to the attitudes and skills of others. Therefore, as the result of learning experiences, individuals make generalizations about the nature of their skills. Such self-observation generalizations may be covert or overt, and, like task approach skills, will influence the outcomes of new learning experiences as well as result from prior learning experiences. Mitchell and Krumboltz divided these self-observations into three categories: (a) self-observation generalizations about task efficacy, (b) interests, and (c) personal values. Examples of these self-observations are listed as follows:

1. **Task efficacy** generalizations are a person's estimations about whether they possess the requisite skills to perform a task adequately, that is, "I may not be a fast reader, but I can hold my own when debating a point" or "I'm good in math but terrible in English." One's observations about task efficacy must be evaluated on the basis of the standards to which they are compared, however. A letter grade of B may be shattering, while a grade of C to a learning disabled student may be cause for jubilation.

2. **Interests** relate to one's life experiences and the conclusions they draw about what they do and do not like. Interest tests given to assess one's career desires are based on the belief that it is possible to express

life experiences as likes and dislikes or indifference to certain occupation related indices.

3. Personal values are assessments individuals make about or their attitudes toward the desirability or worth of certain behaviors, events or outcomes, and results from both associative and instrumental experiences, exemplified by expressions such as "The type of occupation I hold is more important to me than the money I could earn." Mitchell and Krumboltz also advanced that individuals, as a result of their learning experience, hold world-view generalizations. These are used by individuals to predict what will occur in the future and in other related environments. An example would be, "To be good at math, you must be smart" or "To be a professional, you must know the right people." Accuracy of these world views depends on the type and quality of experiences one is exposed to.

Task Approach Skills and Career Decision Making

As was stated above, task approach skills are learned cognitive and performance abilities. They include work habits, mental sets (including emotional responses), perceptual and thought processes and problem orientation. Mitchell and Krumboltz (1984) noted that these task approach skills are used in the process of career decision making and also include coping with the environment, interpreting it in relation to self-observations and world-view generalizations and making overt and covert predictions about future events. The specific task approach skills relevant to career decision making are listed as follows: (a) recognizing an important decision situation; (b) defining the task realistically; (c) examining and accurately assessing self-observation and world-view generalizations; (d) generating a wide variety of alternatives; (e) gathering needed information about the alternatives; (f) determining which information sources are most reliable, accurate and relevant; and (g) planning and carrying out the above sequence of decision-making behaviors (Krumboltz & Baker 1973). As can be seen, these seven skills are very similar to those previously listed by Super and Harris-Bowlsbey (1979).

Coping with Decision-Making Tasks

A systematic attempt to apply one or more of these skills may result in negative consequences (e.g., a decision recently made that, to get ahead, a college education is required, just prior to receiving news that your state college cannot accept you because of your low ACT score).

Such negative consequences, which may also depend on unpredictable events, may convince persons that decision making is not worth the effort. This may result in the adoption of alternative decision-making approaches, that is, relying solely on intuition or leaving the decision to fate. In the above example, the student who decided that going to college was needed to "get ahead" may have relied on intuition that no alternatives existed for circumventing his or her low ACT scores (e.g., failed to find out if a person with a learning disability could retake the ACT under an untimed situation, and by doing so might get a higher score).

In the case of William, he feels that, "I'm an above average football player, good in mechanical drawing classes but failing in history and science courses. A career in drafting using computer aided design (CAD) is an interesting occupation and does not require high reading ability. But also of interest to me is the thought of playing college football, however, the college that's interested in me for playing football doesn't have a CAD program. I must see my high school counselor to see how I can get both a football scholarship and a CAD drafting program at the same college."

Utilizing the task skills approach William has recognized an important decision, assessed his self-observations and world-view generalizations and considered how best to gather reliable information about decision alternatives. As a result of learning experiences and the generalizations and skills that develop from them, individuals participate in various behaviors that lead to entry into an occupational area. These behaviors include applying for jobs, schools or training programs.

Applying the SLT Career Decision-Making Model

The social learning theory of career decision making delineates four outcomes of learning experiences that determine an individual's career decision-making behavior. Those four outcomes are self-observation generalizations, world-view generalizations, task approach skills and one's actions. The SLD person who may be in need of assistance with career decision making (determined, in part, via the *ACDM* process outlined in the previous chapter), can also be identified, according to Mitchell and Krumboltz (1984), by the following warning signals:

1. Persons may fail to recognize that a remediable problem exists. For example, if one believes that, "we must learn to accept things the way they are" or "bosses always act that way," one may assume that one's problem and suffering are a normal part of life rather than a set of circumstances that might be altered.

2. Persons may fail to exert the effort needed to make a decision or solve a problem. For example, if one believes that, "it is easier to avoid than to face decision" or "it is best to do whatever is familiar and easily available," one may fail to take constructive action on a problem, explore alternatives or seek information.

3. Persons may eliminate a potentially satisfying alternative for inappropriate reasons. For example, if one believes that, "living on the East Coast is bad; life is more casual and less judgmental in the West" or "I'd like to be a teacher but I'd have to teach in an inner-city area," one may fail to take advantage of potentially worthwhile alternatives because of beliefs based on misinformation, over-generalizations or false assumptions.

4. Persons may choose poor alternatives for inappropriate reasons. For example, if one believes that "I'd rather succeed in a low-level job than risk failure in a more responsible position" or "becoming a minister will give me the desirable qualities that religious people have," one may foreclose desirable alternatives and choose alternatives that result in years of regret and unhappiness.

5. Persons may suffer anguish and anxiety over perceived inability to achieve goals. For example, if one's goals are unrealistic ("If I can't have the best, I don't want anything at all") or in conflict with other goals ("I don't want a job where I'm supervised, but I don't have the courage to set up a business of my own"), one may again eliminate potentially desirable alternatives or accept less desirable ones because of these perceptions.

Avoidance of Career Decision-Making Behavior

The correction of problems in the SLT model of career decision making must be viewed in the perspective that persons will be more likely to learn and use the task approach skills of career decision making if they are positively reinforced for learning and using the skills or if they observe a model being positively reinforced for using the skills (Mitchell & Krumboltz, 1984). However, many SLD individuals may avoid the decision-making process initially because of the discomfort associated with facing one's problem directly. Anticipation of beginning a career can be a fearful experience for those not yet sure of themselves (self-esteem) or independent (autonomy) in their future outlook. Research by

Saltoun (1980) illustrated the point that those individuals with the highest fear of failure were also least career mature in their planning, while once progress in decision making is under way the activity becomes self-reinforcing. Listed below are causes for stress in approaching career decision making, according to George (1980): (a) **threat to self-esteem,** where decision making involves a threat to one's major values. Because making a decision is an event that can be evaluated by oneself and by others, it is a test of one's ability to succeed and, therefore is also an evaluation of one's sense of self-esteem; (b) **surprise,** where the need for making an immediate decision puts a great deal of pressure to act in a short amount of time; (c) **deadlines,** when needing to apply for job or college entrance, the realization hits that this is the last chance for deciding what to do; and (d) **absence of allocated time,** when applying for employment or college scholarships, one must try to fit this "extra" curricular requirement into daily activities.

Negative Effect of Career Decision-Making Stress

The results of such stress emanating from approaching decision making (George, 1980) can be described as: (a) **impaired attention,** where the decision maker tends to ignore important values, alternatives and information and falls back on old habits; (b) **increased cognitive rigidity,** where creativity is lessened and the decision maker has become less receptive to new information that challenges old beliefs, resulting in short-cutting the search for information in order to reduce the pain; (c) **narrowed perspective,** because of the discomfort the decision maker becomes more concerned with the present and ignores the future, resulting in inability to process any new information; and (d) **displaced blame,** where responsibility for the problem is placed on the environment, resulting in side-stepping the decision to be made or placing the responsibility of it on others.

Assessing these difficulties in decision making can be carried on during the career assessment interview process in discussion with the client and by using the *ACDM* for objective information. Another tool for assessing irrational career decision-making behaviors is *A Questionnaire to Determine Beliefs About Career Decision Making* (see Krumboltz, 1983; Holland, Daiger & Power, 1980).

Furthermore, Krumboltz (1983) noted that decision making involves competition between values, as no one alternative will satisfy values evenly and trade-offs must be considered. For example, decision makers who mentally block out the value of trade-offs may be trying to be consistent with some previously adopted belief, which may foreclose the possibility for exploration, the counselor suggests to the counselee that the results from the career assessment indicated that the counselee would be well suited to a career in business management. The counselee states that businessmen are too conservative. It may be that the avoidance towards business is unrelated to conservatism, but rather is related to the fear that one will have to work a great deal with people and the counselee has a fear for face to face interactions.

Developing a Task Approach Skills Model for Career Decision Making

Task approach skills listed earlier in this chapter, are described as learned cognitive and performance abilities and include work habits, mental sets (including emotional responses), perceptual and thought processes and problem orientation. These task approach skills are used to cope with the environment, to interpret it in relation to self-observations and world-view generalizations, and to make overt and covert predictions about future events. Further, seven specific task approach skills, representative of one's learned cognitive and performance abilities, were noted: (a) recognizing an important decision situation; (b) defining the decision manageably and realistically; (c) examining and accurately assessing self-observations and world-view generalizations; (d) generating a wide variety of alternatives; (e) gathering needed information about the alternatives; (f) determining which information sources are most reliable, accurate and relevant; and (g) planning and carrying out the above sequence of decision-making behaviors. Finally, Mitchell and Krumboltz (1984) stated that "the extent to which persons develop and use the task approach skills of career decision-making depends on the sequence and consequences [negative/positive] of relevant learning experiences" (p. 250).

For example, a systematic attempt to apply one or more of the above seven skills may result in negative consequences, that is, a SLD student who completes career assessment is told and agrees with the finding that he has the interest and aptitudes to become a computer programmer. Upon application to a local state college he finds that his past achievements in English and math courses will prevent him from being able to enter the computer science program. If previous attempts to enter junior and senior high school computer classes have resulted in similar consequences, it is likely that this person will cease to persist in this career objective, unless of course he or she finds an advocate who will encourage him or her to correct related academic deficiencies and continue to pursue this career objective.

Teaching Career Decision-Making Skills

The inclusion of systematic efforts to teach decision-making skills within the educational environment is a recent trend in American education (Super & Harris-Bowlsbey, 1979). The work of Harren (1979) and the recent publication of the test instrument *(ACDM)* by Buck and Daniels (1985) will greatly assist our ability to identify ineffective decision-making strategies. Mitchell and Krumboltz (1984) have further outlined an explanation of how individuals and environments interact to influence career decision outcomes. Based on conceptualization of how the antecedents, behaviors and consequences are reflective of one's learned cognitive and performance abilities, Mitchell and Krumboltz have generated several primary career decision-making skills that are necessary for judging qualitative types of decision outcomes. Similar in scope as Super and Harris-Bowlsbey's (1979) list of nine career decision making steps, these seven decision-making skills can be regarded as critical to the total career development process being successful.

Rationale for Teaching Career Decision-Making Skills

A rather unfortunate but factual observation about the career development of adolescents and young adults with SLD is that this group of individuals is the least likely to be in a specific type of high school curriculum where they would receive some type of career guidance. Data from the U.S. Department of Education (1981) showed SLD students to be the least participative in vocational education when compared to other handicapping conditions, for example, the mentally retarded. Although many more SLDs are attending college (Biller, 1983), they are not, by and large, participating in the mainstream of college preparation curriculums. As was noted in Chapters 3 and 4, SLDs and their controls differed significantly in educational attainment. Clearly, below average educational attainment can be partly understood within the social learning theory model of career decision making. The explanation being that by the time the SLD student reaches his/her senior year of high school, the effects (consequences) of years of negative outcomes have more than likely shaped this student into a state of learned helplessness, with its concomitants of lower self-esteem, external locus of control and career immaturity (Biller, 1985a, b). In other words, while there is little doubt many SLD adolescents and young adults will need to be taught effective decision making, it cannot be automatically expected they will embrace the efforts with acceptance. There will be stiff resistance to this kind of a program and the more occurrences of previous negative decision making, the more difficult the training.

Methodology for Improving SLD Decision-Making Skills: Concentrating on the "How" of Instruction

An additional component of the "what" to teach, that is, career decision making, is the "how" to teach adolescent and young adults with specific learning disabilities. More specifically, "how" should SLD adolescents be instructed so as to more maximize the content learned (Deshler, Alley, Warner & Schumaker, 1980), Deshler et al. explained that there was a need to design a systematic set of learning strategies for SLD students due to the limited time these adolescents have to acquire new material/instruction in a resource room environment, and also because SLD adolescents are expected to apply skills they learn across a broad array of settings, contents and conditions.

In terms of how to teach for skill acquisition, students would be first taught a specific skill acquisition strategy in isolation before they would be allowed to apply it to learning decision-making strategies. The steps for teaching this skill acquisition strategy, according to Deshler et al. (1980) are listed as follows:

Step 1: **Analyze the individual's current learning habit.** The SLD client is first asked to perform a task which requires the target skill. Following that performance, the instructor/counselor affirms what is to be the satisfactory/unsatisfactory performance of the task. This step is critical as it allows the client to evaluate his/her current skill level and, thus, see the difference between the inefficient or ineffective approach and the decision-making strategy that will be taught.

Step 2: **Describe the new strategy.** This step in the teaching process is to describe to the SLD client the steps involved in the new strategy, including the major behaviors in which the student will sequentially engage to complete the strategy correctly. For example, using the first of the seven task approach decision-making skills (recognizing the critical factors of an important decision-making situation), state to the client, "First you will listen to a tape of problem situations of three Riddell

High School male seniors. As you listen to each student's situation you will notice a set of circumstances surrounding a particular problem that each senior has. You will think about the problem each person has as being mild, average or severe. After listening to all the cases you will mark for each case a 1 for mild, 2 for average and 3 for severe problem. If you cannot pinpoint a problem in any of the cases you will reverse the tape and listen again for the particular problem that you think requires a decision to be made." Using the taped situations from Super and Harris-Bowlsbey's (1979) *Guided Career Exploration Curriculum* is excellent for practicing/assessing this step of the strategy. Offer to the student before beginning the tape the following practice example: "John is an art major failing English II. He believes that his problem is that the English teacher doesn't like him, so he begins to look for ways to make the teacher like him. To do this, John offered to decorate the English teacher's office with drawings he has completed over the last several days that he has skipped English class." Ask the SLD student being taught the strategy if he/she believes the real problem to be John's personality, that is, the English teacher does not like him or if it may be something else that the English teacher is disturbed about. If the SLD student responds, "The problem is in making the teacher like John and the action of decorating the teacher's office is the right decision," probe the SLD student with a question like, "Do you suppose teachers get perturbed about students who attend class irregularly? If your answer is yes, what implications would this have for John's problem with his English teacher?" Point out to the SLD student that it is necessary to listen to all of the information and to consider each piece separately before making a judgment. If the SLD student had shown to be an "impulsive decision maker" on the *ACDM*, explain how deciding too quickly may lead to a premature response and subsequently an incorrect decision. Once the SLD student has the idea of what kind of task objective must be completed, one can begin the training of the strategies via listening to the taped examples.

Step 3: **Model the new strategy.** In this step, the SLD teacher/counselor models for the student the strategy or skill in its entirety. Act out verbally with the student the entire sequence of decision-making skills one would go through to analyze John's problem with his English teacher, that is, say out loud, "I know my English teacher does not like me because . . . but why is he always so cross with me? I guess because I'm in the SLD program, I'm just not bright enough for him. Perhaps if I could show him my art work he would see I do have talent. But what if he remembers that I cut class to make those drawings. Hey, could that be why he is cross with me, my missing class? Yes, that must be it and if I offer him those drawings he would only get madder. Perhaps my real problem with this English teacher is not coming to class regularly."

Then after this verbal overview, go through the seven decision-making skills and pair them with each part of your above modeling, that is, (a) **there is a real problem,** "My English teacher yells at me every time I open my mouth;" (b) **defining the decision-making task/situation realistically,** "My English teacher seems to be the most angry with me the day after I have missed a class;" (c) **self-observations,** "I'm lousy in reading and writing but I'm good at drawing, perhaps that's why my English teacher doesn't like me, and anyway I don't care because I don't like writing papers" (self-observation of personal value), and "You have to be a college prep student to be liked by our English teachers" (self-observation-world-view); (d) **generating alternatives,** "However, I could show him my art work, but perhaps coming to class more often would be more effective;" (e) **gathering needed information about the alternatives,** "Does this English teacher like art?" (f) **determining which information sources are most reliable, accurate and relevant,** "My art teacher says going to English class more often will solve my problem, but my best friend says that my English teacher has it in for me;" (g) **carrying out above decision-making steps,** "I think I'll try going to class more often and maybe even try to spend a little more time on my writing assignments."

Step 4: **Verbal rehearsal.** Before the student is asked to demonstrate the seven decision-making skills, he/she must learn the steps of the strategy to an automatic level. This means having the student verbally recite each of the seven decision-making skills in context of the model given in the previous step. The objective of this step should be to have the teacher's/counselor's instruction in Steps 2 and 3 transferred to the SLD student so that he/she will progress from overt verbal rehearsal as the student becomes proficient in the strategy, an exercise important to the learning of higher order cognitive strategies (Flavell, 1976; Meichenbaum, 1975).

Step 5: **Student practices in controlled materials.** After the student demonstrates both an understanding and mastery of the steps or procedures involved in the strategy, the teacher/counselor should choose appropriate level materials for student practice (use of audio tapes of the *Guided Career Exploration* curriculum will work well here). Establish a quantifiable base line of skill acquisition to allow self and teacher evaluation of performance.

Step 6: **Student practice.** Using school-related examples of problem situations that require daily decisions as well as long range decisions, engage the student in practice sessions. Use examples such as the decision to attend class or not to attend or the decision to participate in a school extracurricular activity. Gradually allow students to report only the outcomes of their practice decisions and ask them to discuss how this skill has helped them in other nonschool situations, for example, getting along with siblings, opposite sex and so forth.

Finally, some general steps or aids to generalizing these newly developed decision-making skills are: (a) teach SLD students to take an active role in getting teachers, peers and counselors to recognize their newly developed skills; (b) incorporate a diverse range of examples and settings to practice these decision-making behaviors, that is, community, home and so forth; (c) train SLD students in these decision-making skills using varying formats and instructions to approximate as near as possible real life situations; (d) utilize a variety and number of different school/agency staff members to practice/teach these skills; (e) do not always reinforce every positive emittance of the skill, but rather, reinforce the graduated performance at various intervals; and (f) remind students to apply these decision-making skills to new and daily situations (Stokes & Baer, 1977).

Summary of SLT Decision-Making Model

Social learning theory, with its roots in classical behaviorism and reinforcement theory, describes behavior in a person and environment interaction framework. Four categories: genetic predispositions, special abilities, planned/unplanned conditions or events and tasks or problems, serve as the antecedents of career related overt and covert actions. The consequences of these actions, be they negative or positive, dictate whether such behaviors will increase or decrease. A social learning theory of career decision making is designed to address the question of why people enter particular educational programs or occupations, why individuals may change educational programs or occupations at selected points in their lives, and why they may express various preferences for different occupational activities at selected points in their lives. Constructs that describe their career behavior patterns are known as instrumental, associative and vicarious learning experiences.

Interactions among these learning experiences result in the development of certain task approach skills, such as performance standards and values, work habits, perceptual and cognitive processes (symbolic rehearsal, attention and retention), mental sets and emotional responses. These task approaches are used in the process of career decision making. The following specific decision-making steps are represented in these task approach skills: (a) recognizing important decision situations; (b) defining tasks realistically; (c) examining and accurately assessing self-observations and world-view generalizations; (d) generating a wide variety of alternatives; (e) gathering needed information about the alternatives; (f) determining which information sources are most reliable, accurate and relevant; and (g) planning and carrying out the above sequence of decision-making behaviors. Finally, a "strategies" approach was presented as a means of teaching task approach skills.

REFERENCES

ACLD Scientific Studies Committee. (1982). *ACLD Newsbrief.* (Research update I-X). Author.

Adelman, H. S., & Taylor, L. (1985). The future of the LD field: A survey of fundamental concerns. *Journal of Learning Disabilities, 18,* 423-427.

Anastasi, A. (1983). Evolving trait concepts. *American Psychologist, 38,* 175-184.

Astin, A. W., Hemond, M. K., & Richardson, G. T. (1982). *The American freshman: National norms for fall 1982.* Los Angeles: Higher Education Research Institute.

Azrin, N. H., Flores, T., & Kaplan, S. J. (1977). Job-finding club: A group-assisted program for obtaining employment. *Rehabilitation Counseling Bulletin, 21,* 130-140.

Balow, B., & Blomquist, M. (1965). Young adults ten to fifteen years after severe reading disability. *Elementary School Journal, 66,* 44-48.

Bandura, A. (1971). *Social learning theory.* New York: General Learning Press.

Bandura, A. (1974). Behavior theory and the models of man. *American Psychologist, 29,* 859-869.

Bandura, A. (1977). *Social learning theory.* Englewood Cliffs, NJ: Prentice-Hall.

Bannatyne, A. (1968). Diagnosing learning disabilities and writing remedial prescriptions. *Journal of Learning Disabilities, 1*(4), 28-35.

Bannatyne, A. (1974). Diagnosis: A note on recategorization of the WISC scaled scores. *Journal of Learning Disabilities, 7,* 272-274.

Barrett, T. C., & Tinsley, H. E. A. (1977). Vocational self-concept crystallization and vocational indecision. *Journal of Counseling Psychology, 24,* 301-307.

Bennett, G. K., Seashore, H. G., & Wesman, A. G. (1974). *Differential Aptitude Test technical manual.* New York: Psychological Corporation.

Bennett, G. K., Seashore, H. G., & Wesman, A. G. (1982). *Differential Aptitude Tests, forms V and W* (2nd ed.). New York: Psychological Corporation.

Biller, E. F. (1983). Identifying the career maturity of learning disabled college students. *Dissertation Abstracts International, 43,* 43107-2307A. (University Microfilms No. 7)

Biller, E. F. (1985a). Career development of the learning disabled adolescent: A focus on career maturity. *Career Development for Exceptional Individuals, 8,* 17-22.

Biller, E. F. (1985b). *Understanding and guiding the career development of adolescents and young adults with learning disabilities.* Springfield, IL: Charles C Thomas.

Bingham, G. D. (1974). Career attitudes and self-esteem among boys with and without specific learning disabilities. *Dissertation Abstracts International, 36,* 815A. (University Microfilms No. 75-17,340)

Bingham, G. (1978). Career attitudes among boys with and without specific learning disabilities. *Exceptional Children, 44,* 341-342.

Bingham, G. (1980). Career maturity of learning disabled adolescents. *Psychology in the Schools, 17,* 135-139.

Blau, P. M., & Duncan, O. D. (1967). *The American occupational structure.* New York: Wiley.

Bogue, D. J. (1969). *Principles of demography.* New York: Wiley.

Bordin, E. S. (1968). *Psychological counseling* (2nd ed.). New York: Appleton-Century-Crofts.

Botterbusch, K. F. (1980). *A comparison of commercial vocational evaluation systems.* Menomonie: University of Wisconsin, Materials Development Center.

Brown, D. (1984a). Summary, comparison, and critique of major theories. In D. Brown, L. Brooks & Associates (Eds.), *Career choice and development* (pp. 311-336). San Francisco: Jossey-Bass.

Brown, D. (1984b). Trait and factor theory. In D. Brown, L. Brooks & Associates (Eds.), *Career choice and development* (pp. 8-30). San Francisco: Jossey-Bass.

Brown, D., & Brooks, L. (1984). Introduction to career development: Origins, evolution, and current approaches. In D. Brown, L. Brooks & Associates (Eds.), *Career choice and development* (pp. 1-7). San Francisco: Jossey-Bass.

Brown, L. S. (1982). *Career maturity and learning disabilities at the secondary level.* Unpublished doctoral dissertation, Virginia Polytechnic Institute and State University.

Bruck, M. (1985). Adult functioning of children with learning disabilities: A follow-up study. In I. E. Sigel (Ed.), *Advances in applied developmental psychology* (pp. 91-129). Norwood, NJ: Ablex.

Bruinincks, V. (1978). Actual and perceived peer status of learning disabled students in mainstream programs. *Journal of Special Education, 12,* 51-58.

Buck, J. N., & Daniels, M. H. (1985). *Assessment of career decision making (ACDM) manual.* Los Angeles: Western Psychological Services.

Bueler, C. (1933). *Der menschliche lebenslauf als psychologisches problem* [The human life course as a psychologcial subject]. Leipzig: Hirzel.

Buskin, M. (1868, December 23). A fable for our modern wise men. *Newsday.* .

Carkhuff, R. R., Alexik, M., & Anderson, S. (1967). Do we have a theory of vocational choice? *Personnel and Guidance Journal, 46,* 335-345.

Carter, R. P. (1964). *A descriptive analysis of the adult adjustment of persons once identified as disabled readers.* Unpublished doctoral dissertation, University of Indiana, Bloomington.

Cato, C. E., & Rice, B. D. (1982). *Report from the study group on the rehabilitation of clients with specific learning disabilities.* Little Rock, AR: Arkansas Division of Rehabilitation Services.

Chadwick, O., & Rutter, M. (1983). Neurological assessment. In M. Rutter (Ed.), *Developmental neuropsychiatry.* New York: Guilford Press.

Clements, S. D. (1966). *Minimal brain dysfunction in children* (DPHS Publication No. 1415). Washington, DC: Department of Public Health Services.

Coopersmith, C. H. (1967). *The antecedents of self-esteem.* San Francisco, CA: W. H. Freeman.

Cordoni, B. K. (1981). Project achieve: Mainstreaming the learning disabled at the college level. *Perspectives: Research at Southern Illinois University at Carbondale, 2,* 1-6.

Cordoni, B. K. (1982). Post secondary education: Where do we go from here? *Journal of Learning Disabilities, 15,* 265-266.

Coudroglou, A., & Poole, D. L. (1984). *Disability, work, and social policy: Models for social welfare.* New York: Springer.

Crain, E. J. (1980). Socioeconomic status of educable mentally retarded graduates of special education. *Education and Training of the Mentally Retarded, 15,* 90-94.

Crites, J. O. (1973). *The career maturity inventory.* Monterey, CA: McGraw-Hill.

Dawis, R. V., & Lofquist, L. H. (1976). Personality style and the process of work adjustment. *Journal of Counseling Psychology, 23,* 55-59.

Dawis, R. V., Lofquist, L. H., & Weiss, D. J. (1968). *A theory of work adjustment* (A revision). (Minnesota Studies in Vocational Rehabilitation No. 23). Minneapolis: University of Minnesota Industrial Relations Center.

Deshler, D. D., Alley, G. R., Warner, M. M., & Schumaker, J. B. (1980). *Instructional practices that promote acquisition and generalization of skills by learning disabled adolescents* (Monograph #4). Lawrence: The University of Kansas Institute for Research in Learning Disabilities.

Dinklage, L. B. (1969). *Student decision-making studies of adolescents in the secondary schools* (Report No. 6). Cambridge, MA: Graduate School of Education, Harvard University.

Duane, D. D. (1979a). The dyslexic child: Diagnostic implications. *Pediatric Annals, 8*(11), 4-11.

Duane, D. D. (1979b). Theories about the causes of dyslexia and their implications. *Pediatric Annals, 8*(11), 12-17.

Duncan, O. D. (1961). A socioeconomic index for all occupations. In A. J. Reiss, Jr. (Ed.), *Occupations and social status.* New York: Free Press.

Erickson, E. H. (1959). Identity and the life cycle. *Psychological Issues Monograph* (vol I[1]). New York: International Universities Press.

Fafard, M., & Haubrich, P. A. (1981). Vocational and social adjustment of learning disabled young adults: A follow-up study. *Learning Disability Quarterly, 4,* 122-130.

Finucci, J. M. (1985). Follow-up studies of developmental dyslexia and other learning disabilities. In S. D. Smith (Ed.), *Genetics and learning disabilities.* San Diego, CA: College-Hill Press.

Flavell, J. (1976). Metacognitive aspects of problem solving. In R. Resnick (Ed.), *The nature of intelligence.* Hillsdale, NJ: Erlbaum.

Frauenheim, J. G. (1978). Academic achievement characteristics of adult males who were diagnosed as dyslexic in childhood. *Journal of Learning Disabilities, 11,* 476-483.

Frauenheim, J. G., & Heckerl, J. R. (1983). A longitudinal study of psychological and achievement test performance in severe dyslexic adults. *Journal of Learning Disabilities, 16,* 339-347.

Frey, W. D. (1985). Functional assessment in the 80s: A conceptual enigma, a technical challenge. In A. S. Halpern & M. J. Fuhrer (Eds.), *Functional assessment in rehabilitation* (pp. 11-43). Baltimore, MD: Paul H. Brookes.

Gaddes, W. H. (1985). *Learning disabilities and brain function: A neuropsychological approach* (2nd ed.). New York: Springer-Verlag.

George, A. L. (1980). *Presidential decision making in foreign policy: The effective use of information and advice.* Boulder, CO: Westview Press.

Ghiselli, E. E. (1966). *The validity of occupational aptitude tests.* New York: Wiley.

Ginzberg, E., Ginsburg, S. W., Axelrod, S., & Herma, J. L. (1951). *Occupational choice: An approach to a general theory.* New York: Columbia University Press.

Goldenson, R. M., Dunham, J. R., & Dunham, C. S. (Eds.). (1978). *Disability and rehabilitation handbook.* New York: McGraw-Hill.

Gonzalez, A., & Zimbardo, P. G. (1985, March). Time in perspective. *Psychology Today,* pp. 21-26.

Gottfredson, L. S., Finucci, J. M., & Childs, B. (1983). *The adult occupational success of dyslexic boys: A large scale, long-term follow-up* (Report No. 334). Baltimore, MD: The Johns Hopkins University, Center for Social Organization of Schools.

Gottfredson, L. S., Finucci, J. M., & Childs, B. (1984). *The adult occupations of dyslexic boys: Results of a long-term follow-up and implications for research and counseling.* Baltimore, MD: The Johns Hopkins University, Center for Social Organization of Schools.

Gribbons, W. D., & Lohnes, P. R. (1968). *Emerging careers.* New York: Teachers College Press, Columbia University.

Gribbons, W. R., & Lohnes, P. R. (1969). *Career development from age 13 to age 25.* Washington, DC: U.S. Department of Health, Education, and Welfare.

Hallahan, D. P., & Kauffman, J. M. (1986). *Exceptional children: Introduction to special education* (3rd ed.). Englewood Cliffs, NJ: Prentice-Hall.

Hallahan, D. P., Kauffman, J. M., & Lloyd, J. W. (1985). *Introduction to learning disabilities* (2nd ed.). Englewood Cliffs, NJ: Prentice-Hall.

Halpern, A. S., & Fuhrer, M. J. (1985). Introduction. In A. S. Halpern & M. J. Fuhrer (Eds.), *Functional assessment in rehabilitation* (pp. 1-9). Baltimore, MD: Paul H. Brookes.

Hammill, D. D., Leigh, J., McNutt, G., & Larsen, S. (1981). A new definition of learning disabilities. *Learning Disability Quarterly, 4,* 836-842.

Hardy, M. I. (1968). *Clinical follow-up study of disabled readers.* Unpublished doctoral dissertation, University of Toronto, Canada.

Harren, V. A. (1966). The vocational decision-making process among college males. *Journal of Counseling Psychology, 13,* 271-277.

Harren, V. A. (1979). A model of career decision making for college students. *Journal of Vocational Behavior, 14,* 119-133.

Harren, V. A., & Kass, R. A. (1978). *The measurement and correlates of career decision making.* Carbondale: Southern Illinois University. (ERIC Document Reproduction Service No. ED 147 733)

Harren, V. A., Kass, R. A., Tinsley, H. E. A., & Moreland, J. R. (1978). Influences of sex role attitudes and cognitive styles on career decision making. *Journal of Counseling Psychology, 25,* 390-398.

Hartzell, H. E., & Compton, C. (1984). Learning disability: 10-year follow-up. *Pediatrics, 74,* 1058-1064.

Havighurst, R. J. (1976). *Developmental tasks and education* (3rd ed.). New York: David McKay.

Herjanic, B. M., & Penic, E. C. (1972). Adult outcome of disabled child readers. *Journal of Special Education, 6,* 397-412.

Herr, E. L., & Cramer, S. H. (1979). *Career guidance through the life span.* Boston: Little, Brown.

Hesser, A. (1982). Adolescent career development, family adaptability and family cohesion (Doctoral dissertation, Virginia Polytechnic Institute and State University, 1981). *Dissertation Abstracts International, 43,* 5.

Hogan, R., DeSoto, C. B., & Solano, C. (1977). Traits, tests, and personality research. *American Psychologist, 32,* 255-264.

Holland, J. L. (1959). A theory of vocational choice. *Journal of Counseling Psychology, 6,* 35-44.

Holland, J. L. (1973). *Making vocational choices: A theory of careers.* Englewood Cliffs, NJ: Prentice-Hall.

Holland, J. L. (1975). The use and evaluation of interest inventories and simulations. In E. E. Diamond (Ed.), *Issues of sex bias and sex fairness in career interest measurement.* Washington, DC: National Institute of Education.

Holland, J. L. (1985). *Making vocational choices: A theory of vocational personalities and work environments* (2nd ed.). Englewood Cliffs, NJ: Prentice-Hall.

Holland, J. L., Daiger, D. C., & Power, P. G. (1980). *My vocational situation.* Palo Alto, CA: Consulting Psychologists Press.

Hoppock, R. (1976). *Occupational information* (4th ed.). New York: McGraw-Hill.

Horn, W. F., O'Donnell, J. P., & Vitulano, L. A. (1983). Long-term follow-up studies of learning disabled persons. *Journal of Learning Disabilities, 16,* 542-553.

Hotchkiss, L., & Borow, H. (1984). Sociological perspectives on career choice and attainment. In D. Brown, L. Brooks & Associates (Eds.), *Career choice and development* (pp. 137-168). San Francisco: Jossey-Bass.

Howden, M. E. (1967). *A nineteen-year follow-up study of good, average and poor readers in the fifth and sixth grades.* Unpublished doctoral dissertation, University of Oregon, Eugene.

Humes, C. W., & Brammer, G. (1985). LD career success after high school. *Academic Therapy, 21,* 171-176.

Hunter, C. S. J., & Herman, D. (1979). *Adult illiteracy in the United States: A report to the Ford Foundation.* New York: McGraw-Hill.

Jabes, J. (1978). *Individual processes in organizational behavior.* Arlington Heights, IL: AHM.

Jastak, J. F., & Jastak, S. R. (1965). *The Wide Range Achievement Test* (rev. ed.). Wilmington, DE: Guidance Associates.

Jencks, C., Bartlett, S., Corcoran, M., Crouse, J., Eaglesfield, D., Jackson, G., McClelland, K., Mueser, P., Olneck, M., Schwartz, J., Ward, S., & Williams, J. (1979). *Who gets ahead? The determinants of economic success in America.* New York: Basic Books.

Jencks, C., & Brown, M. (1975). The effects of high schools on their students. *Harvard Educational Review, 45,* 273-324.

Jencks, C., Crouse, J., & Mueser, P. (1983). The Wisconsin model of status attainment: A national replication with improved measures of ability and aspiration. *Sociology of Education, 56,* 3-19.

Jencks, C., Smith, M., Aclaud, H., Bane, M. J., Cohen, D., Ginitis, H., Heyns, B., & Michelson, S. (1972). *Inequality.* New York: Basic Books.

Jepsen, D. A., & Dilley, J. S. (1974). Vocational decision-making models: A review and comparative analysis. *Review of Educational Research, 44,* 331-349.

Jepsen, D. A., & Grove, W. M. (1981). Stage order and dominance in adolescent decision-making processes: An empirical test of the Tiedeman-O'Hara paradigm. *Journal of Vocational Behavior, 18,* 237-251.

Jepsen, D. A., & Prediger, D. J. (1981). Dimension of adolescent career development: A multi-instrument analysis. *Journal of Vocational Behavior, 19,* 350-368.

Jordaan, J. P. (1963). Exploratory behavior: The formation of self and occupational concepts. In D. E. Super, R. Starishevshy, N. Matlin, & J. P. Jordaan (Eds.), *Career development: Self-concept theory* (pp. 42-78). New York: College Entrance Examination Board.

Jordaan, J. P. (1977). Career development: Theory, research, and practice. In G. D. Miller (Ed.), Developmental theory and its applications in guidance programs [Special issue]. *Pupil Personnel Services Journal, 6*(1).

Jordaan, J. P., & Heyde, M. B. (1979). *Vocational maturity during the high school years.* New York: Teachers College Press.

Kavale, K., & Forness, S. (1985). *The science of learning disabilities.* San Diego: College Hill Press.

Kessler, J. (1966). *Psychopathology of childhood.* Englewood Cliffs, NJ: Prentice-Hall.

Kirk, S. A. (1962). *Educating exceptional children.* Boston: Houghton Mifflin.

Kirk, S. A., & Elkins, J. (1975). Characteristics of children enrolled in the Child Demonstration Centers. *Journal of Learning Disabilities, 8,* 630-637.

Kirk, S. A., & Gallagher, J. J. (1983). *Educating exceptional children* (4th ed.). Boston: Houghton Mifflin.

Kirk, S. A., & Kirk, W. D. (1983). On defining learning disabilities. *Annual Review of Learning Disabilities, 1,* 17-18.

Klein, K. L., & Wiener, Y. (1977). Interest congruency as a moderator of the relationship between job tenure and job satisfaction and mental health. *Journal of Vocational Behavior, 10,* 91-98.

Korman, A. (1966). Self-esteem variable in vocational choice. *Journal of Applied Psychology, 50,* 479-486.

Korman, A. (1967). Ethical judgments, self-perceptions, and vocational choice. *Proceedings of the 75th Annual Convention of the American Psychological Association, 2,* 349-350.

Korman, A. (1970). Toward a hypothesis of work behavior. *Journal of Applied Psychology, 54,* 31-41.

Kozol, J. (1985). *Illiterate America.* Garden City, NY: Anchor Press/Doubleday.

Krumboltz, J. D. (1979). A social learning theory of career decision making. In A. M. Mitchell, G. B. Jones, & J. D. Krumboltz (Eds.), *Social learning and career decision making.* Cranston, RI: Carroll Press.

Krumboltz, J. D. (1983). *Private rules in career decision making.* Columbus, OH: National Center for Research in Vocational Education, Ohio State University.

Krumboltz, J. D., & Baker, R. D. (1973). Behavioral counseling for vocational decisions. In H. Borow (Ed.), *Career guidance for a new age.* Boston: Houghton Mifflin.

Krumboltz, J. D., Becker-Haven, J. F., & Burnett, K. F. (1979). Counseling psycology. *Annual Review of Psychology, 30,* 555-602.

Krumboltz, J. D., Scherba, D. S., Hamel, D. A., & Mitchell, L. K. (1982). Effect of training in rational decision making on the quality of simulated career decisions. *Journal of Counseling Psychology, 29,* 618-625.

Lacey, D. (1975). Career behavior of deaf persons: Current status and future trends. In J. S. Picou & R. E. Campbell (Eds.), *Career behavior of special groups.* Columbus, OH: Charles C. Merrill.

Laing, J., & Farmer, M. (1985). *ACT assessment results for specially-tested examinees with learning disabilities* (ACT Research Bulletin No. 85-1). Iowa City, IA: American College Testing Program.

Lerner, J. (1981). *Learning disabilities: Theories, diagnosis, and teaching strategies* (3rd ed.). Boston: Houghton Mifflin.

Levin, E. K., Zigmond, N., & Birch, J. W. (1985). A follow-up study of 52 learning disabled adolescents. *Journal of Learning Disabilities, 18,* 1-7.

Levinsohn, and others (1978). *National Longitudinal Study: Base year, first, second, and third follow-up data file users manual* (2 vols.). Chapel Hill, NC: Research Triangle Institute.

Mann, L. (1979). *On the trail of process: A historical perspective on cognitive processes and their training.* New York: Grune & Stratton.

Marqalit, M., & Schuchman, R. (1978). Vocational adjustment of EMR youth in a workstudy program and a work program. *American Journal of Mental Deficiency, 82,* 604-607.

Masterson, J. F. (1967). The symptomatic adolescent five years later. He didn't grow out of it. *American Journal of Psychiatry, 123,* 1338-1345.

McKinney, J. D. (1984). The search for subtypes of specific learning disability. *Journal of Learning Disabilities, 17,* 43-50.

Mead, G. H. (1934). *Mind, self, and society.* Chicago: University of Chicago Press.

Meichenbaum, D. (1975). Self-instructional methods. In F. Kanter & A. Goldstein (Eds.), *Helping people change* (pp. 357-391). New York: Pergaman Press.

Miller, M. J. (1983). The role of happenstance in career choice. *Vocational Guidance Quarterly, 32*(1), 16-20.

Miller-Tiedeman, A. L. (1980). Explorations of decision making in the expansion of adolescent personal development. In V. L. Erickson & J. M. Whiteley (Eds.), *Developmental counseling and teaching* (pp. 158-187). Monterey, CA: Brooks/ Cole.

Mitchell, L. K., & Krumboltz, J. D. (1984). Social learning approach to career decision making: Krumboltz's theory. In D. Brown, L. Brooks & Associates (Eds.), *Career choice and development* (pp. 235-280). San Francisco: Jossey-Bass.

Montagna, P. D. (1974). *Certified public accounting: A sociological view of a profession in change.* Lawrence, KS: Scholars Book.

Montagna, P. D. (1977). *Occupations and society: Toward a sociology of the labor market.* New York: Wiley.

Neff, W. S. (1968). *Work and human behavior.* New York: Atherton Press.

Osipow, S. H. (1975). The relevance of theories of career development to special groups: Problems, needed data and implications. In J. S. Picou & R. E. Campbell (Eds.), *Career behavior of special groups.* (pp. 9-22). Columbus, OH: Merrill.

Parsons, F. (1909). *Choosing a vocation.* Boston: Houghton Mifflin.

Pellegrino, J. W. (1985, October). Anatomy of analogy: The key to understanding our mental capabilities lies not in our answers to IQ tests but in how we arrive at them. *Psychology Today,* pp. 48-54.

Peter, B. M., & Spreen, O. (1979). Behavior rating and personal adjustment scales of neurologically and learning handicapped children during adolescence and early adulthood: Results of a follow-up study. *Journal of Clinical Neuropsychology, 1*(1), 75-92.

Phillips, S. D., Strohmer, D. C., Berthaume, B. L. J., & O'Leary, J. C. (1983). Career development of special populations: A framework for research. *Journal of Vocational Behavior, 22,* 12-29.

Phillips, S. D., Friedlander, M. L., Pazienza, N. J., & Kost, P. P. (1985). A factor analytic investigation of career decision-making styles. *Journal of Vocational Behavior, 26,* 106-115.

Phillips, S. D., & Strohmer, D. C., (1982). Decision making style and vocational maturity. *Journal of Vocational Behavior, 20,* 215-222.

Prediger, D. J. (1974). The role of assessment in career guidance: A reappraisal. *Impact, 3-4,* 15-21.

Preston, R. C., & Yarrington, D. J. (1967). Status of fifty retarded readers eight years after reading clinic diagnosis. *Journal of Reading, 11,* 122-129.

Rawson, M. B. (1978). *Developmental language disability: Adult accomplishments of dyslexic boys* (Hood College Monograph Series No. 2). Cambridge, MA: Educators Publishing Service.

Reynolds, C. R. (1984-1985). Critical measurement issues in learning disabilities. *Journal of Special Education, 18,* 451-476.

Robinson, H. M., & Smith, H. K. (1962). Reading clinic clients—ten years after. *Elementary School Journal, 63,* 22-27.

Roe, A. (1956). *The psychology of occupations.* New York: Wiley.

Rogan, L. L., & Hartman, L. D. (1976). *A follow-up study of learning disabled children as adults* (Final Report). Evanston, IL: Cove School Research Office. (ERIC Document Reproduction Service No. ED 163 728)

Rosenberg, M. (1965). *Society and the adolescent self-image.* Princeton, NJ: Princeton University Press.

Rotter, J. B. (1966). Generalized expectancies for internal versus external control of reinforcement. *Psychological Monographs, 80*(1, Whole No. 609).

Saltoun, J. (1980). Fear of failure in career development. *Vocational Guidance Quarterly, 29,* 35-41.

Sarason, S. B. (1949). *Psychological problems in mental deficiency.* New York: Harper and Row.

Satz, P., & Morris, R. (1980). Learning disability subtypes: A review. In F. J. Pirozzola & M. C. Wittrock (Eds.), *Neuropsychological and cognitive processes in reading* (pp. 109-141). New York: Academic Press.

Schalock, R. L., & Harper, R. S. (1978). Placement from community-based mental retardation programs: How well do clients do? *American Journal of Mental Deficiency, 83,* 240-247.

Schonhaut, S., & Satz, P. (1983). Prognosis for children with learning disabilities: A review of follow-up studies. In M. Rutter (Ed.), *Developmental neuropsychiatry* (pp. 542-563). New York: Guilford.

Sewell, W. H., Haller, A. O., & Portes, A. (1969). The educational and early occupational attainment process. *American Sociological Review, 34,* 89-92.

Sewell, W. H., & Hauser, R. M. (1975). *Education, occupation, and earnings: Achievement in the early career.* New York: Academic Press.

Silver, A. A., & Hagin, R. A. (1964). Specific reading disability: Follow-up studies. *American Journal of Orthopsychiatry, 34,* 95-102.

Smith, F. (1985). *Reading without nonsense* (2nd ed.). New York: Teachers College Press.

Sperry, R. W. (1973). Lateral specialization of cerebral function in the surgically separated hemispheres. In F. J. McGuigan (Ed.), *The psychophysiology of thinking* (pp. 209-229). New York: Academic Press.

Spreen, O. (1982). Adult outcomes of reading disorders. In R. N. Malatesha & P. G. Aaron (Eds.), *Reading disorders: Varieties and treatments.* New York: Academic Press.

Spreen, O. (1983). *Learning disabled children growing up: A follow-up into adulthood* (Grant MA-6972 and 81/2). Toronto: University of Victoria.

Spreen, O. (1984). A prognostic view from middle childhood. In M. D. Levine & P. Satz (Eds.), *Middle childhood: Development and dysfunction* (pp. 405-432). Baltimore, MD: University Park Press.

Stabler, E. M. (1974). Follow-up study of retarded clients. *Mental Retardation, 12,* 7-9.

Statistical Abstract of the U.S., 103rd ed. (1982). Washington, DC: U.S. Department of Commerce, Bureau of the Census.

Steidle, E. F., Sheldon, K. L., Hoffmann, F. J. Sautter, S. W., Minskoff, E. H., Baker, D. P., Echols, L. D., & Bailey, M. B. (1985). *Demographics: Survey research respondents.* Fishersville, VA: Woodrow Wilson Rehabilitation Center.

Sternberg, R. J. (Ed.). (1985). *Human abilities: An information-processing approach.* New York: W. H. Freeman.

Sticht, T. (Ed.). (1985). Understanding readers and their uses of text. In T. M. Duffy & R. Waller (Eds.), *Designing usable texts.* Orlando, FL: Academic Press.

Stocking, C. (1984). *Who are the handicapped students in American high schools?* Paper presented at a meeting at the National Center for Education Statistics, Washington, DC.

Stokes, T. F., & Baer, D. M. (1977). An implicit technology of generalization. *Journal of Applied Behavior Analysis, 10,* 349-369.

Strauss, A. A., & Lehtinen L. E. (1955). *Psychopathology and education of the brain-injured child.* New York: Grune & Stratton.

Strauss, A. A., & Werner, H. (1942). Disorders of conceptual thinking in the brain-injured child. *Journal of Nervous and Mental Disease, 96,* 153-172.

Super, D. E. (1951). Vocational adjustment: Implementing a self-concept. *Occupations, 30,* 88-92.

Super, D. E. (1953). A theory of vocational development. *American Psychologist, 8,* 185-190.

Super, D. E. (1957). *The psychology of careers.* New York: Harper & Brothers.

Super, D. E. (1977). Vocational maturity in mid-career. *Vocational Guidance Quarterly, 25,* 294-302.

Super, D. E. (1980). A life-span, life space approach to career development. *Journal of Vocational Behavior, 16,* 282-298.

Super, D. E. (1982). Comments on Herr, Good, McCloskey, and Weitz: "Career behavior." *Journal of Vocational Behavior, 21,* 254-256.

Super, D. E. (1983). Assessment in career guidance: Toward truly developmental counseling. *Personnel and Guidance Journal, 61,* 555-561.

Super, D. E. (1984). Career and life development. In D. Brown, L. Brooks & Associates, *Career choice and development* (pp. 192-234). San Francisco: Jossey-Bass.

Super, D. E., & Crites, J. O. (1962). *Appraising vocational fitness by means of psychological tests* (rev. ed.). New York: Harper & Row.

Super, D. E., & Harris-Bowlsbey, J. A. (1979). *Guided career exploration.* New York: Psychological Corporation.

Super, D. E., & Nevill, D. D. (1984). Work role salience as a determinant of career maturity in high school students. *Journal of Vocational Behavior, 25,* 30-44.

Super, D. E., Starishevsky, R., Matlin, N., & Jordaan, J. P. (1963). *Career development: Self concept theory.* New York: College Entrance Examination Board.

Tiedeman, D. V., & O'Hara, R. P. (1963). *Career development: Choice and adjustment.* New York: College Entrance Examination Board.

Tinto, V. (1980). College origins and patterns of status attainment: Schooling among professional and business-managerial occupations. *Sociology of Work and Occupations, 7,* 457-486.

Tyron, W. W. (1979). The test-trait fallacy. *American Psychologist, 34,* 402-406.

U.S. Department of Education (1981). Washington, DC: National Center for Education Statistics.

U.S. Office of Education (1977, December 29). Assistance to states for education of handicapped children: Procedures for evaluating specific learning disabilities. *Federal Register, 42,* 65082-65085.

U.S. Office of Special Education and Rehabilitative Services (1985). *Seventh annual report to Congress on the implementation of The Education of the Handicapped Act.* Washington, DC: U.S. Department of Education.

University of Kansas Institute for Research in Learning Disabilities, & Lawrence School District #497. (1985). *Final report: An investigation of the impact of the Kansas guidelines for identifying children and youth with specific learning disabilities.* Topeka, KS: Kansas State Department of Education.

Unruh, W. R. (1979). Career decision making: Theory construction and evaluation. In A. M. Mitchell, G. B. Jones, & J. D. Krumboltz (Eds.), *Social learning and career decision making* (pp. 5-18). Cranston, RI: Carroll Press.

Vanfossen, B. E. (1979). *The structure of social inequality.* Boston: Little, Brown.

Vetter, A. A. (1983). *A comparison of the characteristics of learning disabled and non-learning disabled young adults.* Unpublished doctoral dissertation, University of Kansas.

Vocational Evaluation Project Final Report (1975). Menomonie, WI: Materials Development Center.

Vogler, G. P., DeFries, J. C., & Decker, S. N. (1985). Family history as an indicator of risk for reading disability. *Journal of Learning Disabilities, 18,* 419-421.

Warnath, C. F. (1975). Vocational theories: Direction to nowhere. *Personnel and Guidance Journal, 53,* 422-428.

Warner, W. L., Meeker, M., & Eells, K. (1949). *Social class in America.* Chicago: Science Research Associates.

Weinrach, S. G. (1984). Determinants of vocational choice: Holland's theory. In D. Brown, L. Brooks & Associates (Eds.), *Career choice and development* (pp. 61-93). San Francisco: Jossey-Bass.

West, W. D. (1980). In W. H. Gaddes (Ed.), *Learning disabilities and brain function: A neuropsychological approach* (2nd ed.). New York: Springer-Verlag.

Westbrook, B. W. (1976). Criterion-related and construct validity of the career maturity inventory competency test with ninth grade pupils. *Journal of Vocational Behavior, 9,* 377-383.

Wigdor, A. K., & Garner, W. R. (1982). *Ability testing: Uses, consequences, and controversies: Part II: Documentation section.* Washington, DC: National Academy Press.

Will, M. (1985). Foreward. In U.S. Office of Special Education and Rehabilitative Services, *Seventh annual report to Congress on the implementation of The Education of the Handicapped Act.* Washington, DC: U.S. Department of Education.

Winer, J. L., Cesari, J., & Haase, R. F. (1979). Cognitive complexity and career maturity among college students. *Journal of Vocational Behavior, 15,* 186-192.

Wittrock, M. C. (1978). Education and the cognitive processes of the brain. In J. S. Chall & A. F. Mirsky (Eds.), *Education and the brain: The seventy-seventh yearbook of the National Society for the Study of Education.* Chicago: University of Chicago Press.

Ysseldyke, J. (1983, August). *Generalizations from research on assessment and decision making.* Report presented at Leadership Conference for Learning Handicapped, Sacramento, CA.

AUTHOR INDEX

SUBJECT INDEX